E

Cuba

www.baedeker.com

Verlag Karl Baedeker

TOP ATTRACTIONS ✶✶

There's much more to Cuba than sun, salsa, rum and cigars! The island has picturesque colonial towns with historic quarters protected by Unesco, while some 100 nature reserves appeal to lovers of the outdoors. And the beaches, which come close to many visitors' idea of paradise, are well worth coming for. We reveal the must-see destinations!

1 ✶✶ Varadero
Cuba's number one holiday destination offers an endless range of entertainment.
▶ **page 314**

2 ✶✶ Havana
Everybody falls under the spell of the capital city, and spending some time seeing the »grand old lady of the Caribbean« should be on the itinerary of every trip to Cuba. Explore the restored historic quarter, tread in the footsteps of the great Hemingway, enjoy the Tropicana cabaret and see the crumbling façades where ocean waves pound against the waterfront promenade.   ▶ **page 197**

3 ✶✶ Valle de Viñales
One of the most impressive landscapes on Cuba   ▶ **page 304**

4 ✶✶ Cayo Coco · Cayo Guillermo
A shimmering turquoise sea, radiant white sand, and coral reefs – in other words, the dream of every holidaymaker.   ▶ **page 175**

Mojito
The essence of Cuba, made with rum, sugar, lime juice, soda water and mint

Many different species
Thanks to a diversity of ecosystems, many plants and animals are found only on Cuba.

1 Varadero
2 Havana
3 Valle de Viñales
4 Cayo Coco · Cayo Guillermo
5 Valle de los Ingenios
6 Trinidad
7 Cayo Largo
8 Santa Lucía
9 Guardalavaca
10 Santiago de Cuba

©Baedeker

Rare & unique
The colourful snail Polymita picta was used by the original Indian inhabitants as a medium of exchange like money.

5 ✷✷ Valle de los Ingenios

6 ✷✷ Trinidad

7 ✷✷ Cayo Largo

Heaven for divers and snorkellers
The crystal-clear waters reveal a wealth of sights for trippers with flippers.

8 ✷✷ Santa Lucía

9 ✷✷ Guardalavaca

10 ✷✷ Santiago de Cuba

In spite of socialism
The Cubans' proverbial love of life can't be suppressed by the lack of material goods.

BAEDEKER'S BEST TIPS

From all the Baedeker tips in this book, we have gathered the most interesting for you here. Experience Cuba and enjoy the island at its best!

🔳 In the footsteps of »Che«

Guests come to the La Rusa hotel not so much for its comforts as because Che Guevara once stayed in room 203.
▶ **page 162**

🔳 Top-class dancing!

The Teatro Principal in Camagüey is famous for its performances and holds a ballet festival every two years.
▶ **page 173**

🔳 Swim with dolphins and seals

If you've always wanted to swim with these friendly sea creatures, Cayo Jutía island is just the ticket! ▶ **page 192**

🔳 Un, dos, tres – learn salsa!

There are several good dancing schools, where the teachers are professional dancers, especially in Havana.
▶ **page 201**

In the end it all goes up in smoke
But before that, it takes nimble fingers to roll a fine Havana.

🔳 Cigar museum and Casa del Habano

An excellent museum about cigars in Havana tells the iconic story, from growing the tobacco to having a smoke.
▶ **page 215**

🔳 Off to Casablanca!

The small settlement named Casablanca has a superb view of Havana and its harbour. ▶ **page 232**

🔳 Liberty boat

In Nueva Gerona you can see the old boat on which Fidel Castro returned to the mainland after his release from prison in 1955. ▶ **page 243**

Climb an elephant's back!
The limestone hills in the Valle de Viñales look like a herd of pachyderms at rest.

🔲 Finca Fiesta Campesina

Stretch your legs beneath hibiscus, mango and avocado trees, pay a call on the crocodiles and watch a kind of show cockfight – all available in the bohíos of Batey de Don Pedro on the Zapata Peninsula. ► **page 250**

🔲 Vegas Robaina

Cuba's best-known private tobacco plantation in the Vuelta Abajo at the edge of the Sierra de los Órganos mountain range is a destination for connoisseurs from all over the world. ► **page 257**

🔲 »Hello my friend ...«

We reveal how to find a reasonably priced private room in Santiago de Cuba without paying a commission to the touts.
► **page 278**

🔲 Overwhelming panorama

The most breathtaking view in all of Cuba can be enjoyed from steep heights east of Trinidad. ► **page 303**

🔲 Heaven for climbers

Fearless climbers find the right terrain in the Valle de Viñales. ► **page 307**

🔲 Into the »jungle«

By kayak or motor boat into the jungle-like landscape on the banks of Río Canímar.
► **page 322**

Cuba's best-looking revolutionary
Che Guevara left traces all over the island.

Meet the family
Stay in private accommodation to get an impression of Cuban everyday life.

Not just a spicy sauce
Cubans love to dance, and salsa is their number one export.

Havana feeling: bands play everywhere, street life is vibrant.
▶ **page 96**

BACKGROUND

PRAKTISCHE INFORMATIONEN

Price categories

Hotels
Luxury: CUC 80 – 300
Mid-range: CUC 40 – 80
Budget: below CUC 40
For two people sharing a double room

Restaurants
Expensive: from CUC 20
Moderate: CUC 6 – 20
Inexpensive: under CUC 6
For a menu with starter, main course and dessert (excl. drinks)

As the mogotes reminded Spanish seafarers of church organs when they approached Cuba from a distance, they called the range Sierra de los Organos.
▶ **page 304**

Background

PRISTINE BEACHES THAT ARE
A WORLD AWAY FROM EVERYDAY
CUBAN LIFE, A CRUMBLING BUT
PROUD CAPITAL CITY WITH COLONIAL CHARM
PROTECTED BY UNESCO, VETERAN CARS AND
SALSA ... CUBA LIVES UP TO THE CLICHÉS.

VIVA LA REVOLUCIÓN!

Like the mint in the mojito, some knowledge of the revolution is an essential part of the tourist programme in Havana. In the Museo de la Revolución in the former presidential palace, for example. But what's that sound? Between Che's blood-soaked shirt and Castro's field telephone, all of a sudden you hear the sound of romantic boleros. The heart-rending singing comes from the patio.

In the shady courtyard of the museum a woman in a housecoat is singing the unforgettable »La Gloria eres tu« as if she had been doing nothing else for the last 80 years, and a trio of 70-year-old women, got up to the nines in chiffon dresses and holding fans, perform a song a cappella. One Saturday a month, Fidel's old comrades-in-arms dance to classic sounds in the museum – and they have just as much groove as the younger generation.

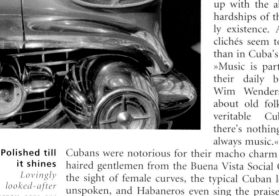

Music and rum, laughter and sensual pleasures, not to mention the foreign currency provided by relatives in exile and tourists, help them put up with the absurd difficulties and hardships of their post-socialist daily existence. And nowhere do the clichés seem to exceed reality more than in Cuba's capital city.

»Music is part of life in Cuba, it's their daily bread«, said director Wim Wenders, whose 1998 film about old folk's bands triggered a veritable Cuba boom. »When there's nothing to eat here, there is always music.«

Polished till it shines
Lovingly looked-after veteran cars are a familiar sight on the streets of Havana.

Cubans were notorious for their macho charm long before the grey-haired gentlemen from the Buena Vista Social Club shot to fame. At the sight of female curves, the typical Cuban leaves no compliment unspoken, and Habaneros even sing the praises of their city as if it were an enchanting woman: »La Habana«. At the age of 500, this Caribbean lady may be a bit wobbly on her legs, but she remains as seductive and romantic as ever. Following Unesco's efforts at resuscitation, at least »Habana Vieja«, the old quarter, is reasonably easy on the eye. The prettiest results of the face-lift can be seen at Plaza de Armas with its columns, arcades and green patios. Plaza de la Catedral and the lively Obispo shopping street are equally photogenic. A walk along Obispo leads inevitably to the Parque Central, where Cuba's finest buildings engage in a beauty contest: the wonderfully or-

Timeless
Che, the eternal revolutionary, smiles from posters and the walls of houses, and the Cubans keep faith with him.

Leafy wealth
The Cuban economy would be ailing even more without this source of foreign currency. In drying sheds the tobacco leaves are only exposed to indirect sunlight.

Caribbean dreams
Sun, sand and sea: more than 300 beaches and 4000 islands, and who can say which is the most beautiful?

Architectural treasures

Since Havana, »the old lady of the Caribbean«, was spruced up with help from Unesco, not only the Capitol is resplendent in the moonlight.

Enjoy life!

If you think the old man with the tanned face smoking a cigar is a worn-out cliché – well, maybe, but it's a likeable one.

Dexterity

A good Havana cigar has to be perfectly rolled. Jobs in the cigar factory are coveted, and not every trainee is up to the mark.

nate Gran Teatro with its turrets and winged figures, obviously unable to decide whether to be neo-Baroque or Art Nouveau, the colonial-style Plaza and Sevilla hotels, the neo-Classical Inglaterra and the Capitolio with its broad flight of steps and white dome towering over everything else.

Travellers in Cuba have much to marvel at, whether it's the ubiquitous revolutionary slogans (»We are working for victory«) beneath royal palms that rise as high as 40m/130ft, or a 5700km/3500-mi coast with more than 4000 offshore islands and islets. Sunbathing beneath coconut palms, bright sand as fine as powder, tempting seawater shimmering turquoise, and an azure tropical sky at destinations such as Cayo Largo or Cayo Coco. On these two idyllic islands, visitors are as far removed from everyday Cuban life as the average Cuban is from buying a Rolls Royce: the only Cuban citizens who come here are hotel employees. Of course holidaymakers in Cuba can easily spend a full three weeks on one of its 300 beaches, lazing on the sand with a Cuba libre in their hand – included in the price after all – but they are missing the best the country has to offer.

Take a trip round the island to see delightful towns with colonial charm and breathtaking scenery, for example Valle de los Ingenios with its ruined sugar-cane mills near Trinidad, the mountainous Alejandro de Humboldt rainforest near sleepy Baracoa (Cuba's first settlement, at its far eastern tip), or the wonderful coast road from Santiago to Granma province, following the steep cliffs of the Sierra Maestra with stunning views over the Caribbean Sea. But be warned: the road might be blocked here by a whole herd of cattle. Would Che Guevara have been happy at the idea that a song in his praise (»Hasta siempre, Comandante«) is sung every evening to entertain tourists as they eat beef and lobster by candlelight, while most of the Cuban population can scarcely afford to eat a chicken leg with rice? Now that's a good question.

The rhythm's in the blood
In bars, on the street – music and dancing everywhere

Facts

Find out about Cuba's miles of superb beaches, tobacco and sugar-cane plantations, and the role of tourism in supplying foreign currency to a post-socialist state where a two-class system emerged long ago.

Nature

Cuba's coastline has a total length of 5745km/3570mi with some 300 **gently shelving sandy beaches** of fine coral lime. The most famous, including Varadero and Playas del Este, are on the north coast. Most of the Cuban coast, however, consists of **steep cliffs**, often of jagged karst limestone, which sometimes make a wild, at other times a romantic impression. Long stretches of coastline, especially at river estuaries, consist of **extensive swamps** with mangrove forests. The natural caves near the coast served as places of refuge in the past for the island's original Indian inhabitants and for pirates. Today they are populated by bats.

Coast

Cuba consists of one main island and a **multitude of smaller off-shore islands**, the low-lying »cayos« that are made up of coral lime and coral reefs. The largest, Isla de la Juventud (Isle of Youth), along with the Archipiélago de los Canarreos lies to the southwest of the main island in the Gulf of Batabano. Further east, the Archipiélago de los Jardines de la Reina (Archipelago of the Queen's Gardens) is the termination of the Gulf of Ana Maria. Its eastern continuation is the Gulf of Guacanayabo with its numerous coral reefs. Off the north coast lie the large islands and peninsulas of the Camagüey Archipelago in the east, and in the centre those of the Sabana Archipelago. The islands off the northwest coast form the Archipiélago de los Colorados, while to the north of the Guanahacabibes Peninsula you'll find the gulf of the same name. Even relatively close to the coast of Cuba, the sea bed falls away to depths of 4000–8000m/12,000–25,000ft.

»Archipiélagos« and »cayos«

About 200 rivers, most of them short with a gentle gradient, flow across the main island, but in the dry season they usually carry no water. Only Cuba's longest river, the Río Cauto (370km/230mi), the Río Tao, also in the province of Oriente, and the Río Cuyaguateje (province of Pinar del Río) have water all year. Practically none of the Cuban rivers are navigable, as most of them have their source in the mountains and flow a short distance to the sea. Many Cuban rivers have a subterranean mouth, which makes them of great interest to divers.

The reservoirs of Cuba not only have the task of compensating for the unreliable level of river water, above all they serve as a precaution against the **floods of the rainy season**. Thus they simultaneously serve as basins for catchment and retention, and as reservoirs for the cities. Only the second-largest, the Hanabanilla Reservoir south of Santa Clara, is used to generate electricity. Presa Zaza near Sancti

Rivers and reservoirs

←*Sugar cane swaying gently in the wind – but harvesting it is a tough job, once done by tens of thousands of slaves.*

? DID YOU KNOW ...?

■ Cuba possesses no fewer than six regions that have been declared World Biosphere Reserves by Unesco: from west to east, these are the Guanahacabibes Peninsula and the Sierra del Rosario mountains in the west, the swampland of Ciénaga de Zapata in the south, Buenavista on the north coast, the Baconao Park near Santiago and the Cuchillas del Toa in the east of the country (also the site of the Alejandro de Humboldt National Park). There are about 100 nature reserves altogether.

Spíritus holds more than one billion cubic metres (265 billion US gallons) of water, which makes it the island's largest reservoir.

The Landscape

Most of Cuba consists of flat lowland plains with intensive monoculture (especially sugar cane) and pasture for cattle, especially in the east of the island. The plains are interrupted by chains of hills up to 500m/1600ft high, called »alturas«. The mountains on Cuba are characterized by rugged, steeply rising cone formations and reach heights of almost 2000m/6500ft.

Sierra de los Órganos The western mountain country of the Cordillera de Guaniguanico is divided into the Alturas Pizarrosas del Norte and del Sur,, and the Sierras de los Órganos and del Rosario. The highest summit is Pan de Guajaibón at 699m/2293ft.

Lush green vegetation, red alluvial soil and hills called »mogotes« characterize

The conical limestone towers of the Sierra de los Órganos have interesting formations resembling organ pipes. Steep karst rocks called **»mogotes«** rise out of the fertile red alluvial earth of the Gulf of Mexico. The deep green of the tobacco that is cultivated here is the third colour that marks this impressive landscape. In the **Güira National Park**, you'll have the chance to admire primeval trees and tropical forests.

On the south coast north of Trinidad, the Escambray mountain range is subdivided into the Alturas de Trinidad and de Sancti Spíritus. Here, amidst beautiful scenery, the Hanabanilla Reservoir presents an opportunity for taking a boat trip to observe coffee, cocoa and tobacco cultivation, as well as natural vegetation: the forests and the highest summit, Pico de San Juan (1140m/3740ft), provide good terrain for long hikes past rare giant ferns and impressive waterfalls.

Sierra del Escambray

The Sierra Maestra occupies the whole southeast coast of Cuba from Punta del Inglés to the Bay of Guantánamo. These rugged mountains, inaccessible in places, consist of the Cordillera del Turquino to the west and the Cordillera de la Gran Piedra to the east of Santiago de Cuba. At 1974m/6477ft, the **Pico Turquino** is the highest peak not

Sierra Maestra

the magical landscape of the Sierra de los Organos.

The royal palm is one of the best-known kinds of palm tree, but many other species thrive on Cuba.

A MAJESTIC APPEARANCE

European visitors associate palm trees with beaches and sunny holidays, but in the lands where they grow, palms are valued above all as an important natural resource. On Cuba they provide building materials, food for humans and animals, wax, fat, sago and other starches, material for weaving and, last but not least, palm wine, the basis for distilling arak.

Palms are astonishingly resilient, and their usefulness can hardly be praised too highly: a wax palm (Copernicia) yields up to 160kg/350lb of special wax, and a single coconut palm produces 50 to 80, and sometimes up to 120 coconuts in a year.

Cuba is blessed with an unusual variety of palms. In addition to common types such as the coconut palm, several endemic species grow on Cuba – palms, that is, which grow nowhere else, as Cuba became an island at a very early stage, enabling certain species to survive and others to develop only there.

The **royal palm** (Roystonea regia) grows to a height of up to 40m/130ft and can be seen on all parts of the island, but especially in the west. It flowers for only one or two days, but not until it is 15 or 20 years old. When this happens, an inflorescence opens below the crown of the tree with thousands of yellow-white flowers which produce so much nectar that countless bees and butterflies swarm round them. As they ripen, the decorative-looking fruit change colour, from green at first to red and then finally to black.

The royal palm has a wide range of uses: while the fruits are fed to animals, the tender palm hearts form the basis for tasty soups and salads. The hard wood of the trunk is made into furniture. The lower, harder leaf sheaths are material for weaving, and the palm fronds of the crown have been used for centuries as roofing material for bohío huts in rural areas. The royal palm has spread from its original home on Cuba to all tropical countries.

The species Colpothrinax wrightii is known locally as **»palma barrigona«**, meaning the fat-bellied or pregnant palm, on account of the swelling of its trunk. It grows only in the west of Cuba and on the Isla de la Juventud. This type of palm reaches a height of 8–15m/25–50ft, and thickens in this curious way as it ages. The belly of the tree probably serves as storage for nutrients and liquids, and is used on the island for the same purpose: the

trunks are split lengthways and used as water containers, as they keep water fresh for a long time.

Botanical rarities

Another rare Cuban species, the **cork palm** (Microcycas calocoma), is in danger of extinction and is only found in the tobacco-growing areas of Pínar del Río province. It is a type of cycad, a living fossil that has little connection to either palm trees or to cork. However, its approximately 10m/ 30ft-high, smooth, single-stem trunk and crown of feathered leaves gives it the appearance of a palm tree.

Among the further peculiarities of Cuban palm vegetation, the **sabal palmetto** is worthy of mention. As a relic of the original flora of the island, it is a protected species. Its fan-like leaves are still used as roofing material. The machete-wielding desmochadores skilfully cut off only as many fronds from the trunk, which can attain a height of 30m/100ft, as will enable the tree to continue growing. The **bottle palm** (Acrocomia armentalis), like the palma barrigona, has a belly-like thickening of the trunk,

covered with a dense layer of thorny rudimentary leaves, a prickly protection that gave it the name »armentalis«, meaning »armed«.

A further endemic species is the **fanpalm** known as palma petate (Coccothrinax crinita). Its stem is surrounded by long fibres, which are initially interwoven in a cross pattern and then dangle down. This covering can become four or five times as thick as the trunk itself.

The best places for admiring the diversity of Cuban palms are the botanical gardens in Havana and nearby Cienfuegos, where all species are represented and avenues of royal palms have been planted which are among the most beautiful and impressive rows of palm trees anywhere in the world.

A single coconut palm can produce up to 120 nuts per year.

Cuba owes a lot to sugar cane – not least rum, a by-product of sugar production and a vital ingredient of mojitos and many other cocktails.

only of this range but of the island as a whole. The highest point of the Gran Piedra has an elevation of 1214m/3983ft. The Sierra Maestra has a special place in the history of Cuba: it was the region around the former capital city, Santiago de Cuba, from which the revolutionary movement started out. Here rebel forces gathered around Fidel Castro and conquered the whole island with the support of the mountain farmers.

Amongst the several smaller mountain ranges to the northeast of the Sierra Maestra, the Sierras del Cristal, de Baracoa and del Purial have especially beautiful scenery. These mountains reach altitudes of 1170m/3839ft. All the mountain regions of the east produce coffee and cocoa of outstanding quality. Moreover, the largest areas of continuous forest, often boasting rare species of trees, can be found here, for instance in the Unesco-listed **Parque Nacional Alejandro de Humboldt** near Baracoa.

Flora and Fauna

Flora   The Caribbean flora is known for its large number of different varieties. Although only about 20% of the island is still forested, Cuba boasts between 6000 and 8000 botanical species, of which 64% have no leaves due to the extensive dry periods. The botanical gardens in Havana and Cienfuegos document the diversity of vegetation on the island.

Most coastal regions of Cuba are dominated by typical **swamp or coastal vegetation**. The beaches support a variety of palm trees (at least 80 different species of palms grow on Cuba, ►Baedeker Special p. 18), sea grapes and sea almond trees, while the swamps are in the grip of mangroves. There are continuous **areas of forest** in the mountainous regions, in the south of the Guanahacabibes Peninsula, in the Sierra Guaniguanico in the west and in the Sierra Maestra in the southeast, in the Baracoa Mountains, around Pico de San Juan and on the Isla de la Juventud. Conifers, especially firs and pines, of which there are many species on Cuba, are extremely common. The largest Cuban island, Isla de los Pinos, today called Isla de la Juventud, took its original name from the large numbers of pine trees. In colonial times, high-grade timber for shipbuilding and export was a pillar of the economy, and today still, mahogany remains important. Among the deciduous trees, apart from the yaya (ocxandra lanceolata), which supplies the wood for cigar boxes, the white kapok tree (ceiba pentandra) and the guana tree (streculie cubensis), which grows only on Cuba, are of interest to amateur botanists. A species of ficus, the jagüey, is notable for its unusual air roots. The leaves of the strange yagruma tree, which are used to make a tea, have a green upper surface and a silvery underside. When it rains, the silver side turns upwards, which is why people who change their minds easily are known as »yagrumas« on Cuba.

◄ Vegetationzones

In addition to various fruits such as pineapples, bananas, papayas, mangos and avocados, citrus trees are a conspicuous feature of the Cuban landscape. Common vegetables are beans, potatoes, maize, manioc, tomatoes and peppers. The cultivation of rice, coffee and cocoa is important to the economy. Cotton and sisal agave are used to make textiles, and the Cubans have even found a way to make a kind of detergent from agave. Cuba's most important crops, and a dominant feature of the countryside in many places, are **tobacco and sugar cane**.

◄ Cultivated plants

Flowering plants delight the eye everywhere on Cuba, and the variety and array of colours are especially beautiful before the start of the rainy season when most of them come into bloom. One of the loveliest trees and shrubs is the decorative, red-flowering flamboyant. Other common plants with luxuriant flowers are the hibiscus and oleander, the hydrangea and the climbing bougainvillea. Flowering tropical plants include the African tulip tree (spathodea campanulata), the golden shower tree from India (cassia fistula) and the jacaranda.

◄ Flowering plants

Many species of orchid are native to Cuba. They can be admired in the orchid garden of Soroa. One invasive species of orchid has become a pest: the common water hyacinth (eichhornia crassipes), a floating plant, obstructs shipping and hinders fish farming in the delta of the largest Cuban river, the Río Cauto.

◄ Orchids

Approximately 3000 species of plants and animals are endemic, i. e. they are native only to Cuba. Among these are a rare kind of iguana

Endemic plants and animals

An artist of flight in a colourful habitat: the hummingbird.

called Cyclura nubila, the freshwater fish known as manjuari and the Cuban manatee. Many of the countless species of insects, bats and snails on the island are encountered only on Cuba.

Fauna   In contrast to its flora, Cuba's animal life is less diverse. However, there is an impressive range of species of fish,, insects and birds.

Marine life ▶   The waters off the Cuban coast are extraordinarily rich in fish. Some 900 species, 300 of them edible, flourish in the warm seas and make Cuba a paradise for sea angling – and that started long before Hemingway's day.

Cuban waters have plentiful seafood,, corals, sea anemones and starfish, shellfish and crustaceans. The great variety of species, and their diverse shapes and colours, mean that snorkelling is rewarding almost everywhere. The size of its langoustines has made Cuba a major exporter. Living in the lagoon of Guamá, the rare and ancient **manjuari** is an endemic freshwater species. About as big as a pike, the manjuari has a crocodile-like snout. Because it is a coveted delicacy, the caguama or giant sea turtle has become a rarity, and the Cuban **manatee**, which can weigh up to 500kg/over 1000 lb and measure 5m/16ft in length, is almost extinct. Being vegetarian, it is unique among marine mammals.

Reptiles ▶   Reptiles are common in Cuba, especially various kinds of lizards and geckos, as well as iguanas. The Zapata Swamps shelter shy giant iguanas, which like the non-poisonous species of snakes are not dangerous. The largest snake found on Cuba, the maja de Santa María, a kind of boa, can grow to a length of 4m/13ft. Crocodiles are more spectacular. As their meat is regarded as a delicacy, they have been almost completely exterminated in the wild, but can still be seen in the Zapata Swamps nature reserve and on state crocodile farms in Guamá.

Over 400 bird species can be found on Cuba, many of them migratory birds that are present only at certain times of the year. 21 species of bird live only on Cuba, amongst them the world's smallest species, the zunzuncito. Visitors to the island are often amazed by the colourful and exotic birds they see. Flamingos in their natural habitat can be spotted on the Río Cauto, canaries in many mangrove swamps and diving pelicans off the south coast. The Isla de la Juventud is a bird-watchers' paradise. The Cuban trogón or tocororo, with its plumage in the national colours of red, white and blue, is regarded as the national bird. Two extremely useful species are the black vulture (Coragyps atratus) and the white heron, which has a symbiotic relationship with cattle by freeing them from insects.

◄ Birds

When the Spanish conquered Cuba, the island was probably home to only two species of land mammals: a rare insect eater and the jutía conga, a kind of rat that is now almost extinct and was prized for centuries by Indios and farmers for the taste of its meat. Bats are common. 30 different species find ideal habitats in the numerous caves of the island. Another endangered species is the stinking **almiquí**, which looks like a mole but has the size of a cat.

◄ Mammals

Population · Politics · Economy

Population

During the first century of colonization, the **Indian aboriginal population** was almost exterminated. Most of the few survivors mixed with the Spanish settlers and African slaves. Today, Cubans of Indian origin are few and far between, mainly to be encountered in rural areas to the east of the island.

Ethnic groups

Cubans living in exile in the USA are an ambivalent issue for the island. On the one hand, politicians associated with Castro fear the propagandistic influence exerted by opponents of the regime based in the USA, which finds expression in media outlets controlled by exiled Cubans. On the other hand, since exiles were first allowed to enter the country in 1978, the gifts and remittances sent to relatives on the island have been important to the economy, as every inflow of foreign currency helps. Exiled Cubans have been successful in their at-

Population structure

 DID YOU KNOW ...?

■ ... that the population of Cuba increased fivefold in the 20th century? Approximately 2 million inhabitants in 1900 were joined by 1936 by half a million immigrants from Spain, as well as hundreds of thousands from Haiti and Jamaica. Improvements in the health system and social security after the revolution of 1959 brought about a further increase of 20% by 1970.

Facts and Figures Cuba

©Baedeker

Island group
▶ Largest island in the Antilles

Area and territory
▶ 110 860 km²/42 800sq mi (1250 km/
777mi east to west, between 31km/
19mi and 200km/124mi wide)
▶ Capital city: Havanna (La Habana)

Population
▶ 11.4 million, population density: ca.
100 people/km² (263 people/sq mi;
Germany: 231 people/km² (608 people/
sq mi)), Havanna 2.2 million residents
(ca. 3050 people/km² (8026 people/sq
mi))
▶ ca. 51 % mulattos, 37 % white, 11 %
black; many exiled Cubans in the USA

Religion
▶ 40 % Christian, ca. 2 % followers of
Santería, 55 % non-confessional

Language
▶ Spanish

Government
▶ Socialist republic with a one-party
system (Communist Party of Cuba)
▶ Head of state and military commander
in chief: Raúl Castro Ruz
▶ Parliament: National Assembly with
589 members, elected every five years,
elects the 31 member Council of
Ministers

▶ Administrative structure: 14 provinces
and one special municipality (Isla de la
Juventud)

Tourism
▶ about 2.1 million visitors/year (2007)

Economy
▶ Gross national product (GNP): US$ 25.9
billion (about 16.1 billion GBP)
▶ Gross domestic product (per capita):
1327 Pesos (official figure, the average
official monthly salary is US$ 12
(8 GBP), about 250 – 300 Cuban pesos)
▶ Annual per capita income: US$ 3300
(2005, amount stated by the CIA
including transfers from overseas, black
market dealing and tips)
▶ Unemployment rate: about 3 % (2007)
▶ Employment structure: about 60 %
service industry and trading, 30 %
industry and skilled trades, 7 % agricultural and fishing
▶ Economic growth 2005: about 3.5 %
▶ Export: 42 % sugar and sugar products,
18 % nickel ores and concentrates, 9 %
seafood, 13 % tobacco
▶ Chief trading partners: Spain (14 %),
Russia (12 %), Mexico (9 %)
▶ Import: 25 % petroleum, 13 % chemical
products, 10 % food, 6 % machines,
5 % raw materials
▶ Income from tourism:
2.2 billion US$
▶ Money transferred fron abroad by
exiled Cubans: about 1 billion US$

tempts to influence American government policy towards Cuba, as the political collapse of Cuba would be in the interest of both parties. Economic pressure, in the shape of the embargo policy and the Helms-Burton Act is designed to bring about the fall of a crumbling system.

◄ Women

Many Cubans marry at a very young age, partly in the hope of getting their own flat. The result is a high divorce rate. Women on Cuba have the same access to education and professional advancement as men. Many Cuban women try to escape poverty by marrying foreigners. A problem associated with this is the increase in prostitution in recent years. Many men and women are available as escorts or for other dubious services in return for payment.

»Achievements« of the Revolution

Housing

Since the revolution in 1959, the state has been trying to provide adequate housing for a growing population. Due to the shortage of building materials, however, this has not been achieved. Especially in the towns and cities, and above all in Havana, housing is a major problem, partly in terms of conserving historic buildings: its colonial architecture make Havana a Unesco World Heritage site. It is common for several generations to live together in cramped accommodation. Again and again houses fall down, as alterations carried out without planning permission weaken the structure of old buildings in need of renovation.

Health system

A dense network of health centres has been established across the whole island to provide medical care in rural areas. In every community, doctors live in special, immediately recognizable housing above their surgeries in order to be easily accessible for their patients. Central provincial hospitals are available for operations and special-

---

Provinces Map

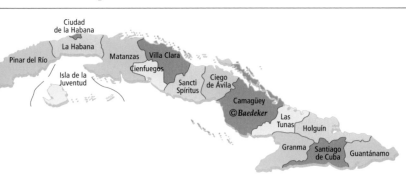

ized treatment. Medical care, including abortions, is free of charge for all Cubans. They have to pay for medicine themselves, at relatively low prices, but often have to wait a long time for certain medications, unless they are able to pay in dollars or another foreign currency. The standard of equipment and availability of medicines has been affected by the economic crisis, and more recently also by **social inequality in medical care** resulting from preferential treatment of tourists and Cubans who have foreign currency. Nevertheless, a focus on health education and preventive measures by means of health passes, regular vaccinations and check-ups reduced the rate of infant mortality within a few years to levels below those in the USA for example. Polio, diphtheria, malaria and diseases such as measles and rubella were almost completely eliminated many years ago. Thanks to a **health system unique in a developing country** and Latin America, life expectation on Cuba is as high as in industrialized western countries.

? DID YOU KNOW ...?

■ ... that you can meet famous people from all historical eras in just one week on Cuba? For example Jesús, a captain of a sailing boat in the south, or Lenin, the husband of a good friend and definitely not dictatorial. Aristotle and Ulysses can also be met often enough, and Julius César came, saw and conquered as a salsero on the dance floor. And what woman would not love to meet an Adonis? When Cubans name their children, the whole history of the world is their oyster.

Education for all   The improvement of the education system was one of the priorities of domestic policy after the revolution. Large-scale literacy campaigns reduced the rate of illiteracy from 24% in 1961 to a stable level of 2% since then. In Cuba, nine years' attendance at school is compulsory. Many pupils attend **boarding schools**, where they get both accommodation and food free of charge. The curriculum in these schools includes up to three hours of work a day in agriculture. This is intended not only to provide food for the boarders, but also to combine schooling with practical work. Attendance at a secondary or vocational school is the pre-requisite for studying at university, which is made possible for many by state scholarships. Havana, Santa Clara and Santiago de Cuba are university cities. Practical work programmes are organized for students in the same way as for school pupils.

State and Society

One-party state   The first merger of political and revolutionary groupings in 1961 resulted in the formation on 3 October 1965 of the **Communist Party** of Cuba (Partido Comunista de Cuba / PCC), since then the only legal party on Cuba. Its leadership role is enshrined in the constitution. The aims of the party were the struggle against injustices inherited from the past and against the consumer society. The party at-

Many pupils attend boarding schools. Cuba has an excellent education system.

tached particular importance to friendship with the Soviet Union and support for the revolutionary liberation movements of other peoples. In **1991 the party underwent reform**, with many new appointments made both to the Central Committee and the Politburo. To this day, most positions are occupied by party members. Miami is the base of the exiles' party, the Party of Democratic National Unity (Partido de Unidad Nacional Democrático/PUND), which has been held responsible for many »subversive« activities on Cuba, some of them violent, and for controlling exile propaganda.

In terms of numbers, the **committees for the defence of the revolution** (Comités de la Defensa de la Revolución/CDR) form the strongest association on Cuba, with five million members. They originated after the revolution as a defence against counter-revolutionary activity, and are today a security and monitoring organization to protect the country and its coastline. The CDR also employs supervisors of housing blocks and is responsible for the ideological monitoring and political education of the people of Cuba, as well as for social services, protection of the environment and cultural programmes.

Cuban mass media are controlled by the government or Communist Party and owned by the state. Because of the economic crisis, the only national daily is the party newspaper *Granma*. All other press publications have ceased or appear weekly.

◄ Mass media and censorship

SANTERÍA – THE CUBAN VERSION OF PSYCHOTHERAPY?

The scene is a flat somewhere in Havana. Beneath a large wooden cross, several black dolls in gaudy clothing are seated. One of them is clothed all in white: this is Obotalá. A few candles flicker. A colourful cake, three coconuts and biscuits have been placed on the altar, next to them shells in a glass of water. A crucified Christ seems to be looking at a half-empty bottle of rum and an offering of rice pudding, the favourite dish of many African gods.

Peso coins jingle in a dish when the faithful pay a visit to their Santero (priest) and show their appreciation by leaving money, prostrating themselves in front of the altar and murmuring their wishes in the presence of the god Obotalá. After this, each person rings the little bell, and then **with Obotalá's blessing the jolly part of the evening can begin**. Michael Jackson's *You Are Not Alone* resounds from the next room.

This Santero »birthday party« has been going on since the afternoon. 14 years ago Alfredo, now 30 years old, became a lay priest in the Cuban Santería cult by completing the highly secret week-long initiation ritual, during which he was »born again, like a child«. All his guests are »sons« (ahijados) and »daughters« (ahijadas) whom he has taken in and converted. Through Alfredo the god familiar to him, Obotalá, told the future of his spiritual children and took cognizance of their wishes, some of which came true.

A few decaying houses further on, a family pays homage to Elegguá, the **god of destiny**, at a similar shrine: he

A domestic altar to San Lazaro, the patron saint of the sick, who heals those who make offerings to him. It is difficult to say whether thanks are really given to Saint Lazarus or to the African god of mercy, Babalú Ayé.

has enabled their daughter to walk again after an accident. An old man in white clothes – he himself is black as night and wears chains – is flapping around his visitors in a hectic manner. The spirit of Elegguá has entered him, say the others: he is speaking a strange tongue in a whisper. He bares his teeth and defiantly sticks out his lower lip. »He's speaking the African Lucumí language – he doesn't usually do that,« say two white-clad old women, who are sitting on stools in the corner puffing on fat cigars.

The gods are numerous and charitable

As black slaves were not allowed to practise their religious cults in the 19th century under Spanish colonial rule in Cuba, under the gaze of their supervisors they venerated, for example, Saint Barbara, but in their eyes she never ceased to be Changó, the god of war – in Catholic garb, as it were. The »orishas« of the African

An old man in white clothes – he himself is black as night and wears chains – is flapping around his visitors in a hectic manner.

pantheon are numerous and charitable, and some of them are especially powerful: Obotalá (the god of peace who created humankind), Elegguá (the god of paths), Ochún (the goddess of love and gold), and Ye-mayá (the goddess of fertility). The god who comes out top in the popularity stakes with Cuban male chauvinists and machos is **Changó**, the god of virility – who else?

A motley assortment of Christian images, African deities and all sorts of knick-knacks can be seen in many Cuban homes. Sometimes the altar is extremely inconspicuous or even hidden, sometimes it is in an expensive glass case that occupies a whole corner of the room, or it may have a place of honour on top of the television: it all depends how serious

This mysterious black woman clad in white is an adherent of the Santería cult.

the Santero is about his Afro-Cuban gods. A doll is almost always used to represent the saint, and there is a soup bowl with a lid, in which other »secret« symbols are kept. Some believers carry a stone that holds the god within itself in their handbag or when they go on a journey.

For those who want to experience Santería and its wonders, the encounter that makes the most profound

given the coup de grace. Santeros and Santeras sit along the wall with their eyes half-closed and accompany the feast of sacrifice with traditional chants sung to the African god Babalú Ayé. The Babalao, the high priest, leads the singing. The air is heavy and sweet. The monotonous singing rises above the shrieks of animals in mortal fear; the smell and the fresh gleam of their blood and their twitching ob-

Santeros and Santeras sit along the wall with their eyes half-closed and accompany the feast of sacrifice with traditional chants ...

impression takes place on the night of 16–17 December, the day of Saint Lazarus. The scene is a large warehouse in the pitch-black middle of nowhere near Trinidad: at the front is the usual altar with an image of Lazarus and a bowl of coins. From a tiny, windowless back room, the sounds of squealing and panting can be heard. The sacrificial animals, a kid goat, chickens and doves, are quickly

viously have a hypnotic effect. After the blood lust, the batá drums pound outside and a 98-year-old priestess dances herself into a trance, shaking wildly. Many of the faithful willingly explain why they are here: only through the help of the merciful Babalú Ayé, patron of the sick, have they regained their health, and in return they offer him their animals – a truly valuable sacrifice in Cuba.

Santería booms in times of crisis

For a long time the socialist government banned the Afro-Cuban religion and its rituals. From the 1980s, however, Fidel Castro adopted a more tolerant attitude to the gods of Santería. Perhaps every last atheist Marxist member of the Politbureau had become aware of the psychotherapeutic value of **superstition as a means of letting off steam**. Santería booms in times of crisis. Cubans of all skin colours and tourists too are increasingly going to fortunetellers. Some credulous gringos travel a long way and pay $ 100 for some fresh flowers, a few herbs and a wise oracle made by casting stones or shells while the »spirit« slowly but surely becomes intoxicated on the rum that was also brought along. Foreign visitors should on no account invest more than $ 10 and some payments in kind for a boozy look into their future.

Black sheep

Branches of African religion that are not without danger are the **Regla de Palo Morte** or **Mayombe** and the Nigerian secret cult **Abakuá**. The Palero priests do not always confine themselves to rites that bring good fortune, but also resort to black magic or »brujeria«, in order to put a curse on people. The ceremonies involve the mixing of soil from cemeteries, human bones and animal blood in a cauldron.

A case in Santiago de Cuba made the headlines a few years ago when a child was killed during a Palo ceremony. The voodoo murderers found their way to hell without delay, as they were sentenced to death.

Information and dates

Many travel operators take their customers to Babalaos and Santeros, who perform a folklore ceremony (see tour agencies, page 127).

A museum and folklore ensembles in Guanabacoa and the Casa de Africa in the old quarter of Havana are specialists on the Afro-Cuban religion.

Every year feast days and pilgrimages take place, for example on 17 December in Havana and on 8 September near Santiago de Cuba.

In addition to several national and regional radio stations, there are four national TV channels. The programming is to a large extent controlled by the party. Cubans in exile in the USA produce their own publications and broadcasts, many of them for propaganda purposes.

Elections ► The **last elections in 1993** confirmed Fidel Castro in office and were regarded as the first direct elections by secret ballot since 1959. According to official figures, 99.2% of Cubans voted. However, the elections were neither free nor democratic, as only members of the Communist Party were candidates.

Foreign policy ► Since the collapse of the Soviet bloc, a close cooperation partner for Cuba cooperated until 1990, Cuban foreign policy has increasingly concentrated on the surrounding region of Latin America and the Caribbean. Strengthening political and economic relations with the countries of this region is currently seen as extremely important. Relations with the USA continue to be characterized by mutual distrust, obstacles, enmity and propaganda.

Dependence on foreign countries ► Cuba is highly dependent on imports and therefore on foreign states. Close ties to the Soviet Union, which lasted until 1990, are now gradually being replaced by other dependencies. In the face of high foreign debts, lack of foreign currency and the economic crisis, efforts

Cuba is far from a free market economy. Despite liberalization there are shortages of many everyday items – or they are only obtainable in exchange for foreign currency.

are being made to create incentives for investors from abroad. Apart from **opening the economy to joint ventures** in the last ten years, especially in the field of tourism, there have been no great changes in Cuban policy. The only hope for the people is that small changes in the law will make their daily lives easier. At times restrictions are reduced by new regulations, but then tightened up again. For example, the possession of dollars was legalized in 1993, but then they were abolished again as an official means of payment in 2004. Or take the licensing of private restaurants – followed by the removal of their concessions a few years later.

Economy

The economy and trade were first built up in the unilateral interests of Spain as the colonial ruler, and later of the USA. The resulting dependence on sugar monoculture led to Cuba's severe dependence on the Soviet Union after the USA enforced an embargo in 1960 (and from 1962 a total economic blockade). Subsidized by the Soviet Union, Cuba's production, exports and imports were set according to the demand existing in the countries forming part of the »Council for Mutual Economic Assistance« (Comecon).

◄ Dependencies

The collapse of the Soviet bloc left Cuba suddenly standing at the edge of the abyss. As the supply of goods deteriorated dramatically, the economic crisis from 1990 onwards was a severe trial for all Cubans. Rationing, the cutting-off of electricity and water supplies at times, and a rise in unemployment as whole industries came to a standstill through a lack of electricity, raw materials or spare parts, led to a rise in emigration but was also countered by new initiatives and an astonishing talent for improvisation.

◄ Intensifying economic crisis

The announcement of the **»período especial«** (Special Period) was intended to revive the economy by making everyday savings. Of greater importance for the re-orientation of the economy have been the partial privatization of agriculture, trade and small businesses, the legalization of the private ownership of dollars and support for joint ventures. It is hoped that foreign investors will help the struggling country back onto its feet, especially in the fields of energy, industry and **tourism**.

◄ Privatization

Although economic liberalization has improved the supply of goods, the cost of living has increased at the same time. Second jobs, private initiatives and the tiring process of coming to terms with a state of decay have been whittling away the strength and patience of most Cubans. At present it would not be correct to speak of a social market economy, but rather of a post-socialist state of affairs.

As hardly any reliable recent figures are available, the economic situation of Cuba can only be outlined in the shape of general trends. Following a severe recession in the first half of the 1990s that affected all sectors of the economy, there has been a gradual improvement since 1995. Gross national product and gross domestic product have

◄ New means of payment

Hard physical labour, but they still manage a smile for the camera: many sugar cane fields are still harvested laboriously by hand.

grown in real terms, with a simultaneous reduction of the budget deficit. Until November 2004, the dollar became a more widespread currency alongside the Cuban peso for business and increasingly for everyday transactions. The US dollars transferred by Cubans in exile to their families also benefit the economy. However, since November 2004 the dollar has no longer been an official means of payment, and can only be changed into a »peso convertible« at the cost of ten per cent in fees.

Food supplies and consumer goods are rationed. In exchange for a voucher (libreta), every Cuban – whether sick, unemployed, a baby or an old person – receives an allocation of monthly rations, which ensure basic subsistence for everyone. »Luxury goods« such as soap and cooking oil, by contrast, are only available in exchange for the »peso convertible« or the euro. In order to mitigate the worst shortages, since autumn 1994 free farmers' markets have been permitted, where meat, fish, vegetables and fruit can be bought for pesos without a rationing voucher.

Agriculture Sugar cane became the Caribbean's most important agricultural product after its introduction to the region by Columbus **sugar cane**. The whole economy was organized around sugar, especially on

Cuba. Sugar was the basis for many other products. For example, its by-product, molasses are used to make the famous Cuban rum, which gains its characteristic colour and aroma from ageing in oak casks and is used for many Cuban cocktails. Bagasse, the fibre that remains after crushing the sugar cane for juice, is used to make paper, cellulose, plywood sheets and now even biofuel.

Although sugar production has fallen steeply since 1990, reaching a historic low in the 2002–03 season with some 2 million tons, it now stands at approximately 2–3 million tons per year. Although most of the crop can be harvested with special machinery that was developed on Cuba, in some places whole fields still have to be harvested laboriously by hand using a machete. The areas of sugar cultivation, like the sugar mills and factories, are scattered across the whole island with the exception of the mountainous terrain in the far west and east.

On Cuba, Columbus discovered not only tobacco, but also the cigar. **Tobacco** The Indios smoked tobacco either by inhaling through a pipe or rolling the uncut leaves to make »tabacos«, cigar-like rolls. Smoking soon became fashionable in Europe and made tobacco cultivation a profitable business for Spanish settlers on Cuba.

To this day, tobacco, or the famous Havana cigar, represents the most important sector of the economy after tourism, on the same level as sugar and nickel. In order to achieve higher profits, even Fidel Castro, who once himself had a passion for smoking, resorted to capitalist methods, beginning to sign boxes of valuable cigars which fetched extremely high prices at auctions, usually from Americans.

On Cuba, tobacco is cultivated on an area of about 70,000 ha/170,000 acres, for the most part by small farmers working for themselves. Growing and harvesting are labour-intensive activities, carried out with great care to ensure high quality. The principal areas of tobacco cultivation lie in the west and the centre of Cuba. After the harvest, tobacco is sorted and dried in sheds. The tobacco-processing industry is mainly based in the Havana region, in the centre of the island and in the Holguín region (►Baedeker Special p. 310).

> **? DID YOU KNOW ...?**
>
> ■ ... that Cuba gained a place in the *Guinness Book of Records* with a 14m/46ft-long cigar? Cigar maker José Castelar, who produced this specimen in 2002, had already set an official record the previous year with a cigar measuring 11m/36ft. Tobacco production is an important source of foreign currency (approx. 200 million US $), but Fidel Castro gave up smoking in 1989 on medical advice. Since early 2005 smoking has been banned in Cuba in public buildings, cinemas, theatres etc ...

Tourism has now displaced sugar as the **leading sector of the economy**. Following steady growth since the mid-1970s, tourism has enjoyed a genuine boom since the early 1990s, with a rise not only in income (in 2005 some 2.2 billion US $) and employment but also in   **Tourism**

A WINNING EXPORT

Genuine Havana cigars are sought-after all over the world. All cigars made in Cuba, over 150 million per year, are marketed exclusively by the state-run Habanos S.A., which has 30% of the world market in »puros«, premium cigars (Baedeker Special, p. 310).

The cigar
Every cigar, whether machine-made or rolled by hand, consists of three parts:

① Filler
The composition of the filler is the secret behind the taste of the cigar, the work of the blender. This is why the filler consists of whole leaves taken from all parts of the plant. The upper leaves have a heavier taste because they are oilier, the leaves from the middle are lighter, and the lower ones have hardly any taste but burn well. The essential difference between hand-made and machine-made cigars is that instead of whole leaves, chopped leaves are used in machine production.

② Binder
The binder (»capote«) has to be tear-resistant in order to hold the filler together.

③ Wrapper
The wrapper (»capa«) presents the cigar. It has to be smooth and the colour, which can vary of course from one brand to another, must be uniform.

Size and shape
The length and ring gauge (diameter) of a cigar determine its size and shape. The length is measured in inches or millimetres, the ring gauge in 64ths of an inch. A cigar with a ring gauge of 43 therefore measures 43/64 of an inch in diameter.
This results in a host of variations: there are no less than 60 different cigar formats. Concentrating on the most usual formats reduces the number to about 20, of which the Gran Corona (235mm, ring gauge 47) is the longest, the Pyramid (156mm, ring gauge 52) the fattest and the Panetela (114mm, ring gauge 26) the thinnest. Cuban cigars are limited to ten different formats.

The tobacco plant
Cuban tobacco farmers divide the plant into a lower section, a middle section and the tip. Leaves from the lower part to the middle are used for wrappers, as they burn best. Leaves from the upper middle part are used as binders. The filler consists of leaves from all parts of the plant. The leaves are harvested from bottom to top at intervals of about a week, and are all classified by special terms:

④ Libra de Pie
»The foot«

⑤ Uno y medio
»One and a half«

⑥ Centro ligero
»Light centre«

⑦ Centro fino
»Fine centre«, the best leaves

⑧ Centro gordo
»Fat middle«

⑨ Semi coronas
»Almost the tip«

⑩ Coronas
»The tip«

Tobacco harvest

The band is not a Cuban invention but was the idea of a Dutch cigar dealer named Gustav Bock, who wanted to distinguish between different brands. Whether it is removed or not makes no difference to the taste.

? DID YOU KNOW ...?

■ The Cohiba, the most exclusive of all Havanas, is a child of the revolution. It was Che Guevara himself who proposed producing a post-revolutionary cigar of unprecedented quality. It was then created by Avelino Lara, the best cigar-maker on the island. The secret of the Cohiba is that its makers have first choice of the leaves from every harvest, the leaves are fermented for 18 months, and only the best cigar rollers are allowed to lay their hands on them.

© Baedeker

visitor numbers, which have now reached about 2 million per year. **The touristic hubs**, apart from the capital Havana, are the long beaches in Varadero and the surroundings of Cienfuegos on the south coast, Trinidad and Santiago de Cuba. A tourist infrastructure has however spread over the whole island, especially on the coast and some islands.

Expansion of tourism ► In accordance with its importance as the leading source of foreign currency, tourism is promoted more than any other branch of the Cuban economy. Most **joint-venture projects** are connected with tourism, and have resulted in successful collaborations. New holiday resorts have been built and new tourist attractions created. In doing so, the renovation of old houses and hotels, many of which have a long tradition, is not neglected. Efforts are being made to restrict tourism to certain suitable areas, peninsulas and islands (e.g. Varadero, Cayo Coco and Cayo Largo). This is intended to mask the **economic and social discrepancies between the world inhabited by the tourists and everyday life on Cuba**. In many cases only a small number of monitored persons and employees have access to the tourist centres. Employment in the tourist sector is in great demand, even among graduates, as it offers good salaries and opportunities to access coveted goods.

The other side of the coin The average Cuban can only get hold of vital foreign currency (euros or pesos convertibles; CUC) by means of a job in tourism or black-market dealing, through relatives in exile or prostitution. The prostitutes are medical students or doctors, musicians or librarians – **nowhere in the world is the level of education among prostitutes higher than in Cuba**. Most Cubans officially earn an average monthly salary of 250 pesos cubanos, the practically worthless »moneda nacional« – this is equivalent to about US $10 or CUC 15, and doesn't even cover the cost of a good pair of jeans. In Cuba almost all manufactured goods have to be paid for in pesos convertibles or euros: lipstick, shampoo or chocolate bars, Cuban »Tropi-Cola« or a trip by taxi. There is a good deal of occasional prostitution, or alternatively just offering an escort or entertainment for tourists, in return for a few pesos convertibles and a smart new dress from a hotel boutique for the otherwise unaffordable price of US $70.

In 1999 the socialist state took strict measures against prostitution, which was increasing as tourism boomed: »jineteras«, as sex workers are known, face a spell in a re-education camp in the country and up to 20 years imprisonment if caught repeatedly. In private accommodation (casas particulares), no mixed foreign-Cuban couple can stay overnight officially unless they produce a marriage certificate.

These measures had clearly become necessary as the number of prostitutes working in cities and beach resorts conspicuously rose, the first cases of child molestation by holiday-makers became

Vital for the Cuban economy: tourism and cigars

known and finally a Mexican travel agency quite openly marketed »sex trips« to the island. In a television address, Fidel Castro condemned the »antisocialist behaviour« of the many families who were said to be selling their daughters.

The marriage market, too, is booming: families with young daughters will pay out US $ 5000 in order to marry them to an unknown Mexican, Canadian or European so that they can leave the country by legal means (Peruvians are cheaper at a reported US $ 1000). The longest queue of nubile »mulatas« is said to be the one outside the Italian embassy.

◄ Marriage market

History

Since its discovery, Cuba's history has been dominated by the interests of foreign powers. The islands of the Greater Antilles, whose lush vegetation and pleasant climate seemed to offer ideal conditions for living, soon became coveted goods. Influence from abroad led to continuous and changing dependence, which has made self-determination difficult to this day.

Pre-Columbian Cuba

| approx. 2000 BC | Settlement on the island by Guanahatabey Indians |
| approx. AD 300 | The Taínos are dominant on Cuba |

The first **settlement of the island** for which archaeological evidence exists was the arrival of the Guanahatabey Indians, whose culture is little known. They are thought to have led a nomadic existence in caves near the coast and to have possessed primitive tools and weapons made from shells or stone. Spanish colonists found only a few members of the tribe in the extreme west of Cuba, especially on the peninsula of Guanahacabibes, which is named after them.

Guanahatabey

The more advanced Ciboney came from the region that is now Venezuela. As this originally numerous Indian people had astonishingly well-built canoes, they settled the Antilles little by little, making tools from stone and living in caves, or sometimes extremely simple huts. Originally the Ciboney were **hunters and gatherers**, learning about agriculture and making pottery from the culturally superior Taínos, who later displaced them from most Caribbean islands. However, on Cuba a small number of Ciboney held on until the Spanish conquest in the west and centre, in places as a mixed society.

Ciboney

The Taínos, who are thought to have come from northern South America, took over on Cuba, as they did on the neighbouring islands of Hispaniola (today Haiti) and Jamaica, from AD 300. In addition to their knowledge of crafts and agriculture, they brought with them **distinctive religious cults** and social structures. Around 1450 saw a second wave of immigration by more advanced Taínos, who settled in the east of Cuba.

Taínos

As hunters and fishermen, the Taínos used weapons and nets, and made the large **sea-going canoes** that the Spanish so admired. They cultivated sweet potatoes (»boniato«), maize, manioc (»yuca«) and pineapples, as well as cotton and tobacco. Their huts consisted of corner posts with woven walls and roofs, and were grouped around the circular caney, the hut of the cacique (chief). This style of building can still be found In rural areas of Cuba.

The craft skills of the Taínos found expression in the production of specialized tools and body ornaments of wood, ceramics and metal. They were able to work with, though not to smelt, gold, from which they made earrings and nose rings. The Taínos succeeded in using manioc as a foodstuff by developing a special press to remove the poisonous juice.

← *When the US ship »Maine« sank off Havanna in 1898 for unknown reasons the USA occupied the island; Spain was quickly defeated.*

Smoking tobacco, which was supposed to lead to a trance-like state, was an expression of their religious cults, as were ball games, music and dancing. Tobacco leaves were also inhaled directly into the nose using tubes or ceramic pipes, a custom that the Spanish at first rejected, but later adopted themselves. Further survivals to the present day are the bohío huts, the hammock, a number of musical instruments and the word »hurricane«, originally the name of a god who brought destruction.

Discovery and Conquest

1492	Columbus discovers America.
1512	Diego Velázquez founds Baracoa, the first Cuban town.
1553	Havana becomes the capital.
1700	Tobacco becomes the main product for export; establishment of the sugar industry.

Discovery by Columbus

Christopher Columbus is regarded as the first European to have discovered America. On 28 October 1492 he set foot on the northeast coast of Cuba. Believing he had found a large island off India, he claimed possession of it in the name of the king of Spain and named it »Juana« in honour of the heir to the throne.

Columbus was fascinated by the vegetation of the island, its variety of trees, exotic fruit and birds. As well as its beauty, he praised the large number of natural harbours, the navigable rivers and the peaceful nature of the Indians. Their modest gold jewellery led him to expect greater deposits of gold and he also hoped to find spices and other valuable raw materials.

After staying for several weeks to explore, Columbus left Cuba in November 1492, returning to Spain after discovering further islands. From there he set off in September 1493 on a second voyage that was intended to secure and exploit the islands. During this and the two succeeding voyages, the Spanish did set foot on Cuba, yet it was spared their aggressive land claims at first, as they initially settled on the neighbouring island of Hispaniola.

Conquest by Velázquez

When conquistador Diego Velázquez was instructed by the Spanish Crown to conquer and exploit Cuba in 1511, about 500,000 Indians were living on the island. Within a few years they were almost completely exterminated by a Spanish force of originally no more than 300 men. As on other Caribbean islands, the **conquest of Cuba was accompanied by needless massacres, rape and the destruction of whole villages.** Many of the Indians who did not commit suicide to escape the cruelty of the Spanish died in the following years from introduced diseases or from starvation and forced labour.

The cacique Hatuey had fled to Cuba from the neighbouring island of Hispaniola after the Spanish conquest there, and reported to the Indians on Cuba about Spanish atrocities. In 1511 he and a small band of followers began to resist, but due to the military superiority of the Spanish he was captured and executed. By 1515 the conquerors had taken the entire island and founded the most important towns: Baracoa, Bayamo, Trinidad, Sancti Spíritus, La Habana (Havana), Puerto Príncipe (Camagüey) and the capital Santiago de Cuba.

◄ Hatuey, the first freedom fighter

Colonial Cuba

In order to settle Cuba, whole swathes of land including their inhabitants were granted to Spanish noblemen and churchmen. These colonial rulers enslaved the Indios, exploiting them mercilessly. Although the Spanish carried on animal husbandry and agriculture, their priority was the **search for gold**. As gold deposits were meagre, however, the gold rush of the early colonial years did not last long.

Colonial exploitation (16th century)

The Dominican monk Bartolomé de Las Casas (1474 – 1566) was one of the few to react to the impending extinction of the Indios. The son of one of Columbus' companions, Las Casas came to Hispaniola in 1502 as a conquistador, initially took part in the war to subjugate the Indios and became a landowner. After being consecrated as a priest in 1508, he became sensitized to the atrocities being carried out against Indians in the guise of conversion to Christianity

◄ Bartolomé de Las Casas

How the discovery of the Americas was once seen:
Indios welcoming Columbus.

■ ... that Cuba itself initiated the end of the era of sugar cane in 2002? That year the government decided to close half of all sugar-cane factories (71 of 156 on the island), following a continuous fall in sugar-cane production from 1990 to 2002, when the harvest (»gran zafra«) reached a historic low of approximately 2 million tons. Cuba was once the world's leading supplier of sugar cane with a volume of up to 8 million tons per year.

though a sermon by the Dominican monk Montesino. During the conquest of Cuba, which he accompanied as a military chaplain, Las Casas became increasingly committed to defending the rights of the Indios. He was the author of many writings that expounded the fundamentals of human rights and the rights of peoples, and spoke out for these in public and at court in Spain. He proposed to transport more resistant black slaves from Africa to the colonies in order to relieve the Indians, in danger of being wiped out, but was later to regret deeply the even more inhuman treatment of the slaves.

Although Las Casas, who was controversial and had enemies, was made bishop of Chiapas in Mexico in 1544, he abandoned his efforts for the cause of human rights in the face of his lack of success, returned to Spain in 1547 and died there in 1566. The many writings and reports he left are regarded to this day as important critical sources on the history of colonization.

Base of the colonial fleet The conquest of further colonies in Latin America lent Cuba strategic importance. **Havana** became the principal base and supply station of the Spanish fleet, a commercial port with the largest harbour in the Caribbean. The town prospered and in **1553 was expanded into a capital city**, while other towns on the island such as Santiago de Cuba, the former capital, sank into decline. However, strict Spanish trading laws restricted the economic growth of Cuba in comparison with other colonies in the region.

Piracy ► Increasing trade and the transport of great riches to and from Havana attracted many pirates, who found suitable hideouts on the islands. They looted and destroyed towns, which the Spanish tried to protect by building fortifications.

To this day, sunken ships and tales of buried gold fire the imagination of many treasure hunters. For example, the Isla de la Juventud (Isla de los Pinos) off the Cuban coast is thought to have been the inspiration for Robert Louis Stevenson's *Treasure Island* – a claim disputed by other Caribbean islands however.

Tobacco and sugar cane Columbus was the first to introduce tobacco and smoking to Europe. Received with suspicion at first as a heathen practice, soon the new cult of smoking spread all over Europe and beyond. Within a short time **an expanding market for tobacco** emerged and became a significant source of revenue for the Spanish Crown thanks to the taxation of tobacco imports.

The Spanish colonies were not only the lands from which tobacco originated, but also possessed a highly advantageous climate and soil, and were able to draw on slave labour: conditions which enabled them to become the world's main producers. In 1717, royal monopolies of cultivation, processing and trade made tobacco the main pillar of the Cuban economy.

However, because of the Spanish monopoly, the price of tobacco in Europe was outrageously disproportionate to the living conditions of the slaves and the income of the Cuban tobacco farmers, who subsisted on the poverty line. This resulted in social discontent and armed uprisings.

Sugar cane was introduced to Cuba immediately after the Spanish conquest, because the climatic conditions seemed favourable. The **extensive cultivation of sugar cane** necessitated great effort and intensive use of labour for harvesting and processing, leading to the enslavement and death of millions of black Africans.

In accordance with the rising demand for labour, in the course of the 17th and 18th centuries the number of **slaves** on Cuba also increased, but slavery did not reach its peak on Cuba until the 19th century, by which time it had already been abolished in other colonies (►Baedeker Special p. 290).

English occupation

The 18th-century conflicts between Europe's great powers in the Old World and their struggle for supremacy in the New World also affected Cuba: in 1762 the island was conquered by Britain following a siege of Havana, then swapped for Florida almost a year later and handed back to Spain.

Industrialization in the 19th century

In 1763 the Spanish permitted trade with North America. After a revolt of slaves in 1791 and the founding of a republic in 1804 in Haiti, the French part of Hispaniola, some 30,000 planters, whites and mulattoes fled from there to Cuba, not only bringing a new plant for cultivation, coffee, but also serving as **a reservoir of labour** for the booming sugar-cane business.

The rapid industrialization of sugar processing, the large number of slaves taken to Cuba each year and the cultivation of greater areas of land raised the **profits of the small upper class** of plantation owners immeasurably. By 1868 Cuba was the world's richest colony.

Social discontent

Whereas almost 30,000 Africans lived in slavery on Cuba in 1760, their numbers rose to over 400,000 by the early 19th century. This rapidly led to growing social discontent. More and more slaves fled to remote mountain areas or organized revolts (1812 and 1844), which failed however. After the official abolition of the slave trade by Britain in 1807 and Spain in 1817, slaves had to be smuggled to Cuba.

The emancipation of slaves as a result of the American Civil War meant that Cuba was isolated in this respect from 1865. Furthermore, dissatisfaction with social ills grew among white Cubans too. Corrupt officials born in Spain were the representatives of a paradoxical colonial system contrasting with the new national identity of the Creoles, Cuban-born descendants of Spanish immigrants.

Liberation Movements and Dependence on the USA

1868 – 1878	First War of Independence
1886	Abolition of slavery
1895 – 1898	Second War of Independence, end of the colonial period, US military rule until 1902
1940 – 1944	First regime of dictator Batista
1952	Establishment of Batista's second dictatorship with the support of the army

First War of Independence (1868 – 1878)

Although Spain was able to hold onto its profitable Cuban colony, in contrast to the loss of its other Latin American colonies, the Spanish rulers lived in fear of the strengthening movement for independence, of revolutionary change and a consequent economic decline.

The first attempt at liberation was made by **Carlos Manuel de Céspedes**. His revolutionary manifesto demanded **independence for Cuba, the emancipation of slaves and the recognition of human rights** as well as comprehensive free trade. 26,000 rebels, many of them armed only with machetes, had initial successes in the east of Cuba, but then the conflict turned into a guerrilla war, which dragged on until 1878 under Antonio Maceo and Máximo Gómez. Despite the **defeat of the rebels**, the emergence of Cuban national feeling can be considered a success of this uprising.

Second War of Independence (1895 – 1898)

A circle around Maceo, exiled in America, became the seed of the Second War of Independence, which was also to be the last anti-colonial war in Latin America. The thoughts and works of **José Martí** underpinned the independence movement in political terms. Martí demanded true freedom, including freedom from other powers such as the USA, and a return to Cuba's own traditions.

Although Martí was killed at the very start of the fighting in May 1895, he is regarded in Cuba to this day as the »apostle of freedom« and the man who paved the way for revolution. The rebels were soon fighting in all parts of the island, but their lack of supplies and poor armaments again denied them a final victory. The revolutionaries controlled the interior, Spanish forces the towns.

As various attempts by the USA to buy the island from Spain had been unsuccessful, the USA eventually decided to intervene. Under the pretext of protecting US property, in 1898 the cruiser *Maine* was sent to Havana and sank there following an explosion, for reasons that have never been ascertained. The USA used this as an excuse to occupy the island, defeating Spain within four months.

Occupation by the USA

In 1898 the colonial era ended on Cuba, to be **replaced until 1902 by US military rule**. During this period the USA incorporated Cuba into its sphere of interests. Spanish industrialists who were engaged in the tobacco and sugar industries, as well as leading merchants joined forces with American companies, many of which established branches in Cuba and boosted its war-torn economy by opening up new markets in the US. However, purchases of land and investments by US citizens made Cuba ever more dependent. The **Platt Amendment** to

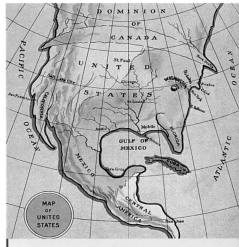

»*I've had my eye on this tasty morsel for a long time …*«, as the cover of the American magazine »*Judge*« stated in 1895.

the constitution of the USA, passed in 1901 by Congress, declared that the USA had a right to military intervention to »protect the government and the independence of Cuba«. This and the lease of the **Guantánamo military base** formed the basis for the USA to enforce its position on Cuba. A hundred years later, the US used its extra-territorial base in Cuba following the attacks of 11 September 2001 to hold 600 prisoners, mainly from the Arab world – alleged Taliban fighters and members of Al Qaida – who for years didn't have (and still don't have) access to legal counsel.

The Pseudo-Republic (1902 – 1959)

The republic that was proclaimed to be an independent Cuba in 1902 can only be described as a pseudo-republic until 1959, as it was subject to **political and economic domination by the USA**. The US ambassador ruled the country together with presidents who were American puppets (Palma, Gómez, Menocal and Zayas); corruption, fraud and violence undermined democratic principles.

Cuba under US control

The extent of economic dependence was such that the sugar industry, railways and mining on Cuba were controlled by American firms. The **sugar boom** from 1914 to 1918, a result of the fall in

Guerrilla forces led by Fidel Castro aiming to topple the dictator Batista hid out in the Sierra Maestra mountains in 1957.

European production of sugar beet during the First World War, triggered the »dance of the millions«, bringing untold wealth to the sugar barons and making the divide between extremely rich and extremely poor social classes even greater. American investments intensified the monoculture of sugar plantations. With its trade deficit, Cuba was hit particularly hard by the world economic crisis and the fall in sugar prices during the 1920s.

Dictatorships under Machado and Batista (1924 – 1959)

Worsening social conditions in the 1920s, and fear on the part of wealthy Cubans and the USA that unrest and revolts would result, paved the way for dictatorship.

Gerardo Machado, who earned the nickname of »butcher« during his term of office from 1924 to 1933, led a **bloody reign of terror,** accompanied by political repression and social exploitation. In 1933, with the support of the American special ambassador, he left the country following a general strike, taking the contents of Cuba's state treasury with him.

After a 30-day interim presidency, a military coup put Fulgencio Batista in power for the next 26 years. Officially, Cuba was ruled by the president, but real power lay in the hands of Batista, the **supreme commander of the armed forces**. He made sure that American interests were served. During his own periods of office from 1940 to

1944 and 1952 to 1959 he accumulated wealth for himself and set up a totalitarian state. Opposition was banned and a gigantic web of spies controlled the country. Corruption, gangsters, arbitrary rule and up to 600,000 unemployed marked the life of the country. Two worlds that were poles apart met on Cuba: on the one hand, a holiday paradise where rich Americans took their pleasures with fine houses, luxury hotels and prostitution – on the other a Cuba marred by poverty, repression and unemployment.

The Cuban Revolution

1953	Attack on the Moncada Barracks
1959	Victory of the Cuban Revolution
1962	Cuban missile crisis, USA declares a total economic embargo
From 1980	The economic situation deteriorates

The Cuban Revolution

The history of the Cuban Revolution began on 26 July 1953 with the defeat of a rebel group that attempted to storm the Moncada Barracks in Santiago de Cuba. A chain of unfortunate circumstances thwarted the small band of poorly equipped revolutionary students and intellectuals, who included the 27-year-old **Fidel Castro Ruz**. The survivors were put on trial, a public platform which Castro used to hold a plea in defence that became famous: »History will acquit me.« His next stop, however, was the prison island Isla de los Pinos (now Isla de la Juventud) and exile in Mexico after an amnesty in 1955. In Mexico, along with other opposition members including his brother Raúl, and the Argentinean doctor Ernesto »Che« Guevara, he founded the **»Movement of 26 July«**, the cradle of the Cuban Revolution, named after the date of the Moncada Barracks attack.

Revolutionary movement

On 2 December 1956, the old, overloaded, leaky yacht *Granma* took 82 inadequately armed revolutionaries ashore in the east of Cuba. Most of them were killed by government troops. Only twelve of them, including Che Guevara and the Castro brothers, succeeded in fighting their way through to the Sierra Maestra, where little by little they found support among the peasants. In 1957, resistance to the Batista regime grew across the island. In the following year, when Batista tried to stamp out the rebel movement with military force that was also turned on the civilian population, the time had come for a nationwide revolution.

Fall of the Batista regime

The number of »guerrilleros« guerrilla fighters increased, many soldiers defected from the army, the presidential elections of November 1958 were boycotted, and the revolutionaries were able to conquer the island from east to west. On New Year's Eve, Batista fled with state funds and a general strike prevented the army from taking power. The climax of the Cuban Revolution came when **revolutionaries under Fidel Castro triumphantly entered Havana** on 8 January 1959.

Reforms under Castro

As head of government Fidel Castro first of all emphasized the social character of the Revolution. The first actions of his government were to reduce rents, start a programme of housing construction, introduce social insurance and take measures against racial discrimination.

Over the course of the following years a large-scale literacy campaign and an extensive free health and education system raised the country to a level that could stand comparison in these fields with standards

The invasion of Cuba planned by US secret services was a failure: the anti-Castro Cuban exiles who landed in the Bay of Pigs in 1961 were taken prisoner.

in the world's most developed states. The real core of the changes, however, was **land reform**, which confiscated the estates of big land-owners and leased the land free of charge to agricultural labourers.

Land reform affected a small class of rich Cubans, and above all American citizens who had invested on Cuba or bought property at low prices. The USA applied pressure by reducing sugar imports. Cuba responded by turning to new trade partners such as the Soviet Union and China. When American oil refineries on Cuba refused to process crude oil supplied from the Soviet Union, they were expropriated by the Cuban government.

From then onwards, **see-saw policies** characterized Cuban-American relations, culminating in 1960 in a trade embargo imposed by the USA. Many intellectuals, as well as the economic and academic elite, left the island and formed influential circles in Florida, from where they continue to play a major role in shaping American policy towards Cuba to this day.

Confrontation with the USA

In the years immediately after the revolution, **antirevolutionary actions** took place repeatedly on Cuba, and contra groups supported by the USA held out in some areas. In 1961 1500 Cuban exiles and mercenaries, guided by the CIA and massively supported by the US Air Force and Navy, landed in Cuba at the Bay of Pigs.

Although certainly inferior in terms of technology, the Cubans repulsed the invasion within a mere three days. The result of this debacle was that the USA imposed **a total commercial embargo** in 1962 that still applies today. Cuba responded by moving closer to the Soviet Union, and in 1962 Castro proclaimed that Cuba was a socialist state.

Bay of Pigs Invasion

In April 1962 Khrushchev stationed medium-range nuclear missiles in Cuba – capable of hitting any target in the USA, only 150km/95mi away as the crow flies. President John F. Kennedy put in place a naval blockade against Soviet ships on 22 October 1962, and **for 13 days, the world held its breath**. When Kennedy made assurances in a secret agreement not to invade Cuba and to withdraw missiles from Turkey, Khrushchev removed the nuclear warheads from Cuba. The world had never come so close to nuclear war. In 2000 the American director Roger Donaldson made these dramatic events into a film entitled *Thirteen Days*, starring Kevin Costner as an adviser to Kennedy.

Cuban missile crisis

Socialist Cuba

The alignment of Cuba with socialist countries under the leadership of the Soviet Union initially brought economic growth to the island, but soon resulted in new dependencies. Sugar, the island's principal export, was bought in planned quotas at subsidized prices, in return

New dependency

for which the Soviet Union supplied cheap crude oil that not only covered Cuba's own needs but could also be resold at a profit. A new **planned economy based on the Soviet model** was introduced – and soon showed the symptoms of socialist economic mismanagement.

1970s and 1980s
In the 1970s it proved impossible to achieve the aim of a super-harvest bringing in 10 million tons of sugar, the »gran zafra«), although all resources were mobilized. After this Cuba turned away from sugar monoculture, expanding other branches of agriculture and industry. The **political realignment** of Cuba was reflected in its membership of the Council for Mutual Economic Assistance (Comecon) in 1972, newly established diplomatic relations and the constitution of 1976 with elected representatives of the people.

The deteriorating economic situation came to a head in 1980 when Cubans wishing to emigrate occupied the Peruvian embassy in Havana. This first major exodus of thousands of Cubans to the USA was followed by further emigration, which Castro used as a means of getting rid of unwanted persons. Rationing and the continued repression of any opposition showed that the **situation was increasingly critical**.

1990s: »Período especial« and boom on Cuba

1995–96	The US intensify economic sanctions.
1997	Transfer of the mortal remains of Che Guevara to Cuba
2000	Relaxation of the US commercial embargo
2003	Severe prison sentences for 75 critics of the regime
2004	The US dollar is replaced by the peso convertible and euro.

Economic crisis and new trade partners
The collapse of the Soviet bloc had a drastic effect on Cuba. The guaranteed markets for sugar and oil imports that were vital to the island fell away. The already **crisis-ridden economy** deteriorated fast due to a rapidly increasing shortage of foreign currency and the trade deficit. The consequences were rationing, power cuts, shortages of fuel and disrupted production. Domestic political developments such as the **constitutional reform of 1991** and the first direct elections in 1993 were signs of change. Furthermore, the conditions that had to be met for emigration were relaxed and the proclamation of a »período especial« was an appeal to the people to hold out.

Although since 1993 Cubans had been permitted to own dollars privately, and free farmers' markets run as private businesses improved

In 1994, tolerated by the government, 30,000 Cubans left the country in home-made boats, marking the peak of the wave of emigration.

the supply situation, in summer 1994 a **mass flight to Florida took place**. Embarking in home-made boats that were mostly unseaworthy, thousands of Cubans tried to cross over to the USA. Those who made it were first interned, then taken back to Cuba to the American naval base at Guantánamo.

Hoping to speed up the collapse of its worn-out socialist neighbour, the USA stepped up sanctions in 1995. The **Helms-Burton Act** of 1996, which attracted much criticism, stipulated sanctions against those who made foreign investments on Cuba. However, it has never taken effect in law. Pope John Paul II made a clear statement against American sanctions when he visited Cuba in January

Ry Cooder made their music famous, and Wim Wenders honoured the stars of Cuban son musician in his film »Buena Vista Social Club«.

1998. Castro based his policy on strengthening trade with Central and South America and liberalizing the economy, especially by means of joint ventures in tourism.

Tourism on Cuba

In 1996 the American musician Ry Cooder flew to Havana to make recordings with the great Cuban stars of the past. The recording of the Afro-Cuban All Stars under the name **Buena Vista Social Club** not only garnered a coveted Grammy award, but also brought a large number of other productions in its wake. The documentary film of the same name by director Wim Wenders also contributed to the success. Thanks to the marketing of romantic son and groovy salsa, rum and cigars, beautiful beaches and lovely women, with a pinch of romantic revolution thrown in, Cuba boomed as a destination for sun-seekers on package holidays and independent tourists from all over the world looking for an adventure.

In 1997 the mortal remains of **Che Guevara** and six of his comrades were found in Bolivia and taken to Cuba to be interred in Santa Clara.

On 25 November 1999 the six-year-old Cuban **refugee Elián González** was pulled out of the sea. His mother had drowned off the coast of Florida while trying to flee from Cuba. The ensuing tug-of-war between relatives living in the USA and the boy's father on Cuba led to a months-long conflict between Fidel Castro, the American judicial authorities and the Cuban exiles' opposition in Miami.

Cuba in the New Millennium: Signs of Hope?

At the start of the new millennium, even relations with the USA showed signs of returning to normal: in 2000 the US Senate decided to **relax its commercial embargo**, and after severe damage done by Hurricane Michelle Cuba imported food from the USA in 2001 for the first time since the 1960s – a development which President George W. Bush blocked again, as he regarded Cuba as part of the »axis of evil«, and almost as bad as Iraq and North Korea. Despite this some half a million Cubans applied for a visa to enter the USA (20,000 were approved).

Socialism enshrined in the constitution

In May 2002 the Cuban opposition's Varela Project presented a petition with 11,000 signatures to the People's Congress – the first mass protest against the Communist Party, **demanding free elections and freedom of speech**. Castro's reaction was not long in coming: in June 2002 socialism was permanently enshrined in the constitution by the »decision of the people« as »unalterable«. In 2003 Cuban courts sentenced **75 dissidents** for alleged participation in »conspiratorial activities« in the representation of the USA in Havana to long terms in prison, the total sentence reaching 1454 years. One of the prisoners is the well-known journalist and poet Raúl Rivero.

Unusual escape attempts

2002 saw the start of a wave of escapes from Cuba by unconventional methods: one person was found in the undercarriage of a Canadian plane, there were several attempted armed hijacks of planes and ships (e.g. a passenger ferry in Havana), trucks converted into amphibian vehicles that headed for the US coast, and refugees who were abandoned on a tiny Bahaman island by human traffickers. Several people died in the hijacks, and the ship hijackers were executed after summary justice in 2003. In November 2004 51 artistes, dancers and musicians of the Havana Night Club show defected while on tour in Las Vegas. Only two members of the ensemble returned home, and the others were granted asylum in the USA.

Revolutionaries don't retire

Dissidents such as writers and journalists critical of the regime continued to suffer from **repression by state security forces** in the form of house searches and confiscations, defamation as being »mad«, »counter-revolutionary« and »worms« (»gusanos«), bans on working, censorship and long prison sentences. Despite his increasing frailty, Castro held on to power, stating that »revolutionaries don't retire«.

Elián was a pawn in a power game.

However, in 2006 after undergoing an operation for intestinal problems, Castro was too ill to attend the 50th anniversary of the *Granma* boat landing. He handed the post of president to his brother **Raúl Castro** in 2008, and has rarely appeared in public since. Raúl's inaugural speech announced a **process of transition** that would reduce some restrictions on the liberty of the people without abandoning the path of socialism. Raúl replaced some of his brother's closest supporters in order to put his own stamp on the government. Since 2011 there has been a good deal of discussion about economic liberalization, including speculation that private buying and selling of property may be permitted, but little real progress has been made to expand the private economy. The octogenarian leadership fears that economic reform will make it impossible to prevent political change. With the US commercial embargo remaining in place, the Cuban economy lags behind those of its capitalist neighbours.

Raúl Castro

The visit to Cuba of Pope Benedict XVI in March 2012 put the spotlight on a situation that follows old patterns of behaviour. Before arriving in Cuba, Benedict XVI said that Marxism was out of place in the contemporary world and urged Cubans to find »new models«. Raúl Castro nevertheless took the step of meeting the pope, but his vice-president responded by saying that »there will be no political reform in Cuba«. A dissident shouting »Down with the revolution!« as crowds greeted the Pope was arrested, while Cuban exiles from the USA welcomed Benedict XVI by setting off fireworks from a flotilla in the safety of international waters twelve miles from Havana.

Papal visit

Arts and Culture

The architecture typical of Cuba derives from the colonial period: beautiful wrought-iron grilles and wooden window-shutters. The infectious rhythms of Cuban music are part and parcel of life on the island: the sounds of son and salsa come from almost every doorway.

Architecture

While the Indians' round huts (caneyes) disappeared over the centuries, the rectangular type of house, called a bohío, became the prototype of a Cuban farmhouse and agricultural labourer's accommodation. Today, **bohíos** are still common in rural areas. Built from local materials without an upper storey and with a low-reaching roof, they are ideally adapted in terms of appearance and climatic qualities to conditions on the island. The walls consist of panels of palm wood or a kind of half-timbering with woven lianas stretched between the posts and covered with clay.

Indian domestic buildings

Spanish settlers founded towns following a **uniform pattern**, at least in the early decades, with a rectangular open space called Plaza de Armas, Plaza Mayor or simply the plaza forming the centre of colonial towns. This site would hold important public institutions, especially government buildings and places of assembly: a church, the governor's residence, dwellings and commercial buildings. A decree of King Philip II specified exactly what these squares should look like: rectangular in shape, one and a half times as long as wide, in order to provide enough space for public parades and celebrations. Wide boulevards called Paseo or Prado led to the plaza and formed the basis of a grid structure of streets at right angles. As residents preferred to stay out of the sun, houses were built close together with arcades on the ground floor. In the 19th century these **arcaded walks**, which remain a feature of Cuban towns, were built of stone instead of wood.

Colonial period

The prosperity resulting from cultivating sugar cane and tobacco in the late 18th century permitted the construction of many public buildings. Churches were enlarged and adorned in the Spanish Baroque style. Typical examples of this period in Cuban architecture are the church of the Franciscan monastery (1738) and the **cathedral in Havana** with its curving Baroque façade, completed in 1777. In the early 19th century the Baroque style went out of fashion; elements of Renaissance architecture and classical forms such as colonnades or features of ancient temple architecture dominated the design of showcase buildings until well into the 20th century. One of the most original designs is the **Gran Teatro García Lorca** in Havana, where a lively Art Nouveau façade represents a return to Baroque traditions.

Spanish colonists employed stone and bricks of fired clay not only for public buildings and churches, but also for the houses and commercial buildings of landowners, merchants and government officials. The usual model was **the patio house** common in Spain and

Domestic buildings

←*Decorative wrought-iron grilles and railings on façades are a hallmark of the colonial architecture of Trinidad, a World Heritage site.*

other southern European countries. The courtyard (patio), surrounded by three wings with arcades, formed the centre of the estate. Featuring shady plants, it ensured a pleasant climate in the rooms and gave residents the option of being outdoors without showing themselves in public. The arcades connected separate rooms; when they were large enough they were also an agreeable place for the family to spend time and meet, half outdoors and half inside the house.

The whole house presented a closed façade to the street. The tall, heavy wooden doors were opened only for coaches. Otherwise a small door within the gates sufficed as an entrance. On the ground floor the windows, which reached down almost to ground level, were closed by wooden grilles known as barrotes, which were often attached like little bay windows in front of the façade itself. Later, more durable and **skilfully made wrought-iron grilles** became fashionable.

Pastel colours and wooden window-shutters: a typical scene in Santiago de Cuba.

They are as much a characteristic of Cuba as the two-part **wooden window shutters** in the upper storeys of the house (persianas), as high as doors and used to regulate the temperature in the room behind by means of adjustable slats. The semi-circular or rectangular areas above doorways reveal a love of decoration and an opulent variety of forms. In the case of windows with round arches, slats radiate around the semi-circle or – as can frequently be seen in Havana – the semi-circle is filled with a floral pattern of coloured glass (vitrales). In the 16th and 17th centuries, many fine residences were constructed in the **Mudéjar style**. In the period of prosperity at the end of the 18th century more expensive building materials were used, and many houses acquired two or even three storeys. Ostentation was evident both inside and on the façades: marble gateways, decorative tiles on the walls, small balconies in front of the windows and stone balustrades made dwellings into little architectural gems.

As the Cuban population moved from the country into the towns in the 1940s and 1950s, slum quarters sprang up on the urban fringes. The Cuban solution for increasingly urgent housing problems since the early 1970s has been »microbrigadas«, the temporary allocation of some of the employees of large factories for construction work. By the late 1970s some 80,000 flats had been built in this way. At the edge of Havana huge suburbs of uniform, plain-looking prefabricated buildings were raised from nothing within a decade in order to accommodate 100,000 people. As this collective self-help was a success, it was revived after 1986 in a modified form – the difference being now that workers not only built housing for themselves and other employees of their factory, but thanks to the microbrigadas, social projects (e.g. accommodation for the elderly) and communal institutions were completed.

20th century
◄ Microbrigadas

Visual Arts

Painting as an independent art form was not established on Cuba until the early 19th century, when the first art schools were founded: the Academy S. Alejandro in Havana, for example, initiated by the French history painter Jean-Baptiste Vermay (1784 – 1833) in 1818. As was the case in the European academies on which these institutions were modelled, painters concentrated on subjects that fulfilled their patrons' wish for ostentation and thirst for knowledge: portraits, history and mythology. Later, landscape painting and (pleasant) motifs from everyday life became acceptable themes.

The **reception of European avant-garde art** is generally considered the most important driving force behind an artistic reorientation **in the 20th century**, but **revolutionary art from neighbouring Mexico**

Beginnings in the 19th century

Lam's synthesis of European influences and his own roots: The Third World, 1966

also played its part in the rejection of academic tradition by such painters as Amelia Pélez (1896 – 1968), Carlos Enríquez (1900 – 1957), René Portocarrero (1912 – 1985), Mario Carreno (1913 – 1999), Victor Manuel (1897 – 1969) and Wifredo Lam (►below). As in other Latin American countries, the beginnings of modern art on Cuba were closely linked to the emergence of a national identity. Art started looking to its Afro-Cuban and Indo-Cuban roots and started to take an interest in the social situation and to criticize social ills. The most prominent representative of that generation of modern artists, and also the island's best-known painter, is **Wifredo Lam**(1902 – 1982; ► Famous People). In Europe Lam made the acquaintance of the leading Cubist and Surrealist artists, and with them discovered African art. The Cuban Revolution also had an impact on artistic life. A national school of art, the Escuela Nacional de Arte, was founded in Havana, and in provincial cities **peoples' studios** (talleres populares de arte) were established to promote art by non-professional artists.

1980s and 1990s ► A move away from the »fathers« of Cuban art took place in the 1980s, when a legendary exhibition entitled Volumen Uno, organized by the Pintura Fresca group in 1981, caused a furore. For the first time a range of art was shown that was not preoccupied with bowing to the ideals of the revolution but took a critical, proactive and provocative look at the present. This included emancipation from content in favour of conceptual art. In Europe and the USA the rebels of young Cuban art did not attract attention until many of them left Cuba.

Son, Rumba and Salsa

Cuban music arose from a mix of Spanish and African traditions. Spanish colonists brought their own melodies and genres to Cuba, as well as instruments like the guitar and violin. Dance music was especially popular, both in the country and towns, especially the guajira, bolero, zapateo, habanera and danzón.

Spanish and African traditions

With the arrival of the first slaves from Africa, completely different but nevertheless fitting musical elements were added. African songs with lyrics in the Yoruba language were usually accompanied by drums, including the egg-shaped bata. They were played at dances, religious festivals, parades on holidays and during carnival. Over time, African and Spanish music blended, especially after independence and the consequent removal of racial divisions. White musicians played drums and adopted African forms of song, while the trumpet, trombone and piano were integrated into the music of the black population.

The rumba, perhaps the best-known Cuban dance, has African roots and originally served a ritual purpose. It is characterized by syncopated, varied rhythms and a moderately lively to fast tempo. Its start is always signalled by a roll of the claves and a call by the singer, who then improvises. The chorus repeats the refrain as the drummers produce ever more complex rhythms. The dance begins only after this. The three most popular forms of rumba – though with completely different rhythms – are yambú, columbia and guaguancó.

Rumba

In the 1920s son evolved from the dances of black labourers on the sugar-cane plantations. This kind of music is the best symbol of the newly created creole culture, with which blacks and whites could identify equally well. To this day Santiago de Cuba boasts that it is the »cradle of son«, which developed on the east of the island and was taken to Havana by migrant sugar-cane workers. »Sonero Mayor«, the best son musician of all time, was the title awarded to **Benny Moré** (1920 – 1963), the most popular singer in the Caribbean.

Son

? DID YOU KNOW …?

■ … that in the Hospital Psiquiátrico in Havana, professional musicians play for the patients: 79 trained musicians and two conductors – a level of personnel that even cultural institutions in Europe can often only dream of.

He also composed, was a bandleader and lent his own unmistakable touch to every piece of music. He was considered a master of son montuno, the fastest and liveliest genre of son, which is usually played by a large orchestra.

In the 1940s Cuban dance music, especially son, was strongly influenced by **Arsenio Rodríguez**, who performed it with large orchestras

Cuban dance music

using congas, pianos and various wind instruments. In New York in 1947 he caused a sensation with this new style. Many well-known pieces of Latin music, especially salsa, were written by him.

Bandleaders constantly innovated with dance music. Orestes López, for example, transformed danzón into **mambo** by lengthening the pieces and introducing solos for percussion, piano and flute. Mambo was then made famous beyond Cuba by **Dámaso Pérez Prado**, who had enormous success in Mexico and the United States with this style.

The invention of cha-cha-cha is attributed to the bandleader **Enríque Jorrín**. In 1951 Jorrín composed a song by this name, inspired by the sound that dancers' feet made in special, slightly delayed mambo rhythms.

Cha-cha-cha ▶

Filin

Composers such as Ernesto Lecuona began to combine new rhythms with traditional forms of Spanish song. In the 1950s the style known as »filin« (feeling), which was strongly influenced by Nat King Cole, evolved from this.

Trova

The quieter trova, a kind of romantic or political ballad, accompanied only by a guitar, also emerged in the 1940s. This typically Cuban kind of song is still performed in Casas de la Trova, where amateur musicians play together and **everyone is welcome to come and listen**. The most famous of these establishments are in Santiago de Cuba, Sancti Spíritus and Camagüey.

Cuban anthems

In 1967 the North American folk singer Pete Seeger made a recording of the song *Guantanamera*, based on a poem by José Martí and orchestrated by Joseíto Fernández. This made it equally well known in North and Latin America, and brought it back to Cuba. Today this song almost has the status of the island's unofficial anthem.

Carlos Puebla, who died in 1989, was *the* revolutionary singer of Cuba. Puebla's songs, for which he wrote both lyrics and melodies, are strongly influenced by Cuban folk melodies, taking up and varying their typical rhythms, such as guaguancó, son, bolero and guajira. His most famous song is without doubt a hymn to Che Guevara: »Hasta siempre Comandante«, which can often be heard on Cuba.

Nueva trova

In 1967 Cuba's music scene gained new life through the appearance of two singers at a festival: **Pablo Milanés** and **Silvio Rodríguez**, who used their guitars to accompany songs that praised revolutionary Cuba but with a slightly critical attitude. They told stories of love and life, sometimes with a touch of surrealism, and put poetic texts to music. This style, today known as nueva trova, made them known across Latin America and even in Europe. Their songs have now become a part of the national musical heritage; almost all Cubans know them by heart, and they can be heard everywhere on the streets and in bars.

Today people talk of a **second generation** of nueva trova. Its exponents include Carlos Varela, Gerardo Alfonso and Xiomara Laugart.

The dominant music in the nightlife of Havana is however **salsa**, with a catchy beat that has now caught on in the USA and Europe. At venues such as the Palacio de la Salsa, Café Cantante and the garden of the restaurant Cecilia, the leading lights of the salsa scene perform: Los Van Van, Son 14, Manolín – El Médico de la Salsa, Adal-

Never leave home without your double bass: happy musicians on the street are not just a cliché, but reality! No-one is immune to this infectious atmosphere.

❓ DID YOU KNOW ...?

■ ... that Cubans don't dance salsa, but »casino« or »timba«? These are the Cuban names for the hot »sauce« mixed from the basic rhythms of son and mambo, with a touch of rumba and cha-cha-cha. Cubans do not necessarily dance salsa or casino as couples, but as a group dance in a ring: in »rueda de casino« commands are shouted (»Saccala!«, roughly meaning: »get it!«, and »botala« »get rid of it!«) as jointly agreed figures are danced in a circle and partners are whirled around with gusto.

Paulito. Few Cubans are in the audience at their relatively expensive concerts, preferring matinees where admission is paid in pesos.

The blend of styles that is salsa (the word means »hot sauce«) evolved in New York, where homesick Latinos mixed it from the Cuban rhythms of son, rumba, cha-cha-cha, mambo, Dominican merengue and the Puerto Rican plena. Among the founding fathers of salsa, mention must be made of the blind tres player Arsenio Rodríguez, while one of its foremost performers is without a doubt **Celia Cruz**, the »queen of salsa«, with her Sonora Matancera orchestra. Both of these musicians have left the island, but salsa seems to have remained a domain of Cubans, even though new variations with influence from reggae, samba, rock and jazz have emerged.

A dance floor is never hard to find – sometimes it's the street on a balmy summer night.

Film

Since 1979 a big international film festival, the Festival of New Latin American Cinema, has been held each December in Havana, quickly becoming a leading forum for Latin American films. Although fewer international and Latin American guests can be invited nowadays, the film festival remains the most important regional event in the business. Star actors such as Antonio Banderas, directors such as Pedro Almodóvar from Spain, Fernando Solanas from Argentina and Werner Herzog from Germany have made their way to Havana to watch the most significant releases of the year.

Film festival

The financial difficulties that have dogged Cuba ever since the revolution have had a severe impact on the film industry since the 1980s. Whereas the **Cuban film institute** (Instituto Cubano del Arte y Industria Cinematográficos, ICAIC) was able to produce up to 17 films per year during its heyday in the 1960s and 1970s, by the 1980s only two or three could be financed annually, and the institute now functions at best as a co-producer of international film projects. In response the ICAIC has recently sought a role as a provider of services for the cinema business – competing directly with established companies from the USA – to offer staff, development, editing and sound services to Latin American film makers, seemingly with success.

Current situation

In the cinema of the ICAIC, the Cinemateca Charles Chaplin in Havana, however, the programme consists almost entirely of Latin American films. In the foyer, visitors can admire and purchase a byproduct of the movie business: the famous silk-screen-printed film posters displayed here are coveted collectors' items for cineastes.

A film that shaped our view of Cuba: in Wim Wenders' Buena Vista Social Club, Compay Segundo and other aged musicians conquered our hearts with macho charm.

MAKING HARDSHIPS BEARABLE WITH AFRO-CARIBBEAN HUMOUR

»Committed cinema means cinema that isn't perfect«: this was the motto of the father of post-revolutionary Cuban film, Julio Garcia Espinoza. This led to the evolution of a cinematic vocabulary that was a counterweight to technically perfect North American films.

By means of creativity and imagination, Cuban film makers were able to compensate their viewers for many technical shortcomings. The generation of directors that made Cuban films globally famous set itself the aim of defining an authentic national cinema that was grounded in the themes and goals of Cuban reality. For these cineastes, several of whom had fought in Castro's rebel armies, the focus lay on contributing to the establishment of socialism by cinematic means. In this way a number of documentary films on contemporary issues were made, especially in the 1960s and 1970s, which gained international recognition. For example *Hanoi, Tuesday 13th* by Santiago Álvarez (1966), a film about the history and situation of Vietnam that won multiple awards, or Pastor Vega's *The Fifth Border* (1973).

By means of creativity and imagination, Cuban filmmakers were able to compensate their viewers for many technical shortcomings. The genera-

tion of directors that made Cuban films globally famous set itself the aim of defining an authentic national cinema that was grounded in the themes, struggles and achievements of Cuban reality. For these cineastes, several of whom had fought in Castro's rebel armies, the focus lay on contributing to the establishment of socialism by cinematic means.

In this way a number of documentary films on contemporary issues were made, especially in the 1960s and 1970s, which gained international recognition. *Hanoi, Tuesday 13th* by Santiago Álvarez (1966), for example, was a film about the history and situation of Vietnam that won multiple awards. Another notable example was Pastor Vega's *The Fifth Border* (1973).

In contrast to Russian and some other East European films, which also had a strong political motivation, satire and irony that did not spare their own regime became a hallmark of the work of Cuban directors as early as

the 1960s. In *Death of a Bureaucrat* (1966), Tomás Gutiérrez Alea has the dominance of bureaucracy and the personality cult in his sights. Other films such as *A Day in November* (1972) by Humberto Solás and *The Adventures of Juan Quinquin* (1967) by Julio García Espinoza take a humorous look at the challenges of everyday life in Cuba.

Of course the range of themes explored by Cuban directors is just as broad as in other countries. Love, passion, suffering, murder and persecution are all part of the mix. Women defend themselves against repression by their macho husbands, children dream of castles in the air, doctors fight to save their patients' lives and armies repel attacks by the enemy. However, the storyline is seldom presented as a pure drama, and ironic sideswipes at the reality of socialist everyday life are almost always included.

Treading a narrow path

In the 1980s, however, things went remarkably quiet in the Cuban film world. The reasons for this, alongside the political and financial chaos of the time, undoubtedly lay in a degree of uncertainty among Cuban intellectuals about how much freedom they had to do as they pleased. After many years when Cuban moviemakers were treated like stars at international festivals, in this decade hardly any of their films succeeded in reaching beyond the borders of their country for screenings abroad. The first film that attracted international attention again was the comedy *Alice in Wondertown* (1991) by Daniel Diáz Torres, one of the few directors who are able to make films in which irony and subtle humour express the absurdity of normal Cuban life – above all in times of financial and political difficulties. In Havana the film was booed at its premiere and then not shown for years until finding its way onto the international market.

With two humorous films that were critical of the system, the director Tomás Gutiérrez Alea (1928 – 1996) made Cuban cinema a talking point around the world once again. *Strawberry and Chocolate* (1993), made like *Guantanamera* with his friend and colleague Juan Carlos Tabío (1994), seems at first to be a bizarre gay comedy, but then turns out to be a many-layered description of the state of socialist Cuba and finishes with a plea for cultural and sexual tolerance. The story is told in an amusing way and leaves a lot of scope for impressions of everyday Cuba: decaying houses in Havana, shortages on the peso market and the variety of goods on the dollar market, signs of Afro-Cuban religion in the enlightened socialism of the 1990s. *Strawberry and Chocolate* and *Guantanamera*, also an open, almost sarcastic critique of the excesses of bureaucracy on the island, heralded a new era in Cuba film policy that speaks more of liberalism and openness than of narrow-minded dogmatism.

What is in demand abroad is above all clichés about Cuba: the Hollywood version of the revolution (*Havana* by Sydney Pollack, ► below) or the wave of music films in the wake of Wim Wenders' *Buena Vista Social Club* (► below). Here is a small selection of the internationally best-known films about Cuban themes. *Our Man in Havana* (USA, 1959, directed by Carol Reed): A famous spy film, a classic based on Graham Greene's novel of the same name, with Alec Guinness playing the English vacuum-cleaner salesman Jim Wormold, who makes up espionage reports in order to satisfy the insatiable demands of the British secret service in Havana. *Havana* (USA, 1990, directed by Sydney Pollack): in a dramatic love story from the last days of the Batista regime, Robert Redford plays an American gambler who tries to win

the beautiful wife (Lena Olin) of a guerrilla fighter. The revolution from Hollywood's point of view – but still worth seeing.

Strawberry and Chocolate (*Fresay y Chocolate*, Cuba 1993, directed by Tomás Gutiérrez Alea): this film gained more attention than any other by the famous Cuban director, won several international awards, and was even nominated for an Oscar. It is a comedy about the encounter between David, a young party cadre, and Diego, who is gay, a story of discrimination against homosexuals and tolerance in Cuba. The scenes where it was filmed in Havana, including the Coppelia ice-cream park and the La Guarida paladar, have become cult sites for foreign visitors.

Guantanamera (Cuba 1993–94, directed by Tomás Gutiérrez Alea): A comedy about an absurd attempt to transport a corpse from Guantánamo to Havana and the truly crazy bureaucratic obstacles to the endeavour.

Buena Vista Social Club (Germany 1999, directed by Wim Wenders): the most famous film of recent times about Cuba. The American musician Ry Cooder and the German film director Wim Wenders scored a global success and triggered a boom in Cuba tourism with this wonderful portrait of a traditional band of elderly musicians. It was followed up by the

Havana Centro, Calle Concordia no. 418 is the film set. Tomás Guttiérrez Alea's Oscar-nominated »Strawberry and Chocolate« was made here – in its own way an advertisement for tourism.

French production *Cuba Son* in 2001. Other music films about Cuba: *Lágrimas Negras* (Cuba 1997) and *Havana Girl Orchestra* (1991) about the legendary female band Anacaona. *Waiting List* (*Lista de Espera*, Cuba, Spain, France, Mexico, Germany 2000, directed by Juan Carlos Tabío): a multinational co-production that paints a superb picture of the condition of the transport system in Cuba. Travellers get stuck in a bus station in Granma province in the east of the island – brilliant satire based on real life.*Havana, mi amor* (Germany 2000, directed by Uli Gaulke): The everyday life of Habaneros with all its pitfalls. A sensitive documentary film about loving and being loved, loneliness and abandonment, telenovelas and broken Russian TV sets.

Playing Swede (*Hacerse el Sueco*, Cuba, Spain, Germany 2000, directed by Daniel Díaz Torres): A man purporting to be a Swedish tourist in Havana robs tourists and finally even the Habaneros themselves. A madcap comedy starring many well-known Cuban actors.

Before Night Falls (USA 2000, directed by Julian Schnabel): the eponymous novel (1993) by Reinaldo Arenas (1943 – 1990) relates the life and troubles of the homosexual author in Cuba. Arenas' books are banned in Cuba, and the author died of AIDS in the USA. This biopic, with Johnny Depp playing a double role, was nominated for an Oscar.

Comandante (USA 2003, directed by Oliver Stone): Oliver Stone was permitted to accompany the Cuban head of state for three days. His portrait of Fidel Castro is controversial, as Stone's attitude to Castro is not particularly critical in their talks about politics and power, enemies and women. For this reason the film was not distributed in the USA.

Música cubana – The Next Generation (Germany 2004, directed by German Kral): A musical journey to Cuba, following up-and-coming musicians on their way to stardom.

The Motorcycle Diaries (USA, Germany, Argentina, Great Britain 2004, directed by Walter Saller): Che Guevara is portrayed as the rather naïve and spoiled medical student Ernesto on a nine-month motorbike tour of the South American continent, which first made him aware of the social misery of Latin America and later turned him into Che the revolutionary. The film, impressive not only for its landscape photography, is based on Guevara's diaries.

Barrio Cuba (Cuba 2005, directed by Humberto Solás): seven Habaneros in search of love, with a musical accompaniment that includes the famous Cuban salsa band Los Van Van.

Famous People

People who fought for their country, without exception: Carpentier with the pen, Lam with the paint brush, Quirot on the athletics track, the martyr Che Guevara with armed force, and last not least the untiring Fidel Castro.

Alejo Carpentier (1904 – 1980)

A writer of Russian-French descent born in Havana, Carpentier is one of the greats of Latin-American literature and an exponent of magic realism. Carpentier lived in Paris from 1928 to 1939, became professor of music history in Havana and later worked as a journalist in Venezuela. After the revolution he returned to Cuba and became director of the state publishing house.

Novelist and essayist

As a novelist and essayist Carpentier succeeded in painting an expressive picture of life in the Caribbean region. His most significant work, *El siglo de las luces*, (*Explosion in a Cathedral*), which gained him a nomination for the Nobel Prize for Literature, describes the effects of the French Revolution in the Caribbean. Further well-known books by Carpentier are *The Kingdom of this World*, *Baroque Concerto* and *The Harp and the Shadow*. Although he openly espoused the revolution and was used as an advertisement for the new Cuba, he never signed up to a literary doctrine and remained true to his own way of portraying the workings of society and politics. Carpentier died in Paris on 24 April 1980 at the age of 75.

Novels about society and politics

Fidel Castro Ruz (born 1926)

The legendary leader of the Cuban Revolution was born in Mayarí and was already politically active in his student days. When Fulgencio Batista y Zaldívar carried out a coup in 1952 and established a dictatorship in Cuba, Castro decided to work with like-minded allies to bring about his downfall. The **attack on the Moncada Barracks** in Santiago de Cuba on 26 July 1953 led to Castro's arrest. Two years later in Mexico he organized the Movement of 26 July. On 2 December 1956 Castro landed on Cuba with a guerrilla force. After suffering heavy losses in battles against Batista's troops, he and eleven remaining supporters – including his brother Raúl and Che Guevara – withdrew to the remote Sierra Maestra and continued their struggle from there. At the end of 1958 Batista left the country.

Head of state and party

> **?** DID YOU KNOW …?
>
> ■ … that Fidel Castro has even made a triumphant entry into the *Guinness Book of Records*? The longest speech ever made to the United Nations General Assembly on 29 September 1960 lasted for four hours and 29 minutes!

As prime minister of Cuba from 1959 and máximo líder (supreme leader), Fidel Castro Ruz was able to consolidate his power. After the invasion in the Bay of Pigs (1961) he declared Cuba a socialist republic and established a dictatorship based on the Soviet model, re-

← *The heroes of the revolution are part and parcel of Cuban everyday life.*

The tireless Comandante – always serving the revolution

formed education with a literacy campaign and introduced a planned economy in association with far-reaching agricultural reform. The big American companies that had previously operated on Cuba had their assets confiscated without compensation, which led to a serious **conflict with the USA**. He was able to resist pressure from the United States thanks to the economic and military support from the states of the Warsaw Pact. This resulted in the Cuban Missile Crisis in 1962.

Again and again Castro attempted to end the partial isolation of his country, but his support for revolutionary movements in Central America and Africa (e.g. in Nicaragua, Angola and Ethiopia) were a considerable handicap for this policy. In 1988 he clearly distanced himself from reforming movements in the Soviet Union and as late as April 1989 described himself as the last »guardian of pure Marxism-Leninism«. The collapse of the Soviet bloc and the consequent loss of approximately 85% of Cuba's export markets ushered in the so-called **periodo especial** (Special Period), years characterized by great hardships for the population but also by a gradual opening to the world. In the 1990s the Cuban economy was opened to foreign investors, religious freedom was guaranteed, the US dollar was permitted as a means of payment (until November 2004), free farmers' markets were allowed and a dialogue with Cubans in exile was initiated. Although the shine has come off the myth of Castro in recent years, for many Cubans he is still the hero who tries to make his dream of a just world come true.

For health reasons Fidel Castro handed over his offices and powers to his younger brother Raúl Castro Ruz in 2006, initially on an interim basis. In 2008 Raúl took over the leadership permanently.

Carlos Manuel de Céspedes (1819 – 1874)

Freedom fighter

Carlos Manuel de Céspedes was born on 28 April 1819 in Bayamo to a family that lived off its sugar plantations and thus off slavery too. After studying law in Barcelona and travelling in England, Germany and Italy, Céspedes returned to Cuba.

Working constantly to achieve the independence of Cuba from Spain, he was given several prison sentences for his trouble. His enthusiasm for the libertarian philosophy of Thomas Jefferson made Céspedes a campaigner for freedom and equality. The emancipation of his slaves on 10 October 1868 on his plantation, La Demajagua near Manzanillo, triggered the First War of Independence. The Spanish colonial government took his son hostage and executed him when Céspedes refused to yield. His initial force of 147 men, armed with 47 shotguns, four rifles, a few pistols and machetes, was ridiculed and given the name »mambises« (rebel criminals). They adopted this name as a badge of honour and by the end of the year had grown to a force of 26,000 men. The fighting continued and the rebels took several towns, including Céspedes' home town of Bayamo, which was declared the capital of the Cuban Republic. Céspedes fought to the death at the head of his Mambises, falling on 27 February 1874 in the Sierra Maestra in battle against colonial forces.

Carlos Manuel de Céspedes is regarded in Cuba as a great **freedom fighter** and honoured as »Padre de la Patria« (Father of the Fatherland).

Che Guevara (1928 – 1967)

Ernesto Guevara Serna – better known as Che – was born on 14 June 1928 in Rosario in Argentina. His parents gave him an extremely liberal upbringing, and through his mother he came into contact with Marxist ideas at an early age. With a tendency to asthma, he did a lot of sports and began to study medicine. After completing his studies, he first worked at a leprosy station in Bolivia and in 1954 went to Guatemala to support the government of J. Arbenz Guzmán.

Following Guzmán's fall in 1954 he met Fidel Castro and his brother Raúl in Mexico. On 25 November 1956 he was on board the **yacht**

Doctor, politician and revolutionary

Che Guevara and Fidel Castro in 1969

Granma when it sailed for Cuba, completely overloaded with 82 persons on board. They were tracked down by Batista's soldiers, and after severe fighting only a dozen freedom fighters were left, including the Castro brothers, Camilo Cienfuegos and Che Guevara, who gained a reputation for being a hard but fair commander.

From professional politician ...

After the victory of the revolution he was charged with various political offices in the Cuban government: first as president of the Cuban national bank (1959–1961), while later as minister for industry (1961–1965) he was in a position to take a decisive part in the revolutionary reshaping of the island republic. His dream was to create a »new man«, altruistic and revolutionary, committed to solidarity and renouncing material interests. However, when the island returned to sugar monoculture at the wishes of the Soviet Union in 1964 and Guevara's plans for industrialization were put on hold, he increasingly lost interest in his role as a professional politician. In March 1965 he returned from a journey across Africa and Asia. What then happened is shrouded in mystery. He was not seen for a long time, and there were reports of a break with Castro, of sickness and depression.

... back to revolutionary

Soon afterwards Guevara must have left Cuba to build a revolutionary movement in Bolivia, as on 3 October 1965 Castro read out a farewell letter in which Guevara renounced his citizenship and all offices in order to »dedicate himself to a new field in the struggle against imperialism«. Again the revolutionary went into the mountains to organize the fight, but this time he failed, as he had too little support among the people. His diary ends on 7 October 1967. It is thought that he was shot without trial the next day, and what was said to be his body was shown to the reporters. In the late 1960s Che Guevara was glorified as a **martyr and cult figure** of revolutionary movements. Posters depicting him as the best-looking revolutionary of all time could be seen around the world. Cubans still honour his memory; alongside José Martí he is the best-loved and most venerated national hero.

Christopher Columbus (1451–1506)

Discoverer of the »New World«

Cristoforo Colombo – Cristoval Colom – Cristóbal Colón: these three variants of his name in Italian, Portuguese and Spanish help to cast some light on the biography of the seafarer and explorer Columbus.

Born in 1451 in Genoa, he went to sea at the age of 14. In 1476 he settled in Lisbon and became increasingly preoccupied with the idea of finding a route to India by sea. He tried in vain to convince the king of his plan. Finally he succeeded in finding wealthy backers in Castile and gained the support of Queen Isabella. On 3 August 1492 he set out with the caravelles *Santa María*, *Pinta* and *Niña*, and

In around 1520 Ghirlandaio painted a portrait of the sceptical-looking seafarer who discovered the New World, who was denied fame during his own lifetime.

sighted land on 12 October. Columbus took possession of the island and named it San Salvador – in all probability it was what is now known as Watling Island in the Bermudas. On the same voyage he also discovered Hispaniola (today Haiti) and **Cuba, where he stayed only a few days**, but took several Indians back to the Spanish court. The voyages that followed, however, did not lead to the expected success in Spain, as the new territories were regarded as poor, uncultivated lands inhabited by savages. As a result of denunciation by several participants in his journeys of exploration, he was arrested on his third voyage to Hispaniola and taken back to Spain, where he succeeded however in defending himself before the royal couple. Despite this, Columbus was denied fame during his lifetime.

Wifredo Lam (1902 – 1982)

The painter Wifredo Lam, son of a Chinese father from Guangzhou and a Cuban mother of European and African descent, was born in Sagua la Grande on Cuba. He initially trained as an artist in Havana.

Painter

In 1923 he went to Madrid and 14 years later moved to Paris, where he had close links to Surrealist artists. In 1941 Lam emigrated to Martinique with the so-called **hard core of Surrealists** and shortly afterwards returned to his native Cuba. After 1947 he spent long periods in Italy and Paris.

Mythological and demonic iconography

Lam's paintings are marked by the **awakening self-determination** of the Caribbean region as it freed itself from colonial rule. Much of his work contains interpretations of Afro-Caribbean heritage, for example depictions of the demons that are present in Cuban syncretism. Cubist elements and balanced compositions are hallmarks of his work.

José Martí (1853 – 1895)

Journalist and writer

José Martí, who came from Havana, is the outstanding figure in the Cuban independence movement of the second half of the 19th century – and wrote the lyrics to the famous *Guantanamera* song.

When Martí spoke out for Cuba's struggle for independence at the age of 16 in the journal *Patria Libre*, he was sentenced to forced labour by the Spanish colonial government and deported to Madrid in 1871. After completing his studies of law and philosophy, and travels to Mexico, Guatemala and Venezuela he returned to Cuba in 1878, but a year later was once more exiled to Spain on account of his political activities. From 1881 Martí lived in New York. His articles, which regularly appeared in the Argentinean newspaper *La Nación*, earned him a reputation throughout Latin America.

Fight against injustice and inequality

From 1884 Martí devoted himself to **preparing an invasion** of Cuba and made contact with fighters from the War of Independence, the revolutionary's letters and numerous essays reflecting his political thought. His main concern was the struggle against injustice and inequality, the liberation of Cuba from Spanish colonial rule, rejection of the annexation of Cuba by the USA and the uniting of all political forces. By founding the Cuban Revolutionary Party (Partido Revolucionario Cubano) in 1892 he attempted to put these ideas into practice. Accompanied by Máximo Gómez, he arrived in Cuba on 11 April 1895. Just a month later he fell in battle near Boca de Dos Ríos. José Martí is today revered as a national hero.

Ana Fidelia Quirot (born 1963)

Athlete

The most remarkable winner at the world championships of 1995 in Göteborg, Ana Fidelia Quirot from Cuba, received standing ovations: only one and half years after a severe explosion and months in hospital, she won the 800-metre race in the year's record time.

Six months pregnant, Quirot suffered second and third-degree burns on 22 January 1993 when a gas stove exploded. She lost her baby and was at death's door for several days. With iron will Quirot made an unexpected comeback. A mere two months after the accident she took second place at the Central American championships; her performance at the world championships is regarded as a minor miracle.

Ana Fidelia had always looked to a future in sports, but also in a kind of political mission. Fidel Castro, after whom she was named Fidelia and whom she greatly admired, visited her in hospital a few days after the explosion and made her promise to run again. Letters of encouragement came from all over Cuba. Despite a painful healing process, she restarted training. She trained only in the mornings and evenings, in special clothing and

Proud of her country: an exceptional athlete celebrates victory.

gloves that protected her from sunlight. With her head secured in a corset, she ran her first circuits again. Even before the tragic accident and astonishing comeback she was an exceptional athlete – winning 39 consecutive competitions between 1987 and 1990, and taking the top rung 15 times on the run over 400 metres from 1990. At the Olympic Games in summer 1996 in Atlanta, Quirot won the silver medal, although she had been favourite for gold. In 1997 she gained a gold medal once again, at the world championships in Athens over 800 metres. She ended her sporting career in 2001. Fidel Castro was present at her farewell.

Practicalities

BUENOS DÍAS! HOW TO STRIKE UP A CONVERSATION WITH THIS CUBAN AND OTHER USEFUL INFORMATION IS PRESENTED ON THE FOLLOWING PAGES.

Accommodation

Various alternatives

The range of accommodation includes **basic holiday cottages and luxury apartments** with every conceivable creature comfort and landscaped pools. An all-inclusive holiday is the cheapest option when booking from home in advance. Private guesthouses, **casas particulares**, charge CUC 15 to 30 per night depending on the region and season, and approx. CUC 3 for breakfast. Sometimes guests have a room or apartment to themselves, sometimes they live with the family. The private addresses named in this guide (►Sights from A to Z) are given without guarantee, as there is considerable fluctuation: the owners may have been unable to pay the high taxes, or emigrated, or lost their concession for political reasons, and the casa particular no longer exists.

Cheap, individual and authentic: an overnight stay in a casa particular.

CATEGORIES

HOTEL CATEGORIES

▶ **Prices**
The hotels recommended in this guide in the chapter Sights from A to Z are classified according to the following price categories (double rooms):
Luxury: CUC 100 – 400   (todo incluído, on the beach)
Mid-range: CUC 50 – 100
Budget: under CUC 50
(often only with breakfast)

INTERNATIONAL HOTEL CHAINS

▶ **Horizontes**
www.horizontes.cu (state-run 3- to 4-star hotel chain)

▶ **Cubanacán**
www.cubanacan.cu (state travel agency, with representation in London: http://cubanacan.co.uk: Cubana flight tickets, cars, water sports, spa tourism, restaurants, mid-range hotels ...)

▶ **Gran Caribe**
www.gran-caribe.com (state-run upscale hotel chain, usually 4 stars)

▶ **Gaviota**
www.gaviota-grupo.com (state travel agency, mid-range and high-end hotels, restaurants, water sports, transport, shops)

▶ **Islazul**
www.islazul.cu (chain with fairly basic, state-run hotels, 2-star category)

▶ **Melía**
www.solmeliacuba.com (luxury Melía chain, Spanish-Cuban joint venture)

▶ **Habaguanex**
www.habaguanex.com (beautifully restored colonial hotels, especially in Habana Vieja)

CASAS PARTICULARES

▶ **Internet**
www.casaparticularcuba.org (in English, with photos)
www.homestaybooking.com, www.havanahomestay.com
www.casaparticular.info (lots of addresses and more information about Cuba)

Those searching for private accommodation are often approached by Cubans. In this case a commission has to be paid. All the casas named in this guide offer a room with en-suite bathroom (including hot water) and air-conditioning. However, don't expect everything to be spotless, and there may be power cuts. Details of guests and their passports are entered into an official register.

The extremely basic **»Campismo« holiday villages** were once reserved for Cubans but now take foreign guests too, costing from CUC 5 per bed. The facilities are usually spartan, i.e. cold showers, sometimes no running water, no bed linen provided, frequent power cuts, no decent restaurant or no restaurant at all. Bookings through www.cubamarviajes.cu (Tel. Cubamar agency 07 833 25 23)

Camping in tents for tourists , while officially disapproved of, is possible in some regions.

Proof of a hotel booking, once a requirement on entering the country, is now rarely demanded. If asked, give the customs official the name of a well-known hotel.

Categories

In addition to the renovation of long-established hotels, the building of new ones as joint ventures with international hotel chains has become significant business. While officially Cuba operates a **hotel classification** of 1 – 5 stars, the 4 and 5-star houses do not always meet European standards for 3-star hotels. 2-star accommodation is basic – but that does mean that the necessary basics are provided.

Tarjeta de huésped

When checking in at all-inclusive beach hotels, guests are given a guest card or a plastic wristband that entitles them to enter the hotel, dine in the restaurant and use the hotel facilities. They should always be worn, and to an extent are substitutes for a passport.

»Operación Milagro«

Independent travellers without hotel bookings should be aware of a **campaign of solidarity** named »Operación Milagro«, in which Latin American visitors and patients are invited to Cuba for health or spa tourism. This means that outside the high season (e.g. Sept. – Nov) tourist hotels are often fully booked by Latin Americans. For the high season in winter the hotels are then opened again for visitors from Canada and Europe who pay in hard currency. This applies particularly to mid-range hotels and Cubanacán hotels, as well as remote »eco-hotels« and some high-quality beach hotels such as that in Marea del Portillo or the Sierra Mar and Los Galeones near Santiago.

Arrival · Before the Journey

Travel Alternatives

By air

Havana is the main airport, followed by Varadero. Thomson and Thomas Cook operate charter flights to Air Lingus flies from Dublin via Paris, with Air France, but at a price. The national carrier Cubana has flights from London, Virgin Airlines flies twice daily from Gatwick. Iberia has daily flights from Madrid. The flying time from Europe to Cuba is 10 – 12 hours. Due to restrictions in place (though loosened under Obama), US citizens usually have to fly from Canada or Mexico. Miami, Tampa, Fort Lauderdale and New York have flights for US citizens with permits. American Eagle, for instance, flies from Miami to Havana, Camagüey, Cienfuegos and Santiago de Cuba. **Cuban domestic flights** e.g. to Cayo Largo, Santiago de Cuba, Cayo Coco and Baracoa, should be booked well in advance.

ADDRESSES

AIRLINES

► **Cubana de Aviación**
Havana, Calle 23 no. 64, esq. P
Infanta, Vedado
Tel. 07/83 44 44 6
inform
acion.cliente@cubana.avianet.cu
www.cubana.cu

Unit 50, Skyline Village Limehar-
bour Road, Docklands London
E14 9TS
Tel. 020 75 38 59 33,
Fax 020 70 93 15 38
www.cubana.com

► **American Eagle**
Tel. 1 800 433 73 00
www.aa.com

► **Iberia**
Tel. (0 870 609 05 00
www.iberia.com

► **Virgin Atlantic**
Tel. 08 44 811 00 00
www.virgin-atlantic.com

AIRPORTS

► **José Martí International
Airport**
Avenida Nguyen Van Troi, Ciudad
de La Habana
Tel. 07/266 41 33

► **Juan Gualberto Gómez
International Airport**
Varadero (Provinz Matanzas)
Tel. 045/24 70 15

► **Frank País International
Airport**
Carretera Central, Vía Bayamo,
km 15, Holguín
Tel. 024/46 25 12

► **International Airport of
Cayo Coco**
Cayo Coco, Jardines del Rey
(Province Ciego de Avila)
Tel. 033/30 11 65

On leaving Cuba an airport tax of 25 CUC has to be paid. This pay- ◄ Airport tax
ment is often charged, contrary to the law, from those who have
booked a package holiday and already paid the tax with the ticket
price. In this case simply get a stamp from the separate »airport tax«
desk, do not pay anything and in case of problems refer to the airline
representative at the check-in.

Sailors find excellent facilities at the marinas in Havana (Marina He- By sea
mingway, Tarara), Varadero (Acua, Chapelín, Gaviota and Paradiso),
Camagüey (Santa Lucía), Cienfuegos (Jagua), Guardalavaca (Puerto
de Vita), Holguín (Bahía de Naranjo), Santiago de Cuba (Punta Gorda), Manzanillo, Trinidad (Ancón), Cayo Largo (Marina Gran Caribe), Cayo Santa María and the Isla de la Juventud. In order to sail
within the Cuban twelve-mile exclusion zone, make radio contact
with the authorities on channel 68.

Cruise ships sailing the Caribbean stop at the harbours or off the beaches at Havana, Santiago de Cuba, Cienfuegos, Cayo Largo and the Isla de la Juventud.

Package holidays   Packages including the flight, accommodation and half-board or full board are cheaper than individual trips to Cuba.

Immigration Regulations

Travel documents   To enter Cuba citizens of states of the EU need a passport which must be valid for at least six months. Children need a child's passport with photo. Furthermore, on entering the country a **tourist card** (substitute for visa, costs US$ 15), which is valid for a maximum of 30 days and for most people is included in the travel papers they receive after booking. It can also be obtained from Cuban embassies (▸ Information). While restrictions have been relaxed under the Obama government, US citizens wanting to visit have to fall under certain categories – visiting relatives, educational or research visits. The vast majority travel through Mexico or Canada, where agencies arrange the tourist card. Independent travellers who have only booked a flight usually have to present on arrival at the airport hotel vouchers for at least three nights. Recently it has been enough to name a hotel or a legal casa particular on the tourist card. Business travellers, photographers and journalists need a **visa** from the Cuban embassy.

Pets   For dogs and cats an official veterinary **pet certificate** is required. It includes an official attestation of the animal's health from a government veterinary authority (no more than 30 days old), a vaccination certificate that is at least 20 days old and was issued at most 11 months before arrival (rabies, distemper) and a passport photo. The certificates have to be authorized by the Cuban consulate. The pet must also have a microchip implant or a tattoo.

Customs regulations   At **arrival** in Cuba it is best to have only items for personal use. Larger quantities may be regarded as illegal gifts and confiscated. Fresh meat and dairy products, vegetables and fruit are confiscated as import is prohibited for reasons of public health. Electric devices may only be imported if they are for personal use and not gifts for Cuban nationals. For gifts (non-commercial import) from a value of 100 – 1000 US$ 100% customs duty is charged. For more details refer to a Cuban diplomatic representation (▸ Information). Maximum 10 kg of medicines, 3 litres of alcoholic drinks and 200 cigarettes can be imported. Drugs, pornography, weapons and explosives may not be brought into the country.
Export of food, tortoise-shell, coral and coral jewellery is prohibited. Export of items made of gold, silver and other precious metals as well as of precious stones must be declared. In recent years it has re-

peatedly happened that craft items of no real value that were bought on tourist markets were confiscated by the Cuban customs on the grounds that they are Cuban culture. For information and export permits: Bienes Culturales, Calle 17 #1009, entre 10 y 12, Havana-Vedado, tel. 07/83 96 58, registro@cubarte.cult.cu. A permit costs only a few pesos and saves potential trouble when leaving the country.

Since 28.10.2009 **new export regulations for tobacco products** have been in force: no more than 20 cigars can be exported without presenting proof of their origin and of the purchase. Up to 50 cigars can be exported on the condition that they are in closed, sealed original packaging with the official hologram. For more than 50 cigars an original invoice issued by an officially approved state shop must be presented. This invoice must specify the total amount of tobacco that is to be exported. In this case too it is essential that the cigars are kept in closed, sealed original packaging with the official hologram. For further information see the website of the Cuban customs authorities: www.aduana.co.cu.

When **entering the United Kingdom, Ireland or other EU countries** persons over the age of 17 have the following duty-free allowance: 2 litres of spirits below 22% or 1 litre of spirits above 22% or 2 litres of sparkling of fortified wine or 2 litres of other wine, 200 cigarettes or 100 cigarillos or 50 cigars or 250 g of tobacco, 500 g of coffee or 200 g of instant coffee, 50 g of perfume and 0.25 litres of eau de toilette. Goods not subject to these limits (except gold alloys and gold plating, unprocessed or half-finished) can be imported from Cuba duty-free to a value of € 430/£ 390. The import of food from Cuba is subject to restrictions. In duty-free shops goods for personal use can be bought without paying customs duties up to a value of € 430/£ 390.

Importing living holiday souvenirs and products from protected plants and animals is prohibited. This applies especially to certain products that are sometimes on sale in Cuba: black corals, coral jewellery, crocodile skins, turtle shells and tortoise shell. Infringement of the Washington Convention on endangered species is subject to severe penalties in the European Union.

Protected species

Children in Cuba

The Cubans love children, who are often at the centre of attention, if only for a joke and some horseplay. Cuba is free from malaria and other dangerous tropical diseases against which children would need to be inoculated (an outbreak of dengue fever seems to have been brought under control again thanks to drastic use of chemicals in re-

A carefree childhood in a post-socialist country? Cubans love children.

cent years). Poisonous and dangerous animals do not pose a threat on the island.

Temperatures are pleasant and not to hot, especially in winter at around 25°C/77°F. There are plenty of diversions on tropical beaches, which often shelve gently into the sea, as in Varadero. And if splashing in the water and building sandcastles gets boring, many hotels have **children's clubs** where kids are entertained, excursions organized and games or contests are on the programme. For those travelling with babies and toddlers, it can be difficult to find the preferred food (there is no baby food) and good-quality diapers (very expensive!), so it is best to take plenty of supplies from home. For children below the age of twelve a **generous discount** is frequently offered, e.g. by the bus company Viazul and in many hotels and museums. Families who want to keep costs low by staying the cheap Campismo bungalow villages should be aware that many of them only have cold showers, no bed linen is provided and electric power is not always available.

Crime

Cuba is relatively safe for travellers in comparison to other Caribbean states. Nevertheless, tourists are exposed to pickpocketing and other small-scale swindles, and should take some generally applicable precautions, especially in the cities of Havana (above all in the Habana Vieja and Centro districts) and Santiago de Cuba, in the well-known beach resorts and in tourist hotels.

Leave large sums of cash and valuables in the hotel safe (ideally with a combination lock), don't show off expensive jewellery, always keep the hire car locked and leave nothing inside, carry handbags and cameras close to your body, and avoid lonely areas and unlit streets at night (especially in Havana). Women should not leave expensive underwear lying around in the hotel room, but keep it in the suitcase, as temptation makes a thief, especially in Cuba, where women's underwear is either unattractive or unaffordable. Always check restaurant bills. Warnings have been issued about locks on luggage being broken open at Cuban airports. Valuables such as cameras, money and jewellery should not be packed in suitcases for air transport. To be on the safe side, it is a good idea to travel with a hardside case.

Precautions

Prostitution

Economic hardship is what drives Cubans into prostitution. It is often their only option for getting hold of **coveted foreign currency** and improving their strictly rationed supplies of food, or obtaining some of the luxury goods that can only be purchased with foreign money or pesos convertibles.

Sometimes holidaymakers unintentionally fall into the hands of prostitutes or people who are more interested in their wallet than in the friendship that they claim to be offering. As the boundary between a friendly conversation on the beach, on the street or in a dance club and a business-minded proposition can be fluid, naivety many have consequences. In certain places it is best to be careful, especially at night.

Electricity

The power supply in Cuba usually operates at 110 volts. However, some hotel complexes have an AC supply at 220 volts.

In order to use electric devices that you bring with you (hair dryer, shaver etc), an adapter is needed, but is hard to get in Cuba. Energy shortages occasionally lead to blackouts. It is advisable to take a flashlight.

Please note

Emergency

As emergency phone numbers vary from one region to another, it is best to ask in the hotel or at the tourist agency directly after arriving. Police in Havana: 8 67 77 77, nationwide 116.

Etiquette and Customs

One thing is certain, and it escapes nobody's attention: **Cuba is a noisy place!** If you are sensitive to noise, take ear plugs or avoid Cuban cities, as music is everywhere: it resounds from almost every half-collapsing doorway. When there is a power cut, someone always comes along with batteries for the ghetto blaster, and then the music goes on till the early hours.

The trios who play *Chan Chan* and *Guantanamera* for tourists do their stuff without interruption in every hotel patio and restaurant, by the pool and even on the beach, and those who travel to Trinidad and Santiago de Cuba risk getting a musical overdose. Add in the sounds of hip-hop, techno and merengue, relentlessly schmaltzy Latino hits and boleros that have been crooned since pre-revolutionary times, and a killing mix is complete.

Music

With our without music, Cuban fully live up to their Latino reputation. Women travelling alone should be prepared for »piropos«, the **Cuban way of making compliments**: sometimes shouted to a passing women, sometimes hissed, perhaps a poetic phrase or a verbal bouquet of flowers, perhaps witty or vulgar, or uttered with the kind of revolutionary pathos that could bring Che Guevara in his mausoleum in Santa Clara back to life: »Te quiero – hasta siempre!«, I love you for ever, will you marry me? – after no more than a few swooning glances!

Cuban compliments

»Ay mi madre, mulata, tienes una buena salud«, someone will say with an admiring glance, »My goodness, mulata, you're in good shape! You must be double-jointed.« No doubt about it, Cuban women are world leaders at swinging their hips and swaying along the street. Tourists who want to be left in peace should not attempt to emulate this (it's impossible anyway), should not react to any approaches (which is how most Cuban women play it) and should not wear revealing clothing – and if all this still does not produce the desired effect, a firm »no moleste, por favor« (please don't pester me) often works wonders.

← *The cigar-smoking old ladies and the »Santeras« in white clothing are professionals who make their living by posing for photos.*

Patience is a virtue

Like the Cuban way of walking and the piropos, an inexhaustible supply of patience (or is it fatalism?) is part of Cuban life. This might serve as a good example to hotel guests when, after a long day of hardship on the beach, roasting in the Caribbean sun, they are forced to queue up outside the hotel restaurant (because it's full to bursting at 8pm in the high season) and then find, when they finally get to the sumptuous buffet, that they are still only moving at a snail's pace. Then it's time to feel some solidarity with the locals: Cubans are **world champions** at standing in a queue, whether outside peso shops, in public offices or at bus stops, and often they don't even get what they want in exchange for their food coupons, because it has already been sold on the black market or is reserved for tourists!

»Who was last?«

It therefore comes as no surprise that **a rendezvous with Cubans** may well involve a bit of waiting around. Possibly the bus, which only runs once each evening, failed to arrive again. Or it did come, but did not stop as intended because passengers were already crammed in like sardines. By the way, a tourist who comes to a bus stop, a shop or a bank and cannot tell whether there is a proper queue, should ask the others standing there after »el último?«: »Who was last?« When meeting Cubans in a non-peso restaurant, it goes without saying that the foreigner pays for the Cubans.

What not to mention

For Cubans **politeness and proper dress** are important. It is still usual to give a lady a hand to help her out of a car! In the evening people dress up as a matter of course: shorts are definitely out of place in restaurants. Cubans have a great passion for dominoes and baseball, which always provide **good subjects to talk about** – so long as you speak Spanish and can actually understand Cuban Spanish! The Cubans tend to speak extremely indistinctly. »S« and whole word endings tend to disappear completely (fish, »pescado«, comes out as »pecado«), and »V« is almost always pronounced as »B« (which is how Havana became »La Habana«). **Political topics** should be avoided, or you should at least tread carefully, in order not to embarrass your host or companion. Cubans speak openly to people whom they trust!

Festivals · Holidays · Events

National holidays

On **national holidays** schools, shops and places of work are closed. On **national days of remembrance** celebrations are held, depending on the place and region, but shops are open.

Many events

In Cuba countless events and festivals on the themes of music, sports, literature and of course politics and the revolution are held every year, in addition to many religious holidays and days of pilgrimage. It is unfortunately not uncommon for these events to be cancelled for financial reasons. Information is available from the **Casas de la Cultura**, **Casas de la Musica** and **Casas de la Trova**, which can be found in almost every town.

Information on the internet: www.cubarte.cult.cu (culture, festivals, in English) or www.dtcuba.com and www.cartelera.com (weekly listings magazine in Havana, comes out on Thursdays).

◗ HOLIDAYS & EVENTS

NATIONAL HOLIDAYS

1 January Day of the Victory of the Revolution
1 May Labour Day
26 July Anniversary of the attack on the Moncada Barracks
25 – 27 July Days of the National Uprising
10 October Anniversary of the start of the War of Independence of 1868
25 December Christmas

NATIONAL DAYS OF REMEMBRANCE

28 January Birthday of José Martí
24 February Anniversary of the start of the revolution of 1895
8 March International Women's Day
13 March Anniversary of the storming of the presidential palace in 1957
19 April Anniversary of the victory at the Bay of Pigs in 1961
30 July Day of the Martyrs of the Revolution
8 October Anniversary of the death of Che Guevara, 1967
28 October Anniversary of the death of Camilo Cienfuegos, 1959
17 November Anniversary of the shooting of students,1871
7. December Anniversary of the death of Antonio Maceo

JANUARY

▶ **Nationwide**
1 January (Liberation Day): all over Cuba events, rallies and festivities are held to celebrate the victory of the revolution in 1959 (government offices, museums and many shops are closed).

FEBRUARY

▶ **Havana**
Carnaval (late February/early March): on two weekends the Habaneros give themselves over to carnival frenzy, and parades go along the Malecón and Prado. The true »Carnaval« in Havana and other cities is held in the Cuban holiday season in late July and early August (▶below).

▶ **Havana**
Cuban Cigar Festival: Aficionados meet in Havana amid thick blue smoke, seminars are held and business is done – and sometimes a cigar-smoking Hollywood star puts in an appearance.

MARCH or DECEMBER

▶ **Havana or Santiago (in alternate years)**
Domino world championships: clack, clack, clack – the Cubans are true masters of dominoes. The game is played on every corner, and since 2003 a world cham-

The world championships at dominoes are held alternately in Havana and Santiago.

pionship has been held in which 150 duos from more than 20 countries take part.

MARCH

▶ **Havana**
At the »Festival Danzón Habana« music festival traditional Cuban music and its (mostly deceased) stars are honoured: with lots of concerts, at which young and old join in the dancing.

APRIL

▶ **Havana**
Festival International de Percusión PERCUBA: Percussionists and would-be percussionists should make their way to Cuba in April, when Havana is taken over by drummers, who talk to other artists and craftsmen about their instruments and take part in exhibitions and discussions.

▶ **Havana**
Festival de Rap Cubana Hip Hop: Havana in rap and hip-hop fever, with a host of concerts and stars. Seeing and being seen is all-important.

▶ **Gibara/Holguín**
Festival Internacional del Cine Pobre: In this idyllic little coastal town committed low-budget productions from Latin America are screened in an annual competition.

MAY

▶ **Havana (and nationwide)**
On 1 May Havana is chock-a-block: about one million Cubans gather for rallies on the Day of Labour and a military parade at the Plaza de la Revolución. In past years this was the occasion for the famous speeches of the Comandante en Jefe Fidel Castro.

MAY/JUNE

▶ **Havana**
International fishing tournament at Marina Hemingway: Hemingway himself initiated the tournament in 1950: In May marlins abound in the Gulf Stream, and deep-sea anglers from all over the world come in hope of carrying off one of the world's most prestigious trophies for fishing: the Ernest Hemingway Cup (more tournaments in September and November).

JUNE

▶ **Havana and other cities**
Bolero d'Oro: Romantics travelling in Cuba should not miss this music festival of »golden boleros«. The rhythm of boleros will carry you through Havana.

Anglers who take part in the Havana fishing tournament need a bit of luck.

JULY

▶ **Santiago**
Carnaval and Festival del Caribe (Festival del Fuego): around 25/26 July all of Santiago is at boiling point for eight days and nights during the annual carnival: folklore groups and comparsa bands make up a spectacularly colourful parade through the city. Usually the carnival has a theme country, and participants dress in the appropriate style with elaborate

»capas« – the best capes get a prize.

The second party in July, the Festival del Caribe, is usually held at the start of the month (caribe@cultstgo.cult.cu).

JULY/AUGUST

▶ Carnaval in Habana

The more important of the two carnivals in the capital takes place in the third week of July and the first week of August: parades with colourful costumes and loud music.

OCTOBER

▶ Santa Clara (and elsewhere)

On 8 October the anniversary of the death of Che Guevara is solemnly commemorated in Santa Clara in the mausoleum.

OCTOBER/NOVEMBER

▶ Havana

Festival Internacional de Ballet de la Habana: the Havana ballet, for many years now directed by Alicia Alonso, has an international reputation. Every two years (2014 etc) top-class performances are staged.

Summer carnival in Havana

NOVEMBER

► **Havana**
Festival Jazz Plaza Internacional: each year in late November leading figures of the jazz scene in Latin America and the rest of the world, including some real stars, perform in Havana.

NOVEMBER/ DECEMBER

► **Biennale de la Habana**
Every two or three years, an international rendezvous for artists and art experts, organized by the Centro Wifredo Lam, with exhibitions in museums and private studios.

DECEMBER

► **Havana (and other towns)**
Festival Internacional del Nueve Cine Latinoamericano: the biggest cinema event in Latin America: directors and actors from all over the continent and film fans from the whole world, sometimes including the odd Hollywood star

who keeps faith with Cuba, come to see the latest productions.

► **Rincón (suburb of Havana) and Santiago (El Cobre)**
A major festival with crowds of pilgrims in honour of St Lazarus and rituals for Babalú Ayé, as the Catholic saint is known by adherents of Santería, on 16/17 December.

► **Guantánamo**
Fiesta de la Guantanamera: this annual festival at the start of the month delights Cubans and visitors with concerts and folklore, French tumba and Franco-Haitian traditions and religious rituals, but also readings and discussions.

► **Remedios (and other towns)**
Parrandas: carnival parades with music; in late December drummers and dancers go through the streets of several provincial towns, such as Remedios on the coast near Santa Clara.

Food and Drink

Good tourist hotels have á la carte restaurants and opulent buffets that Cubans can only dream of. Most of them provide international cuisine. Cuban specialities are served in many state-run foreign-currency restaurants and in private »paladares«.

These restaurants, which may only employ members of the family, are often run in the family home with a great deal of improvisational talent. In small restaurants seats for ten diners at most, Cuban dishes can be tried at fairly low prices in exchange for foreign currency or pesos convertibles. Private restaurants (► Sights, Where to Eat) appear and disappear frequently, as »paladares« can be closed down if the owners cannot pay the high tax, or emigrate or commit some political transgression.

International and Cuban food

Most Cubans can afford the food that tourists enjoy neither at home nor in restaurants, as food is still rationed.

Typical Cuban dishes: chicken, rice with black beans, and pork

Price categories The restaurants and private paladares recommended in the chapter
»Sights from A to Z« are mostly in the category »moderate«. With
few exceptions, only basic »cafeterias« are cheap, and in Havana
there are also some expensive restaurants.
Price categories:
Expensive: over 20 CUC
Moderate: 6 – 20 CUC
Inexpensive: below 6 CUC

Creole Food

Basics Typical Cuban, i.e. creole food combines Indian, African and Spanish
influences. Its staples are **rice, beans** and **cooking bananas.** Meat is
usually chicken and pork. Beef is found only in better-class tourist
hotels.
Characteristic features of creole cooking are the use of yuca (manioc), malanga (a tuber), boniato (sweet potatoes) and pumpkin, refined with onions, garlic and many spices and herbs. Good restaurants also prepare creole fish dishes and seafood.

The stew known as **ajiaco** is a Cuban speciality made of pork, yuca, malanga and pieces of pumpkin.

There is hardly a Cuban meal without **moros y cristianos** (Moors and Christians), which means boiled black beans to which rice and a mixture of onion fried in oil, garlic, steamed peppers, oregano and cumin are added. The alternative to moros y cristianos is **arroz congrí**, the same recipe except that red beans are used instead of black beans. **Plátanos** (cooking bananas) are a favourite addition to almost all meals. They are pressed flat and served deep-fried as **tostones**.

Meat dishes

Moros y cristianos or arroz congrí is usually eaten with fried chicken (pollo asado), pork (cerdo asado) or minced meant (picadillo). Meat is truly delicious when it has been steeped in a marinade of fried garlic and sour oranges. Sometimes sucking pig (lechón a la pulla) appears on the menu.

Desserts

Popular desserts are **flan**, a kind of crème caramel brought by the Spanish, ice-cream, fruit salad and pastries (buñuelos). **Guayaba con queso**, a kind of guava jam with fresh curds, is extremely sweet.

Drinks

Soft drinks

In addition to mineral water of the Ciego Montero brand (sin gas: still, con gas: sparkling) there are fruit juices (jugos), usually orange, grapefruit or pineapple juice, and **refrescos** such as malt beer (malta), Tu-Kola etc.

coffee

After a meal or when friends come round, coffee (café cubano/cafecito: black, café con leche: with milk) is always served in Cuba.

Rum

Cuba's national drink is rum, which is available in all quality categories. Many Cubans drink »**chispa-tren**«, the most basic and cheapest kind, which is made in home distilleries and is not exactly smooth on the tongue. It is drunk neat, sometimes a bottle at a time, and before a meal if needed. A better bet for the tourist palate is the famous **Havana Club**, which replaced Bacardi after the revolution. Rum has a white, golden or an almost dark brown colour, depending on its age. The three-year-old Havana Club is white or gold (Añejo 3 Años) and is used above all in cocktails. The five-year-old tastes good neat, and for those who like something more special, the seven-year-old Añejo is just the thing. The top rum and the most expensive one is the 15-year-old Habana Club Reserva. The locals also like to drink

Ron Matúsalem, and there are other brands such as Varadero, Caney, Cubay and Caribbean Club (►Baedeker Special p. 101).

Beer Plenty of beer is drunk, especially **Cristal**, brewed in Holguín. The same town produces the stronger Mayabe. Manacas is a speciality from Santa Clara. The strong local beer called Hatuey is now fairly rare. Popular imported beers include Heineken, Beck's and the Canadian brands Labatt Blue and Molson.

Wine In higher-class restaurants imported wines, usually Spanish, are on offer at high prices.

It doesn't take much to make a daiquirí: ice, sugar-cane syrup, rum of course, a few limes, then give it all a good shake.

HIGH SPIRITS

Rum and rumba, cocktails beneath palm trees, sun, the sea and that Bacardi feeling – these are all part of how we imagine a dream holiday in the Caribbean. Many films and not least the life and work of Ernest Hemingway have created a widespread image of exotic cocktails and barkeepers at work beneath whirling fans.

The basis of these drinks is usually rum, that old sailors' and pirates' liquor which has gained global popularity as an alcoholic ingredient for cocktails, and which originated on Cuba as well as on the neighbouring islands Jamaica and Haiti (Hispaniola).

Rum's road to fame

As rum is a by-product of sugar manufacture, its spread is closely connected to the rise of sugar-cane cultivation. The mistaken belief that drinking this high-octane spirit would boost the courage of conquistadors and seafarers led to its consumption being permitted on ships – with well-known adverse consequences.

The worldwide demand increased, and rum often took on the function of a currency in international com-merce. Only gradually did it attain the status of a product for the enjoyment of well-to-do drinkers, especially as a constituent of cocktails or in higher-quality versions.

The basis for making rum is molasses, a by-product of sugar manufacture. By means of pressing and boiling several times, a viscous sugar-cane juice is extracted and poured into moulds to cool down. As this happens, the raw sugar crystallizes at the surface. The syrup-like molasses sinks to the bottom, and still contains enough sugar to produce alcohol during fermentation. By distilling and purification the alcoholic liquid becomes a spirit known as aguardiente, with an alcohol content of up to 75%. The decisive factor for the aroma and quality, apart from the way it is grown and the type of sugar cane,

Hemingway liked it: his favourite place for drinking a mojito was the Bodeguita del Medio.

is above all the maturation: the rum, originally colourless, is poured into wooden barrels – usually oak barrels – and acquires its characteristic golden-brown colour and its aroma, according to the length of time it is stored and the nature of the wood. One of the biggest secrets of every distillery is the recipe according to which the final blending is carried out: the mixing of different vintages and kinds of rum.

A competitive business

The Spaniard Facundo Bacardi founded the best-known rum distillery in Santiago de Cuba in 1862. What remains of his business empire, abandoned by his heirs in rather a hurry as they headed for Puerto Rico following the revolution, is a museum and a giant-sized Bacardí bottle on the former site of the distillery in Santiago. Today the best-known Cuban rum is Havana Club, which is distilled in Santa Cruz del Norte, about 80km/50mi east of Havana. During Prohibition in the US, the legendary Havana Club bar in the Cuban capital was a favourite haunt of wealthy American tourists and alcohol aficionados, as all drinks containing rum were served free of charge there. This act of generosity was more than compensated by the habit – undoubtedly encouraged by rum consumption – of throwing liberal quantities of silver coins into the fountain in the courtyard in the hope of a happy return to the bar.

The lightest kind of Cuban rum, »light dry«, is matured for three years before being reduced to drinking strength and sometimes coloured by the addition of caramel. It is the commonest basis for cocktails, but is also drunk neat or with water. A longer period of storage in wooden barrels produces »extra aged« and »old gold extra aged«, which become darker and darker in colour during a maturation time of seven to 25 years.

The older the rum, the less often is it mixed with other ingredients and the more often is it drunk neat.

Famous cocktails

Papa Hemingway was a fan of Cuban cocktails: mojito, which he always drank at the Bodeguita del Medio, and daiquiri, for which Floridita was his bar of choice. Of course Cuba libre and other drinks are available in every bar.

Cuba libre originated during the Wars of Independence, when American forces assisted Cubans in their struggle against Spain. They brought a new product with them: Coca Cola, which they mixed with Cuban rum. This concoction was every bit as successful as the war, and Cuba was free: Cuba libre! Take one quarter of a lemon or lime, 6 cl of white rum, four ice cubes and Coca Cola, then squeeze out the lime peel and juice over the glass, add the ice cubes and rum, fill the glass according to taste with Coca Cola, then stir.

Daiquiri is said to have derived from the plight of an engineer near the Cuban town of that name, who had only rum and limes to serve to his guests. A number of versions of this cocktail as made by Constante, the barkeeper at La Floridita in Havana, were immortalized by Hemingway: the juice of half a lime, two spoonfuls of crushed ice, 6 cl of white rum, 1 cl of syrup, chill the cocktail glass in advance, give all the ingredients a good short mix in a shaker, pour through a sieve into the cooled glass and garnish with slices of lime.The mojito in the Bodeguita del Media is an especially famous cocktail. Take the juice of half a lime, one teaspoon of sugar, five mint leaves, 6 cl of white rum, two dessert spoons of ice, and soda water. Stir the sugar in with the lime juice until it has dissolved, add the mint leaves and squeeze them a little with a bar spoon, then add the ice, rum and soda water to taste, give it all a good stir and garnish with some more mint leaves. If no mint leaves are to hand, then there's no need to go without a cocktail: prepare the drink as described and enjoy it under the name Ron Collins.

Health

First aid
The Cuban health system is good. Almost all tourist hotels have an emergency medical service. More serious cases are treated in clinics. Tourists who need medical help in Cuba and buy medication must pay immediately. It is therefore recommended to take out **travel health insurance** with transport back home in case of emergencies.

Vaccinations, medicines
Cuba is currently free of malaria and epidemics. Special vaccinations are not therefore necessary. As supplies on the island are subject to shortages, it is wise to take all medicine needed for personal use. In Havana there is an **international pharmacy**: Farmácia Internacional, Ave. 41 esq. 20, Miramar, Playa.

Those with a sensitive stomach should refrain from drinking **tap water**.

Information

► USEFUL ADDRESSES

INFORMATION IN UK AND CANADA

► **Cuba Tourist Board**
1 st floor 154 Shaftesbury Avenue, London WC2H 8HL
Tel. 020 / 72 40 66 55
www.traveltocuba.co.uk

► **Cuba Tourist Board Canada**
1200 Bay St., Suite 305, Toronto, Ontario M5R 2A5
Tel. 416 36 20 700 through /6799
www.gocuba.ca

INFORMATION IN CUBA

► **Infotur – Información Turística**
Calle Obispo, corner of San Ignacio, Habana Vieja
Terminal de Cruceros, Avenida del Puerto (Habana Vieja), both offices tel. 07/863 68 84
Miramar tel. 07/204 70 76
and other offices at José Martí

Airport (Terminal II and III)
www.infotur.cu

► **Cubatur**
Oficina Central Cubatur, Calle 15 no. 410, entre F y G, Plaza, Havana
Tel. 07/ 836 20 76
dcomercial@cmatriz.cbt.tur.cu, www.cubatur.cu

► **Asistur**
Prado 208 entre Calle Colón y Trocadero, Havana
Tel. 07/866 44 99, fax 866 80 87
asisten@asistur.cu, www.asistur.cu
Medical help, legal counsel, international money transfers etc.

CONSULATES & EMBASSIES

► **In UK**
Cuban Embassy
High Holborn, London WC1V 6PA

Tel. 020 24 88, 74 63 (Visa Office)
Fax 020 78 36, 26, 02, 45 57 (Visa Office)
http://cuba.embassyhomepage.com

► **In the Republic of Ireland**
Embassy of Cuba in Ireland
2 Adelaide Court, Adelaide Road, Dublin 2
Tel. 01 / 47 50 899, or -52 999,
Fax 01 47 63 674
http://cuban.embassydublin.com/

► **In the US**
Cuban Embassy USA
2630 16 St. NW. Washington D.C. 20009, USA
Tel. 202 / 79 78 518, -519
Fax 202 79 78 521
http://www.cubadiplomatica.cu

► **In Canada**
Cuban Embassy Canada
388 Main Street Ottawa, ON, K1S, 1E3, Canada
Tel. 613 / 563 01 41, fax
613 563 00 68, http://www.cuban.embassyottawa.com

► **In Cuba**
UK Embassy Cuba
Calle 34 no. 702 e/7ma y 17, Miramar, Playa
La Habana
Tel. 07 214 22 00
Fax 07 214 22 68
http://ukincuba.fco.gov.uk/en

ROI representation in Cuba via the Irish Embassy Mexico
Cda. Blvd. Avila Camacho, 76-3, Col. Lomas de Chapultepec
11000 Mexico D.F.
Tel. 00 52/55 55 20 58 03
Fax 00 52/55 55 20 58 92
http://www.irishembassy.com.mx
US Interest Section

Calzada between L & M Streets, Vedado
Tel. 07/ 833 35 51 through 59,
emergency/after hours tel.
07 833 23 02
http://Havana.usint.gov/

Embassy of Canada Cuba
Calle 30 no. 518 (esq. 7ma), Miramar (Playa)
Tel. 07/ 204 25 16,
Fax 07 204 20 44
http://canadainternational.gc.ca/cuba

INTERNET

► **www.cubainfo.co.uk**
Detailed official information and addresses in English

► **www.travel2cuba.co.uk**
Website of the tourist offices with general information and prices, in many cases out of date

► **www.cubaweb.cu**
Official website (Spanish/English). Topics: from weather to Castro's speeches and jazz in Cuba

► **www.gocuba.com**
Government website

► **www.canalcubano.com**
Concert dates in Havana, but inquire again when you get there

► **www.desdecuba.com/ generationy**
The diverse musings of Cuba's most famous blogger, Yuani Sanchez, are blocked in Cuba

Language

Useful to know some Spanish	The official language in Cuba is Spanish. Many Cubans also have some knowledge of English, but it is extremely useful for tourists to be able to speak Spanish or at least to know a few basic phrases.
Language courses	►Sports and Activities
Pronunciation	It takes a little while to get used to Cuban Spanish, as it is spoken very fast, and the final syllables are often omitted. There are also Cuban expressions derived from Indian languages. The pronunciation of vowels is short and open.
Stress in words	There are only three rules relating to stress in pronunciation: 1. The second-to-last syllable is stressed if the word ends with a vowel, or with -n or -s: Pedro, Carmen, aficionado. 2. The last syllable is stressed if the word ends with a consonant (except -n and -s): Madrid, español. 3. Deviations from these two rules are marked by an accent: médico, información.

SPANISH LANGUAGE GUIDE

At a Glance

Yes./No.	Sí./No.
Maybe.	Quizás./Tal vez.
All right./Agreed!	¡De acuerdo!/¡Está bien!
Please./Thank you.	Por favor./Gracias.
Thank you very much.	Muchas gracias.
My pleasure.	No hay de qué./De nada.
Sorry!	¡Perdón!
Pardon?	¿Cómo dice/dices?
I don't understand you.	No le/la/te entiendo.
I only speak a little …	Hablo sólo un poco de …
Could you please help me?	¿Puede usted ayudarme, por favor?
I would like …	Quiero …/Quisiera …
I (don't) like that.	(No) me gusta.
Do you have …?	¿Tiene usted …?
How much is it?	¿Cuánto cuesta?
What time is it?	¿Qué hora es?

Greetings and Meetings

Good morning!	¡Buenos días!

Good afternoon!	¡Buenos días!/¡Buenos tardes!
Good evening!	¡Buenos tardes!/¡Buenos noches!
Hello!	¡Hola!
My name is …	Me llamo …
What is your name, please?	¿Cómo se llama usted, por favor?
How are you?	¿Qué tal está usted?/¿Qué tal?
Fine, thanks. And you?	Bien, gracias. ¿Y usted/tú?
Goodbye!	¡Hasta la vista!/¡Adiós!
Bye!	¡Adiós!/¡Hasta luego!
See you soon!	¡Hasta pronto!
See you tomorrow!	¡Hasta mañana!

On the Road

left/right	a la izquierda/a la derecha
straight ahead	todo seguido/derecho
near/far	cerca/lejos
How far is it?	¿A qué distancia está?
I would like to rent … .	Quisiera alquilar …
… a car	… un coche.
… a boat	… una barca/un bote/un barco.
Excuse me, where is …	Perdón, dónde está …
… the train station, please?	… la estación (de trenes)?
… the bus station, please?	… la estación de autobuses/ la terminal?
… the airport, please?	… el aeropuerto?

Breakdown

My car has broken down.	Tengo una avería.
Could you please	¿Pueden ustedes enviarme
send me a breakdown truck?	un cochegrúa, por favor?
Is there a garage nearby?	¿Hay algún taller por aquí cerca?
Where is the nearest petrol station, please?	¿Dónde está la estación de servicio/a gasolinera más cercana, por favor?
I would like… litres of …	Quisiera … litros de …
… regular petrol.	… gasolina normal.
… super./ …diesel.	… súper./ … diesel.
… unleaded./ …leaded.	… sin plomo./ … con plomo.
Please fill up.	Lleno, por favor.

Accident

Help!	¡Ayuda!, ¡Socorro!

If you'd like to know why these girls are so happy, it helps if you're able to ask.

Warning!	¡Atención!
Look out!	¡Cuidado!
Please, quickly call …	Llame enseguida …
… an ambulance.	… una ambulancia.
… the police.	… a la policía.
… the fire brigade.	… a los bomberos.
Do you have bandages?	¿Tiene usted botiquín de urgencia?
It was my (your) fault.	Ha sido por mi (su) culpa.
Give me your name, please, and your address.	¿Puede usted darme su nombre y dirección?

Food

Where can I find …	¿Dónde hay por aquí cerca …
… a good restaurant?	… un buen restaurante?
… restaurant that is not too expensive?	… un restaurante no demasiado caro?

Please book a table for us this evening for 4 people.	¿Puede reservarnos para esta noche una mesa para cuatro personas?
Here's to you!	¡Salud!
Could I have the bill, please!	¡La cuenta, por favor!
Did you enjoy your meal?	¿Le/Les ha gustado la comida?
The food was delicious.	La comida estaba écelente.

Shopping

Where do I find ...	Por favor, dónde hay ...
... a market?	... un mercado?
... a pharmacy?	... una farmacia?
... a shopping centre?	... un centro comercial?

Accommodation

Could you please recommend me ...?	Perdón, señor/señora/señorita. ¿Podría usted recomendarme ...
... a hotel	... un hotel?
... a guest house	... una pensión?
I have booked a room.	He reservado una habitación.
Do you still have ...	¿Tienen ustedes ...
... a single bedroom?	... una habitación individual?
... a double bedroom?	... una habitación doble?
... with shower/bath?	... con ducha/baño?
... for a night?	... para una noche?
... for a week?	... para una semana?
What does the room cost with ...	¿Cuánto cuesta la habitación con
... breakfast?	... desayuno?
... half board?	... media pensión?

doctor

Could you recommend me a good doctor?	¿Puede usted indicarme un buen médico?
I have ...	Tengo ...
... diarrhoea.	... diarrea.
... a temperature.	... fiebre.
... a headache.	... dolor de cabeza.

Bank

| Excuse me, where is ... | Por favor, dónde hay por aquí ... |

… the bank, please?	… un banco?
… the bureau de change, please?	… una oficina/casa de cambio?
I would like to	Quisiera cambiar …
exchange dollars for pesos convertibles.	dollar en pesos convertibles.

Post

How much does …	¿Cuánto cuesta …
… a letter …	… una carta …
… a postcard …	… una postal …
to England cost?	para Inglaterra?
stamps	sellos
Telephone cards	tarjetas para el teléfono

Numbers

0	cero	19	diecinueve
1	un, uno, una	20	veinte
2	dos	21	veintiuno(a)
3	tres	22	veintidós
4	cuatro	30	treinta
5	cinco	40	cuarenta
6	seis	50	cincuenta
7	siete	60	sesenta
8	ocho	70	setenta
9	nueve	80	ochenta
10	diez	90	noventa
11	once	100	cien, ciento
12	doce	200	doscientos, -as
13	trece	1000	mil
14	catorce	2000	dos mil
15	quince	10 000	diez mil
16	dieciséis		
17	diecisiete	1/2	medio
18	dieciocho	1/4	un cuatro

GEOGRAPHICAL EXPRESSIONS

Viewpoint	Mirador
Mountain	Montaña
Summit	Pico
Bridge	Puente
Village	Pueblo
Plain	Llano
Rock	Roque

Garden	Jardín
Harbour	Puerto
Cave	Cueva
Church	Iglesia
Coast	Costa
Country road	Carretera
Lighthouse	Faro
Sea	Mar
Square	Plaza
Spring, well	Fuente
Gorge	Barranco
Reservoir	Embalse
Beach	Playa
Street	Calle

Have the colonial times really come to an end?

Valley	Valle
Tower	Torre
City quarter	Barrio
Path	Camino

Restaurant/Restaurante

desayuno	breakfast
almuerzo	lunch
cena	dinner
camarero	waiter
cubierto	place setting, cutlery
cuchara	spoon
cucharita	coffee spoon
cuchillo	knife
lista de comida	menu
plato	plate
sacacorchos	corkscrew
tenedor	fork
taza	cup
vaso	glass

Sopas/Soups

caldo	consommée
gazpacho	cold vegetable soup
puchero canario	stew
sopa de pescado	fish soup
sopa de verduras	vegetable soup

Entremeses/Starters

ensalada	salad
pan con mantequilla	bread and butter
caldo de pollo	chicken broth
crema/asopao	pureed soup
sopa de pescado/de verduras	fish/vegetable soup

Platos de huevos/Egg dishes

huevo	egg
duro	hardboiled
pasado por agua	soft-boiled
huevos a la flamenca	eggs with beans

huevos fritos	fried eggs
huevos revueltos	scrambled eggs
tortilla	omelette

Pescado/Fish

ahumado	smoked
a la plancha	grilled on a hot iron plate
asado	fried
cocido	boiled
frito	baked
anguila	eel
atún	tuna
bacalao	dried cod, codfish
besugo	bream
lenguado	sole
merluza	hake
salmón	salmon
trucha	trout
almeja	river mussel
bogavante	lobster
calamar	calamari
camarón	shrimp
cangrejo	crab
gamba	prawn
langosta	crayfish
ostras	oysters

Carne/Meat

buey	beef, ox
carnero	mutton
cerdo	pork
chuleta	chop
cochinillo, lechón	suckling pig
conejo	rabbit
cordero	lamb
ternera	veal
vaca	beaf
asado	roast
bistec	steak
carne ahumada	smoked meat
carne estofada	pot roast
carne salada	salted meat
fiambre	assorted cold cuts
jamón	ham

There is no shortage of bananas in tropical socialism. Try them deep-fried or roasted.

lomo	sirloin or chine
salchichón	hard cured sausage
tocino	bacon
pato	duck
pollo	chicken

Side dishes/Guarniciónes

arroz (congrí)	rice with red beans
boniato	sweet potatoes
malanga	tuber
moros y cristianos	rice with black beans
tostones	deep-fried bananas
papas fritas	French fries
yuca	manioc

Postres/Desserts

bollo	sweet roll

dulces	confectioneries
flan	flan
helado	ice-cream
mermelada	jam
miel	honey
pastel	cake
queso	cheese
tarta	gateau

Frutas/Fruit

coco	coconut
fresa	strawberry
guayaba	guava
fruta bomba	papaya
limón	lime
mango	mango
naranja	orange
piña	pineapple
plátano	banana
sandía, melón	water melon
tamarindo	tamarind
toronja	grapefruit

Bebidas/Drinks

agua mineral	mineral water
con/sin gas	sparkling/still
agua de caña	sugar-cane juice
agua de coco	coconut milk
aguardiente (de caña)	(sugar-cane) spirit
batida	mixer with milk
cerveza	beer
café cubano/con leche	coffee black/with milk
cafecito	espresso
cocoloco, saoco	coconut filled with rum
champán	champagne
ginebra	gin
guarapo	sugar-cane juice
jugo de naranja/limón/piña	orange/lime/pineapple juice
leche	milk
refresco	soft drink
ron	rum
té	tea
vino blanco/tinto/rosado	white/red/rosé wine

Literature

Arenas, Reinaldo: *Before Night Falls*, London: Serpent's Tail, 2001
A disturbingly brilliant memoir, made into a successful film, about sexual and artistic freedom in Cuba.

Castro, Alicia: *Queens of Havana. The Amazing Adventures of Anacaona, Cuba's Legendary All-Girl Dance Band*, New York: Grove Press, 2007
Today still, in its younger version, this all-female band is popular in Cuba. In 1930s Havana, Anacaona was made up of eleven sisters, and one of them, Alicia Castro, reveals a story of jazz, mambo and cha-cha-cha, the band's breakthrough and the post-revolution era.

Zoë Bran: *Enduring Cuba*, Melbourne: Lonely Planet, 2008
Illuminating description of the daily struggle in Cuba, originally published in 2002.

Padura, Leonardo: *Tell me something about Cuba*, London: Bitter Lemon Press, 2009
Brilliant biblio-mystery and follow-up to Havana Quartet, this thriller features Havana ex-cop turned-antique book dealer Mario Conde.

Hemingway, Hilary and Carlene Brennan: *Hemingway in Cuba*, NYC: Rugged Land, 2003
Ernesto's niece Hilary and Carlene Brennen take the reader on a voyage through time into history, from the legendary 1930s to the Roaring Fifties.

Fuentes, Norberto: *The Autobiography of Fidel Castro*, New York: W W Norton, 2009
An old close friend of Castro's, today living in the US, slips into his role and tells us of the Cuban day-to-day life of the Máximo Líder.

Leonard, Elmore: *Cuba Libre*: Harper Torch, 2002
The king of the hard-boiled crime novel takes his pen to the still-unexplained explosion of the battleship *USS Maine* that triggered the Cuban-Spanish-American War.

Hemingway, Ernest: *Islands in the Stream*: Brookvale, James Bennett, 2003.
Probably Hemingway's most personal novel, telling of his experiences in the Second World War and adventures at sea. For the musical accompaniment, consider downloading the mp3 of the Kenny Ro-

gers and Dolly Parton song, or the Bee Gees version, from amazon, for instance.

Hemingway, Ernest: *The Old Man and the Sea*, New York: Scribner, 1995.
Nobel-Prize-winning Cuba novel about the near-mythical fight between a fisherman and a swordfish.

Anderson, Jon Lee: *Che Guevara – A Revolutionary Life*, New York, Grove Press, 2010
Groundbreaking biography of the charismatic and iconic figurehead. Following the author's research, Che's remains were unearthed in Bolivia and returned to Cuba in 1997, the year the book was first published.

Miller, Tom: *Trading with the Enemy: A Yankee Travels through Castro's Cuba*: New York, Basic Books, 2008
The knowledgeable American Cuba aficionado and National Geographic travel writer tells of his adventures sustained during many stays on Cuba.

Roy, Maya: *Cuban Music: from Son and Rumba to the Buena Vista Social Club and Timba Cubana*, Princeton: Markus Wiener, 2002
Knowledgeable study of the history and origin of the diverse sounds and bands from Cuba with CD with some historical recordings.

Gutierrez, Pedro Juan: *Dirty Havana Trilogy*, New York: Ecco Press, 2002
A hard look at the dark side of life in Havana during the Special Period; not for the faint-hearted.

Greene, Graham: *Our Man in Havana*, Vintage, 2001
The 1958 classic, made into a memorable film with Alec Guinness and Maureen O'Hara, takes the reader deep into the pre-revolutionary era.

Ramonet, Ignacio: *My Life: Fidel Castro*, New York, Scribner, 2009
The acclaimed Spanish journalist spent over 100 hours between 2003 and 2005 interviewing the Líder Máximo – a fascinating spoken-word testimony of a fascinating character.

Jack Kenny: *Cuba*, Corazon Press, 2005
Atmospheric duo-tone prints, the fruit of over 40 trips to Cuba, providing a glimpse of the Cuban soul.

Coffee-table books

Michael Connors: *The Splendour of Cuba: 450 Years of Architecture and Interiors*, NYC: Rizzoli, 2011
Sumptuous coffee table book on the architectural glory of Cuba.

Media

Television
Most large hotels have satellite TV with CNN and other American channels. For those who understand Spanish, there are four national TV channels: »Tele Rebelde« and »Cubavisión« and two educational channels, as well as regional broadcasters in the provinces.

Radio
The English-language **tourist station Radio Taíno** reports on events and other news that is of interest to tourists. Of the five major Cuban radio stations, the most important are **Radio Rebelde**, which was founded by the rebels during the revolution and is still a mouthpiece for the government, and **Radio Reloj**, which broadcasts news round the clock. There are numerous regional stations in the various provinces.

Cuban newspapers
The official organ of the Communist Party of Cuba is the daily newspaper *Granma* (www.granma.cu; English version also online). *Trabajadores* (www.trabajadores.cubaweb.cu; Spanish and English), a trade union journal, and *Juventud Rebelde* (www.jrebelde.cubaweb.cu; only Spanish), a paper for young people, are published weekly. *Bohemia* magazine is also a weekly publication.

Foreign-language newspapers
Cuban Review is a monthly English-language publication produced in Cuba. It contains a lot of information for tourists. Foreign newspapers are hardly obtainable in Cuba, though weekly magazines can sometimes be found in big hotels.

Money

Official means of payment
Since November 2004 only the peso convertible (and in many tourist areas the euro) has been the official **currency for foreigners**. The US dollar is no longer legal tender, and higher fees are charged for changing dollars than, for example, for the British pound. The **peso convertible (CUC)** is a kind of artificial currency, convertible only in Cuba. Any CUCs remaining at the end of the holiday can be changed back again. The value of the peso convertible is US$ 1, i.e. one pound sterling is worth approx. 1.60 pesos convertibles, one euro approx. 1.30 pesos convertibles (May 2012). When US$ are converted to CUC, a fee of 10% is charged!

The »**real**« **Cuban peso** (1 CUP, equal to 100 centavos) can hardly be used by tourists travelling in groups. Its exchange rate to the peso convertible is about 1:25, i.e. 1 CUC = 25 CUP. Foreigners can use the Cuban peso in city buses (»camellos«), on private markets (»agromercados«), in private pool taxis in cities (»taxis particulares«, which run on certain routes with several passengers), and in rural areas at simple snack bars (for Cubans). Otherwise tourists pay in pesos convertibles or in holiday enclaves like Varadero, Cayo Largo, Cayo Coco, etc. in foreign currency, especially euros!

Most hotels, restaurants, souvenir shops, hire-car and travel agencies accept **the usual credit cards and travellers cheques**, so long as they were not issued by American banks. Credit cards and travellers cheques from American Express and Diners Club and the Citibank Visa Card are not taken in Cuba. It is advisable not to rely on credit cards and travellers cheques, but to take **sufficient cash**.

Changing money

Cash and travellers cheques can be exchanged at many banks, cadecas (bureaux de changes) and hotel receptions. Usually a passport is required for this. As a rule banks are open Mon – Fri 8.30 – 12 noon and 1.30pm – 3pm, sometimes also on Saturday mornings in the main tourist areas, cadecas usually Mon – Sat between 8am and 5pm. Keep **receipts** for every exchange transaction, as it may be necessary to present them when changing back from pesos to foreign currency.

EXCHANGE RATES

1 GB £ = 1.60 CUC
1 CUC = 0.62 GB £

1 US$ = 1 CUC
1 CUC = 1 US$

1 euro = 0.77 CUC
1 CUC = 1.28 euros

CONTACT DETAILS FOR CREDIT CARDS

Bank debit and credit cards and SIM cards that are lost or stolen should be reported and blocked immediately. In the event of lost bank or credit cards, can contact the following numbers in UK and USA (phone numbers when dialling from South Africa):

► **Eurocard/MasterCard**
Tel. 001 / 636 7227 111

► **Visa**
Tel. 001 / 410 581 336

► **American Express UK**
Tel. 0044 / 1273 696 933

► **American Express USA**
Tel. 001 / 800 528 4800

► **Diners Club UK**
Tel. 0044 / 1252 513 500

► **Diners Club USA**
Tel. 001 / 303 799 9000

Have the bank sort code, account number and card number as well as the expiry date ready.

The following numbers of UK banks (dialling from South Africa) can be used to report and cancel lost or stolen bank and credit cards issued by those banks:

► **HSBC**
Tel. 0044 / 1442 422 929

► **Barclaycard**
Tel. 0044 / 1604 230 230

► **NatWest**
Tel. 0044 / 142 370 0545

► **Lloyds TSB**
Tel. 0044 / 1702 278 270

Post · Communications

Post (Correos) All large hotels have a post desk. A postcard from Cuba to Europe costs 0.50 centavos, a letter 0.80 centavos, and can take two to four weeks to arrive.

Telephone connections From larger hotels calls can be made directly or through an »operador« to Europe for approx. 5 CUC per minute. It is a little cheaper to use telephone cards, which are available in many hotels and are increasingly widespread in other place in Cuba.

Reorganization of the phone network ▸ The Cuban telecoms utility is currently reorganizing its system. This means new area codes and extensions of the number. Some of the phone numbers given in this guide could not be researched, or will have been changed after going to print.

Mobile phones In Cuba a GSM network functions, so it is possible to make calls via mobile providers from home – but with high roaming charges. At the time of writer, it was no longer possible to rent a mobile/cell phone.

Internet In some tourist destinations such as Havana and Varadero, as well as in the better hotels, cybercafés and internet connections for checking e-mails exist. All the local offices of the phone company ETECSA have kiosks for checking mails.

 DIALING CODES

TO CUBA

00 53
Omit the following 0 of the Cuban area code.

FROM CUBA

To UK: 119 44
to ROI: 119 353
to US/CAN: 119 1. Omit the following 0 of the area code.

Prices · Discounts

Saving money as a package tourist Compared with other Caribbean countries, Cuba is still inexpensive – for »todo incluido« holidays, i.e. with all costs included. As soon as you start to make trips independently, however, things can get more expensive. With daily prices from CUC 50 to 65, hire cars are not cheap. And those things that are cheap tend to have typical Cuban drawbacks: in the low-cost and basic »Campismo« bungalows – insofar as they are not restricted to Cuban holidaymakers any-

WHAT DOES IT COST?

Übernachtung im DZ
ab 32 CUC

3-Gang-Menü
ab 12 CUC

Mojíto
2 – 4 CUC

Mineral-wasser
1 CUC

Taxifahrt in Havanna
2 – 5 CUC

Einfache Mahlzeit
ab 2 – 4 CUC

Eine Tasse Kaffee
0,50 – 1 CUC

way expect to shower in cold water, and there will be no bed linen – though a power cut is possible. In places where usually more Cubans are to be found than foreigners and tourists, menus and at box offices for admission tickets **prices are often quoted with a dollar sign**; however, the prices refer to peso prices for Cubans. After considering this it becomes clear that beer does not cost »$ 10« and a concert ticket in the Casa de la Musica does not cost »$ 100«, but that this is the price in Cuban pesos – for the Cubans only, however, as foreigners will then pay the equivalent in pesos convertibles, i.e. about CUC 10 for the concert.

Although invoices usually include a service charge, hotel employees, waiters, taxi drivers etc expect an additional tip amounting to about **10% of the bill**, as for most Cubans it is very difficult to get hold of foreign currency. It is recommended to give hotel maids a first tip on the day after arrival, then one tip per week.   *Tipping*

For children under the age of twelve there is often a big discount, e.g. on Viazul buses and in many hotels and museums.   *Discounts*

Shopping · Souvenirs

In comparison with other countries, Cuba is nothing like shopping heaven. Food, clothing and other necessary consumer goods are strictly rationed and available to Cubans in exchange for a ration coupon in specific outlets. Those who can get hold of pesos convertibles or foreign currency can also buy clothing and »luxury items«   *Restricted shopping for Cubans* such as soap or cooking oil in expensive stores, but for Cuban citizens the prices in such shops are extremely high. For tourists, who are not subject to these currency problems, there are several attractive products in particular shops.

Souvenir shops and stalls

In all large hotels and at places frequented by tourists there are state-run souvenir shops (the chains are called Caracol and Artex), where visitors can purchase all manner of items – for example rum, cigars, t-shirts, pottery, music, orisha dolls, wood carvings, maracas, papier-mâché figures, chocolate, biscuits and cosmetics. Here and there, especially in Havana and Trinidad, opportunities exist to buy souvenirs on **street markets** (e.g. naïve paintings).

An inexhaustible variety of souvenirs for sale on the beach

Rum, especially the famous Havana Club, is a favourite purchase to take back home. The light-coloured, three-year-old version is good for cocktails, while the 5- and 7-year old (Añejo) are gold to medium-brown in colour and also taste good drunk neat. Connoisseurs will enjoy the 15-year-old Havana Club Reserva or Matúsalem Añejo Superior, and the brands Matúsalem, Varadero, Caney and Caribbean Club are also worth buying.

> ! *Baedeker* TIP

Cuba feeling at home

Those returning home from their Cuban holiday as a passionate salsera, hip swing and all, as an aficionado inseparable from their cigar and addicted to Havana Club rum, will be glad to hear that they can mail order everything they need from Fidel's Cristal beer and Che Guevara t-shirts, stickly-sweet guava jam or the blackest Cubita coffee through companies such as www.cuba-connect.co.uk and www.cubanfoodmarket.com.

Cuba is known for its excellent tobacco. In den tobacco factories in Havana, Santiago, Pinar del Río and Trinidad the brands Habanas, Monte Cristo, Romeo y Julieta and Partagás or on sale at relatively low prices, and cigars can also be had in souvenir and cigar shops. **Cigars**

There are special shops for rum and cigars, especially in Havana, Pinar del Río, Trinidad and Santiago. Visits to a rum distillery and a cigar factory are combined with an opportunity to buy what is made there ▶Baedeker Special p. 310. ◀ Rum and cigar shops

Che Guevara on a t-shirt, as a key ring, on an ashtray, as a photo or magnet, painted in oils or as a portrait in beaten metal or as pokerwork: fans of the national hero can avail themselves of a huge range of »Che« souvenirs. **Che Guevara merchandise**

Lovers of salsa, rumba and son will find all the best Cuban songs and other music on CD. Leading salsa bands are El Médico de la Salsa, Adalberto Álvarez and the old-established Los Van Van and Celia Cruz. Nueva Trova music by Pablo Milanés, Silvio Rodríguez, Irakere and sons by Benny Moré and many others will also delight fans of Cuban music. Recordings can often be bought directly from the music, but the quality is usually that of a living-room studio. **CDs**

Sports and Activities

Both mass sport and international-level sport receive strong official support in Cuba, as shown by the large number of medals that Cubans win at Olympic Games and in other international competitions. The national sports are boxing and baseball, but cycling, swimming and athletics are also held in high regard. Many sports events take place all year round. **Importance of sport in Cuba**

Angling
Deep-sea angling ▶

Hemingway fished for blue marlin off the north coast of Cuba, and since then an international competition for this fish has been held every May or June in Marina Hemingway in Havana. Deep-sea anglers can also go out for swordfish, barracuda, sailfish, tuna and other prey. The waters that are richest in fish are off the north coast near Pinar del Río (Cayo Levisa), Havana, Cayo Guillermo, Santa Lucía and Guardalavaca, and in the south off Cayo Largo, Isla de la Juventud and in the Gulf of Ana María (Ciego de Ávila province).

Golf

So far Cuba has only two golf courses, in Havana and Varadero. New ones, e.g. on Cayo Coco, are planned.

Bike tours

Bicycles – »bici« for short – are luxury goods in Cuba, the land of tropical socialism with its chronic shortage of petrol. Lucky owners of bikes carry these prized possessions into their flats as a matter of course – even if they live on the 14th floor and the lift is not working once again for lack of power and spare parts. Never mind: »así es Cuba«, this is Cuba. In Cardenás a monument honours the heroic workers in the factory that assembles millions of **Chinese bicycles for Fidel Castro's people** – every one of them without gears or lights. Which is why not one of the 11 million Cubans would dream of spending a holiday pedalling a bike. However, more and more tourists are doing so, as Cuba is a wonderful country for tourists with a reasonable level of fitness: it is fairly flat, the motorways are quiet, there are country roads where more ox-cars and horse-drawn carriages are to be seen than card, and the few Cuban drivers, who are used to masses of cyclist, are considerate (or actually cannot go fast in their 1950s museum pieces). Further advantages are the spectacular scenery, and the odd challenge in the »alturas« or sierras (▶ Tours, p. 142). Those who **bring their own bike** even have a chance of climbing high to the toughest of all Cuban cycling routes: the hairpins of the »Farola« in the east of the island near Baracoa, with jungle vegetation at every turn. Further south near Santiago cyclists take the beautiful coast road or follow the revolutionary trail through the Sierra Maestra around Cuba's highest mountain, Pico Turquino (1974m/6477ft) – a dream for off-road fans and fit mountainbikers.

In Havana a Cuban-Canadian joint venture, Bicicletas Cruzando Fronteras (Edificion Metropolitano, Calle San Juan de Dios, esq. Aguacate, tel. 07/8 60 26 17), **hires out bikes**: second-hand bicycles of different sizes donated from Canada cost approx. CUC 12 per day

> **!** *Baedeker* TIP
>
> **Bring your bike...**
>
> Most airlines will allow and charge for transporting a bike. Easily demountable/spare parts are best carried in hand luggage! Consider donating your bike at the end of the trip – Toronto-based www.bikesforcuba.com could be helpful here, as customs officials don't like the practice. ...

(weekly and hourly rates also available), but it is advisable to have a practice ride before hiring and not to expect an fancy high-tech features. Privately hired bikes cost CUC 3 – 7 per day (make sure there is a lock). Hotels too often supply mountainbikes on an all-inclusive basis, although here too standards may not be very high. With a lot of luck you can buy an overpriced Chinese model (about CUC 150) or even a mountainbike in one of the modern shopping centres in Havana (Galerias de Paseo and Plaza Carlos III).

Signposting in Cuba is a bit haphazard and there are no dedicated maps for cyclists. **The best road maps** to use are Guía de Carreteras and the Mapa Turistico Cuba.

Up to now it was mainly Canadians and Latin American who came to Cuba for health reasons (e.g. the Argentinean ex-footballer Maradona for drug rehab). Cuba has an international reputation in the fields of orthopaedics and neurology. The sanatoria and beauty clinics have varying standards, but they usually have all the necessary equipment and offer services like physiotherapy, acupuncture, herbal treatments: e.g. in Havana the hotel La Pradera (Calle 230 entre 15A y 17, Siboney, Playa, tel. 7/33 74 73, -74, fax 33 71 98, -99, comercia@pradera.cha.cyt.cu.), near Trinidad the newly renovated Kurhotel Escambray (▶Trinidad) and the spa town San Diego de los Baños to the southwest of Havana. More and more **hotels have their own spa** with anti-cellulitis and cosmetic treatments and the like, e.g. Hotel Comodoro in Havana-Miramar (Calle 3 esq. a 84, tel. 07/204 55 51, fax 204 20 89, www.cubanacan. cu), and others in the seaside resort Tarará near Havana and in Varadero.

Spa and health tourism

If you want to learn to dance salsa, book a course in Cuba. Where else? It's the **country where the basic rhythms of this »hot sauce« for dancers originated,** where people sway their hips, gyrate with their pelvis and rotate their spine till you think they must be creaking in every joint. Salsa just has to be learned in Cuba! There are now several good dancing schools with professionals as teachers and partners, especially in Havana. In Havana and in smaller cities like Trinidad or Santiago »dance instructors« even approach tourists offering private instruction.

Salsa dance courses

Crystal-clear waters and countless protected coral reefs around Cuba provide excellent conditions for snorkellers and divers. There are 500 registered diving spots off Cuba, some of which are among the best in the world, e.g. those in María La Gorda, the Isla de la Juventud and Cayo Largo in the south, Cienfuegos (Faro Luna), Playa Ancón (Trinidad), Jardines de la Reina and the coast off Santiago. Santa Lucía in the north has the **world's second-largest coral reef** (after the Great Barrier Reef), and there are further excellent diving waters in Guardalavaca, Varadero and the Cayería del Norte (Cayo Coco, Cayo Guillermo).

Snorkelling – Diving

Sail out to sea and go snorkelling in turquoise and azure waters.

Bring diving goggles, a snorkel and flippers with you, as the choice in Cuba is limited. Those who shun water can see the underwater world from a **glass-bottomed boat**without getting wet (e.g. in Varadero, Cayo Coco).

Sailing Those who cannot sail themselves can **charter a boat with a skipper**: e.g. the single-masted *Niña*, which sails along the south coast of Cuba between the Isla de la Juventud and the port of Cienfuegos, cruising among the countless small, uninhabited islands of the Archipiélago de los Canarreos, such as the tiny Cayo Rosario. The next destination is Cayo Largo, a divers' paradise, where yachts and trippers' boats bob in the marina. *Niña* then sets course for the coast: Cienfuegos, her home port and a 19th-century colonial gem on the Bahía de Cienfuegos, where dolphins escort the ship.

During the six-day trip, the night is not always spent in marinas sheltered from the wind, so for landlubbers who have a tendency to be sea-sick and are not used to rocking in a bunk, the trip is not suitable in windy weather. Also bear in mind that the captains don't always speak much English, and that hurricanes cross the region, especially in September and October.

Language courses If you want to understand the indistinct Cuban version of Spanish and even speak it yourself, there are many providers of language courses.

ADRESSES

FISHING

► **Cubanacán Nautica**
184 no. 123 Flores, La Habana
Tel. 07 33 66 75, fax 07 33 70 20
www.cubanacan.co.uk

GOLF COURSES

► **Havana**
Club de Golf Habana (9-hole, par -35), Ctra. de Vento, km 8
Capdevila, Boyeros
La Habana
Tel. 07/84 54 578
9-hole, 18-hole course

► **Varadero**
Varadero Golf Club (18-hole, par -72) Crta. Las Americas km 8.5
Tel. 045/66 73 88, 66 77 88
Fax 66 84 92
www.varaderogolfclub.com
18-hole course

SPA TOURISM

► **Novasans**
East Ocean Centre 303 98 Grandville Road, Kowloon, Hong Kong
Tel. 00 852 81 91 16 19
http://www.novasans.com/spa-wellness/cuba/ kuba-reisen.de

► **Cubanacán**
► angling

► **Gaviotatours**
Ave. 47 no. 2833 entre 28 y 34
Rpto. Kohly, Playa
Havana
Tel. 07/2 04 57 08, 649 72 68 (airport), or 285 34 80 (airport)
www.gaviota-grupo.com

► **Kuoni**
Tel. 0 844 488 04 17
www.kuoni.co.uk
tour

BIKE TOURS

► **Exodus**
Tel. 020 8 675 55 50
www.exodus.co.uk
The well-known adventure tour operator runs relaxed to more challenging bike holidays for small groups, 8 or 15 days. The company supports sustainable tourism, working with local families and paladares

SALSA COURSES

► **Fiesta Cubana**
Tel. 07 80/288 94 63 03
www.fiestacubana.ca
Traditional and popular dances in Havana, organised through this Canadian operator

► **Club Dance Holidays**
Tel. 020 7 099 48 16
www.clubdanceholidays.co.uk
Professional tuition by day and nights out in the Salsa clubs of Havana and Trinidad. The »Salsa at Christmas in Havana and Varadero« package is the choice for people who like their festive season with a difference.

► **In Havana and Santiago**
Courses are organized at the Conjunto Folklórico Nacional (expensive), the Teatro Nacional in Havana and the Casa del Caribe in Santiago. Introductions to Cuban dances, some of them fairly ambitious, and programmes of entertainment including salsa courses by the pool are held in almost every beach hotel.

For further information on dance courses, see Baedeker Special p. 216

Where will you ever learn to dance salsa, if not on Cuba?

SAILING

► **The Real Cuba Experience**
►Salsakurse
British tour operator in Havana
offering 7-day onboard diving and
sailing expeditions, and options
for the complementary activities.
Tel. 020 72 42 31 31
Tel. in Havana: 07 866 42 21

► **www.gosailcuba.com**
►spa tourism

LANGUAGE COURSES

► **Caledonia Languages**
33 Sandport Street
Edinburgh EH6 6EP
Tel. 01 31 621 77 21
www.caledonialanguages.co.uk

► **In Cuba**
Language courses of various levels
of difficulty are held at the University of Havana.
Edificio de Varona, tel. 07/
870 05 84, 8 73 42 50
elizabeth@rect.uh.cu
www.mes.edu.cu

DIVING

► **The Scuba Diving Place**
Tel. 0 20 76 44 82 52,
www.the scubadivingplace.co.uk

HIKING – CLIMBING

► **Captivating Cuba**
Tel. 0 800 171 21 50
Fax 01 242 77 65 40
www.captivating-cuba.com
Specialist operator for hiking and
salsa holidays
►Salsa courses

Hiking – Climbing Cuba is now being discovered by walkers: after all the country has
100 nature reserves. Because they have the best infrastructure and official guides are provided, the best areas are the **Sierra del Rosario**
(near Pinar del Río, Soroa, Las Terrazas, where there are waymarked
paths), the **Sierra del Escambray** for the Topes de Collantes (here the
four-hour hike to the Caburní Waterfall is possible without a guide,
though 400m/1300ft have to be climbed!) and the area around the
reservoir **Presa Hanabanilla** near Trinidad.

In the **Sierra Maestra** a climb to Cuba's highest mountain, Pico Turquino, follows the trail of revolutionaries. It is best done from the
mountain village of Santo Domingo in the interior and not from the
coast, as many find the coastal route from Las Cuevas too steep. The
mountains here, Pico Martí and La Bayamesa too, rise from sea level

to 1974m/6477ft in the space of only 5km/3mi; those who neverthe-less attempt this tour should plan in 2–3 days, ideally in the period between October and May.

An alternative is the walk to the more accessible **Gran Piedra** in the eponymous national park east of Santiago de Cuba. Further recom-mended trips go to the **Parque Nacional Alejandro de Humboldt** with its rainforest character and the **El Yunque** table mountain, both near Baracoa. The more remote the area, the more likely it is that accom-modation will be extremely spartan.

Organized hikes are often only day trips, which are officially allowed only with a guide. In the »mogotes«, the limestone hills of Pinar del Río and Viñales, **climbers** are now making an appearance – with stunning views to be had, no wonder! Rock climbers should bring their own kit with them. For all walks it is important to have stout footwear and a water bottle, perhaps food supplies too.

Time

Cuba is in the American Eastern Time zone, four hours behind Greenwich Mean Time and five hours behind British Summer Time (in Cuba the clocks are not changed for the summer). When it is 12 noon in London, in Cuba the time is 7am (or 8am) in the morning.

Transport

Expect poor surfaces and sometimes gigantic potholes on all roads. In places low-lying railway tracks cross the road and hinder the flow of traffic. Only on motorways is the condition of the road surface reasonably good, but even here, and in spite of the limited amount of traffic, it is best to drive slowly, as **all sorts of obstacles can cross your path:** cows, pigs, hens, ox carts, cyclists, pedestrians, horse ri-ders, horse carriages and much more. Traffic lights are sometimes suspended so high that they cannot be seen, and road works are not always marked. It is especially dangerous at night, as few vehicles and bikes have working headlamps and lights.

State of the roads and dangers

On Cuba the usual international regulations apply. Breaches of the speed limit and monitored and punished severely. The top speed on motorways and country roads is 90kmh/56mph, in built-up areas 60kmh/37mph. »PARE« means »STOP«.

◄ *Traffic regulations*

All sizeable towns have **Cupet petrol stations** which stay open 24 hours a day and accept pesos convertibles.

Petrol

● USEFUL ADDRESSES

BUS

► **Viazul**
Avenida 26 y Zoologico
Nuevo Vedado, Ciudad de La
Habana
Tel. 07/8 81 14 13, 8 81 56 52 and
8 81 11 08
www.viazul.com
Branches in e.g. Varadero (Calle
36 y Autopista) and Santiago de
Cuba (Avenida Los Libertadores
no. 457 esq. Yaroyo).

RAILWAY

► **Estación Central**
Habana vieja
Tickets: La Coubre Train Station,
Av. del Puerto & Desamparados,
Tel. 07/8 62 21 74, 8 66 00 30,
8 66 02 59 (station information)
www.hicuba.com/ferrocarril.htm

► **PTG**
Tel. 01 235 22 72 88
www.ptg.co.uk

► **Seat 61**
www.seat61.com
Reliable train website run by a
dedicated train UK train enthusi-
ast.

HIRE CAR

► **Cubacar/Transtur**
Tel. 07/273 22 77
www.transtur.cu

► **Havanautos/Transtur**
Tel. 07/273 22 77
www.havanautos.com
booking@ vacacionartravel.com,
http://cubaalquilerdecoches.com

► **Gaviota**
Calle 98 e/9na y 11, Rpto,
Cubanacán, Playa, Habana
Tel 07/206 99 35
Fax 207 95 02
com_tr@via-rentacar.cu
www.gaviota-grupo.com

► **Rex**
Office at Hotel Parque Central
Zulueta, entre Virtudes y Animas,
Centro Habana.
Tel. 07/835 68 30
www.rex.cu

► **Transautos**
Tel. 33 57 63 and
33 57 64 (airport)

On longer trips and when driving across the country by hire car, ensure at all times that there is enough petrol to reach the next Cupet
station, as in rural areas, supplies of petrol are by no means guaranteed.

Public Transport

Be patient!   Due to the shortage of petrol and spare parts, public transport on
Cuba does not always function; crowds of people can be seen at bus
stops and railway stations everywhere, waiting for hours for their
connection or for some alternative to arrive.

Fully air-conditioned tourist buses are provided to take visitors everywhere on the island that is of interest to them (book in hotels).

Bus travel

Viazul operates a good bus service from its base in Havana, with connections to e.g. Pinar del Río, Valle Viñales, Varadero, Santiago de Cuba and Trinidad, as well as from Trinidad to Varadero.

◄ Viazul

City buses, known to Cubans as »camellos« (camels), are always hopelessly overcrowded. If you really want to take one, have enough small change at the ready and leave any valuables and bags in the hotel.

◄ City buses

A few travellers in Cuba use **»camiones«,** a typically Cuban means of transport, cheap but time-consuming. Foreigners usually pay in »moneda nacional«, Cuban pesos, and have to queue and wait like everyone else.

Trucks

Train trips too are something of an adventure, with delays that last for hours or even days. Information: Infotur, Informacion Turística in Havana (►Information) and Estación Central.

Rail

The journey, most of it overnight, **from Havana to Santiago** takes 12–17 hours. There are also connections between Havana and Pinar del Río, Matanzas, Cienfuegos, Las Tunas, Bayamo, Holguín, Santa Clara, Morón, Ciego de Ávila and Camagüey.

For a **picturesque trip** take Cuba's only electric train on the three-hour journey from Havana (Casablanca Station) to Matanzas. The »Hershey Train« passes through the scenic Valle de Yumurí for visits to an old sugar mill. Lovers of steam technology should make their way to the area around Guardalavaca and Santa Clara, where steam trains are still used for transporting sugar cane (for historical information: http://www.tramz.com/cu/hy/hy.html).

A horse-drawn carriage is a romantic and speedy way to get around.

Flying is the most comfortable and reliable way to cover long distances on Cuba, but be sure to book tickets in good time (►Arrival).

Flights

Hire cars

International hire-car companies are not represented on Cuba, but all tourist centres, the airports in Havana and Varadero and large hotels have offices of Cuban hire-car agencies.

Cuban agencies

To hire you need a national driving licence, to be at least 21 (sometimes 25) years old and to provide a deposit in the form of a credit card or CUC 200. Basic daily prices start at CUC 50 plus insurance. Petrol supplies for tourists are available from the Cupet petrol stations in large towns, which open 24 hours a day. When receiving a hire car, check the **spare tyres** and wheel jack.

Recently it became possible to travel around Cuba by **camper van** (with the appropriate national licence or an International Driving Licence); however, since 2010 no camper vans have been available for rent. There are about 27 campsites on Cuba, with electricity, water supplies and garbage disposal starting at approx. CUC 140 per day.

Tourist taxis

Tourist taxis can be recognized by the yellow sign on the roof or a »T«. All have a taximeter and stop at hotels and places of interest to tourists. Elsewhere it is often very difficult to find a taxi, especially at night.

More and more **private individuals** offer their services with the sort of cars that make the trip an experience. Negotiate the price in advance and don't be surprised by breakdowns.

Travellers with Disabilities

Facilities for the disabled

Cubans are very willing to help, but few wheelchair users can be seen on the streets (the pavements are often very uneven, there are few ramps). The state TV broadcasts programmes for those with hearing difficulties using sign language. Travellers with limited mobility should bear in mind that lifts are often out of order.

If a room suitable for a person with disabilities or a wheelchair user is needed, be sure to state this when booking the journey. In theory four such rooms should be available **in every hotel**, especially in more modern hotels. For example in the following Gran Caribe and Meliá hotels (www.gran-caribe. com, solmeliacuba.com): Riviera, Meliá Cohíba, Meliá Habana and Golden Tulip (all in Havana), Arenas Blancas (Varadero), Villa Covarrubias (Las Tunas), Maraguan (Camagüey), Casa Granda (Santiago), all large and new all-inclusive hotels on Cayo Coco and Cayo Largo and in Guardalavaca and Cayo Santa María.

 IMPORTANT CONTACTS

► **Disabled Travel Guide**
Quayside Business Centre, Ouserburn Building
Newcastle upon Tyne, NE6 1LL
Tel. 01 91 275 50 00
www.disabledtravelguide.co.uk

► **Clydegrove Travel**
2351 Dumbarton Road, Yoker
Glasgow G14 0NN
Tel. 08 45 257 01 13, outside office hours Tel. 07 798 91 74 05
www.disabledaccessholidays.com

When to Go

For Europeans the most pleasant time to visit Cuba is from **November to April**, the dry season with average temperatures around 25°C/ 77°C. Most precipitation falls in the rainy period from mid-May to October, when it may rain suddenly and hard, but usually not for a long time, so that the sun comes out again soon and travel is possible. The months of July and August are the hottest and least comfortable. Temperatures then rise to over 30°C/86°F, and the humidity can reach 82%. Moreover, in summer and autumn (especially September/October) there is a danger of hurricanes.

In the provinces Pinar del Río, Havana and Matanzas, unpleasantly cool north winds sometimes blow in winter. The south coast of Cuba is mostly warmer than the north coast, and it rains much less in the east of the island than in the west (except in the moist rain forest region near Baracoa, where 3000mm/120in of annual precipitation is the highest level of rainfall in Cuba).

? DID YOU KNOW ...?

- ...that every year about tropical cyclones are formed in the North Atlantic, of which about half reach hurricane strength? This affects the west of Cuba, especially between July and November: the worst storms were Michelle (2001), Lilly (2002) and Dennis (2005). However, Cuba has an excellent warning and evacuation system, which ensures that less damage is done and fewer lives are lost than on other Caribbean islands such as Haiti and Jamaica.

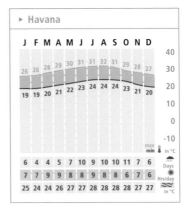

▶ Havana

	J	F	M	A	M	J	J	A	S	O	N	D	
max	26	26	28	29	30	31	31	32	31	29	28	27	in °C
min	19	19	20	21	22	23	24	24	24	23	21	20	
Days	6	4	4	5	7	10	9	10	10	11	7	6	
Hrs/day	7	7	9	9	8	8	9	8	6	6	7	6	
in °C	25	24	24	26	27	27	28	28	28	28	27	27	

Tours

AS IF AIMING TO ACHIEVE NEW RECORD HARVESTS TO FULFIL A FIVE-YEAR PLAN, THE CUBAN SOCIALIST REPUBLIC IS ATTRACTING SOME TWO MILLION VISITORS PER YEAR WITH A GREAT NUMBER OF TAILOR-MADE ACTIVITIES AND THEMED TOURS ACROSS THE COUNTRY.

Sign of quality
The best tobacco grows between the mogotes in the Valle de Viñales.

The Cuban capital
The restored old quarter of Havana contrasts with its other crumbling districts.

Architectural jewel
Authentic restoration of Trinidad's colonial-era historic quarter

Like paradise
The Peninsula de Zapata may not have roast pigeon, but how about coconut?

TOURS OF CUBA

 Four tours through all the regions of Cuba, through cities founded in
colonial times and the capital, Havana, the beautiful scenery of the
tobacco-growing region in the west and the revolutionary east –
with stops at the beach wherever you please.

▬▬ **TOUR 1**   **Tour 1: Grand Tour of Cuba**
This tour across the island takes in the buzzing capital Havana,
sleepy colonial towns and a trip back to the days of the sugar
barons.   ► **page 144**

▬▬ **TOUR 2**   **Tour 2: A Shorter Trip Around Cuba**
A journey back to the days of the revolution and the colonial period, with plenty to interest nature lovers, too.   ► **page 148**

▬▬ **TOUR 3**   **Tour 3: Tobacco and Mogotes in the West of Cuba**
This tour leads to the most beautiful scenery on Cuba: in the Valle de Viñales, overgrown limestone rocks rise from the rust-brown
tobacco fields.   ► **page 150**

▬▬ **TOUR 4**   **Tour 4: In the Footsteps of Revolutionaries**
On this trip to the rebellious east of Cuba, leave enough time for
walking and some relaxation on the beach.   ► **page 152**

Age of the sugar barons
*In the Valle des los Ingenios, slave labour
brought prosperity to the Trinitarios.*

Travelling in Cuba

The Caribbean Coast

Popular beaches

The north ▶ Cuba's coast, 5700km/3500mi long, boasts 300 beaches and more than 4000 islands and islets: fine white sand beneath palms and sea grapes, azure waters and a tropical sky with usually not a cloud in sight. Many of the beaches have not been developed for tourism or are almost exclusively used by Cubans. Others are now internationally known and provide every imaginable tourist attraction, for example **Varadero, Trinidad, Guardalavaca** and the quieter **Santa Lucía**, where divers can go on exciting wreck dives. These places are in the north, where the sea can be rougher than in the south. They offer almost every kind of water sport, international diving bases, bars, dance clubs, restaurants serving international cuisine and an endless range of souvenirs.

Special treats for kids include popular »dolphinariums«, though these are admittedly not cheap, with admission costing 40 CUC per person plus the price of a film permit (dolphinariums can be found in Varadero, Guardalavaca, Cienfuegos in the south and Baconao in the east). New holiday areas on the north coast are **Covarrubias** (near Puerto Padro, Las Tunas province), **Cayo Santa María** (near Caibarién/ Villa Clara province) and **Playa Pesquero** (in the province of Holguín) with their big, luxurious »todo-incluído« (all-inclusive) resorts. The Hotel Playa Pesquero is the largest Cuban hotel to date, with about 994 rooms – perhaps not what everyone is looking for...

Havana ▶ For those who have little time to explore Cuba and prefer to be based in the lively capital city, it is worth knowing that the beaches start just beyond the city limits of Havana at the miles-long **Playas del Este**, where visitors can mingle with Cubans and tourists are in a minority in some places.

Islands ▶ It's a different matter on islands that have been developed for tourism such as **Cayo Largo** and **Cayo Coco/Cayo Guillermo**, and a new destination, **Cayo Santa María**: here foreign tourists keep themselves to themselves, as Cubans are admitted to the holiday zone only when they work there as a barman, chambermaid, travel representative, holiday club entertainer or bus driver (Cayo Largo can be reached only by air, Cayo Coco via a 20km/12mi causeway from the mainland at San Rafael, but only for those who can pay the toll in pesos convertibles!).

Varadero ▶ Although thousands of Cubans live in Varadero town and families spend their free time on the beach, the majority of them are not allowed to swim and sunbathe on the dream beach there – just as it was in the age of the Al Capones and Du Ponts, the rich Americans who populated the beach at Varadero in the 1950s. Only »heroes of labour« who have been invited by the trade unions are allowed to relax with their families in Varadero for a few days, usually in the basic or mid-range hotels. It has more attractions and greater variety than any other holiday town, from glass-bottomed boats to parachute jumps for those who don't like water. It's not surprising that almost half of the foreign holidaymakers on Cuba end up here.

◄ The south

In the south of the island the hotels are more scattered, the sea is calmer and the holiday resorts too are less lively. In winter it is not as cold here in the evenings as on the north coast. Among the well-known places with good hotels and facilities for water sports are **Trinidad-Ancón, Playa Larga** and **Playa Girón** near the Bay of Pigs (close to Guamá), **Playa Rancho Luna** (near Cienfuegos) and the beaches and bays west and east of **Santiago** (for example the quiet Playa Cazonal in Parque Baconao national park).

Quieter spots for swimming ...

The less well-known seaside towns are quieter and tend to have more basic hotels, usually in the lower mid-range category. Some of them are not easy to reach, and patience may be needed, especially if a fer-

So beautiful that it was once reserved for high-ranking party officials: the small island of Cayo Saetía

The west ▶ ry trip is involved. The beaches are largely unspoiled. In the far west of Cuba, the **Guanahacabibes** Peninsula attracts lots of divers. This area is protected as a Unesco world biosphere reserve and consists

Decaying plaster on Trinidad's Iglesia de Nuestra Señora

mainly of mangrove swamps inhabited by many reptiles, but in María La Gorda visitors can lie beneath palms on the beach. A small bungalow hotel caters for guests who want a peaceful time on the idyllic **Cayo Levisa**, half an hour by boat north of Palma Rubia.

The largest island in the **south, Isla de la Juventud**, is attractive to divers, nature lovers and fans of history. The island has a lot of variety to offer, as well as everyday Cuban life. So far the hotels, few in number and fairly basic in standard, are mainly the haunt of divers who book at the Hotel Colony's international diving centre in order to explore the maritime beauty of the Archipiélago de los Canarreos on underwater excursions: about 30km/20mi offshore, where the Cuban island shelf suddenly falls away to a depth of more than 1000m/3300ft, divers find a wonderland of caves, canyons, swarms of fish and plenty of corals.

The north and east ▶ **Cayo Sabinal** in the north is also pleasantly peaceful when the daytrippers from neighbouring Playa Santa Lucía have left again. The beaches near **Baracoa** at the eastern tip of Cuba are pristine and idyllic: Playa Maraguana (to the west) and the coast from Playitas Cajobabo to Playa Yacabo (towards Guantánamo). In some places on Cuba travellers might feel they have been transported to a different continent, for example at the sight of zebras living in the wild! **Cayo Saetía** (95km/60mi from Guardalavaca) might be somewhere in Africa: antelopes, ostriches and wild boar obviously feel at home here. Most foreign tourists fly in for a day by helicopter from Guardalavaca to join a jeep safari, armed with their video cameras and zoom lenses.

The south of the island ▶ In contrast to the endless white beaches of the north coast, those in the south are often dark grey and hidden in lovely little bays with palm groves and steep cliffs, for instance along the wonderful stretch of coast between Santiago de Cuba and the fishing ports of **Chivirico** and **Marea del Portillo**. In some places the road runs barely higher than the deeply indented coastline, with waves washing over the asphalt.

The Interior

Spending two weeks on the beach is not the way to get to know Cuba and the Cubans. A trip to the island's colonial towns by contrast conveys a view of Cuban history and also an impression of Cuba today (the more picturesque the town, the more tourist groups it will attract, and the bolder the begging and offers of various other services; this is particularly noticeable in Trinidad and Santiago). Do visit at least one of the old quarters that have been prettily restored with Unesco funds, as in **Havana (Habana Vieja)**, **Trinidad** and **Santiago de Cuba**, the latter being the site of the oldest building on the island. Less crowded but equally worth seeing are **Camagüey** (with the largest historic quarter in Cuba), **Cienfuegos, Matanzas** and **Sancti Spíritus**. To see a real little gem with the authentic, i.e. in many cases unrestored, charm of a historic town, head for more remote places such as **Baracoa** (the first Spanish settlement in Cuba), **Gibara** and **Manzanillo**.

Revolution pilgrims still come to Cuba in large numbers, following in the footsteps of the great revolutionary heroes. To take a tour of **Havana** without seeing the gigantic Plaza de la Revolución and the Revolution Museum would be like drinking a mojíto without the mint! Situated in the San Carlos de la Cabaña fortress, Che Guevara's former headquarters in Havana is now a museum. Those interested in Fidel Castro will want to pay a visit to his »cell« (actually more like a spacious room) on **Isla de la Juventud** in the Presidio Modelo prison. The famous **Bahía de Cochinos**, the Bay of Pigs, is also an essential stop-off, even though today there is little at Playa Girón and Playa Larga, apart from a museum and a few memorials, to remind visitors of the failed invasion by Cuban exiles in 1961. The highlight for admirers of Che Guevara is the mausoleum in **Santa Clara**, where Che and his comrades-in-arms from Bolivia were buried. Che Guevara drove government troops from this town in late 1958. The region around **Santiago de Cuba** was the birthplace of the revolution in the early 1950s, and it was here that Fidel Castro proclaimed victory on 1 January 1959: the Moncada Barracks, Granjíta Siboney, the spot where the yacht *Granma* landed at Playa Las Coloradas (near Manzanillo) and the Sierra Maestra mountains are all sites that fans of revolutionary heritage should see (►Tour 4).

Cuban eco-tourism is still in its infancy and often appears to be closely regulated – for example, in theory a guide should be present on all walks in nature reserves and on mountains, even though Cuba is free of alpine challenges. Apart from the regions mentioned in »Sport and Activities« (►p. 123), the jungle-like Alejandro de Humboldt National Park and the Sierra Maestra are the pre-eminent destinations for treks. In the **Humboldt National Park**, part of the Cuchillas de Toa mountain range near Baracoa can get very muddy during heavy rainfall (from June to August it rains less). These mountains, which rise to 1200m/3900ft, have been classified by Unesco as a world biosphere reserve and boast an impressive variety of vegetation, from palms, primeval tree ferns and Cuban pine to mahogany and teak trees.

The wild forested terrain around Pico Turquino, the national park of the same name in the **Sierra Maestra** near Santiago de Cuba, can be explored on horseback. From the mountain village of Santo Domingo (64km/40mi from Bayamo) mountain hikers can climb the summit (1974m/6477ft) within a day: first by jeep up a steep road with hairpin bends to the first viewpoint at Alto de Naranjo, then another 13km/8mi or so by foot on rough paths through misty deciduous forest. It is also possible to view the mountains from a helicopter: there are flights above the Sierra Maestra with a stop at the El Saltón waterfall (▶Tour 3).

Tours on a bike

How about a bike tour from the west (Pinar del Río) to Santa Clara in the interior? The route goes up and down a lot of hills that truly test the leg muscles, and there is no guarantee that the Chinese gears will not fail at an altitude of 700m/2300ft in the Sierra del Rosario at Pinar del Río. From time to time a loudly rattling Soviet truck with Cuban passengers clinging on to it roars past the cyclists, enveloping them in black smoke. Around every bend, a new scenic photo opportunity awaits. Continuing east, between Guamá and the famous Bay of Pigs the route at last follows a wonderfully flat country road that seems like an infinitely long final straight for athletes, with nothing but swampland to the left and right. The following day's stage is once again a challenge for mind, body and the bike's gears: Trinidad lies on the other side of the foothills of the Sierra del Escambray, boasting the second-highest mountain in Cuba (Pico Juan, 1156m/ 3793ft). The billboards by the wayside may or may not have an encouraging effect: »Hasta la victoria siempre« (»Until eternal victory«). The midday sun beats down mercilessly on cyclists, the road winds up and down like a path across a giant sheet of corrugated iron, and finally the tempting deep blue of the Caribbean Sea and Trinidad on the south coast provide the motivation for pedalling a last sprint to conclude a daily stretch of some 60km/37mi. On its final day, the tour leads over the alturas towards Santa Clara, the town of folk hero Che Guevara.

Means of Transport

Hard or comfortable

Many of the seaside and colonial towns described in this book are served by daily **Viazul buses**. Many of the tourist islands are reached via a causeway (Cayo Coco, Cayo Santa María), while Cayo Levisa has a twice-daily **ferry** (in the morning and evening), the Isla de la Juventud has ferry and air connections, and Cayo Largo is accessible only by air.

There are many ways to travel on wheels, some of them laborious.

The **rail network** runs different kinds of train (the very slow »lecheros« and »Express« trains) on a regular timetable from Havana to the west (Pinar del Río) and across the centre of the island to Santiago de Cuba, stopping in various provincial towns (Cienfuegos, Santa Clara, Camagüey etc).

The adventurous can try travelling on **»camiones«** (trucks): however, if you want to use this very Cuban means of transport on the back of a truck (the luxury version with benches to sit on is sometimes available!), you should be able to speak some Spanish, and have lots of time, patience and some Cuban pesos.

There are daily **flights** to most large towns, tourist centres and provincial capitals, but it is advisable to reserve a seat well in advance.

To save time and avoid stress, book a trip with a travel agent. In addition to walking and cycling tours, their catalogues include themed trips around Cuba. Some of the walking trips mentioned in this book can be booked locally through Cuban agencies that provide a guide (e.g. at Infotur, Asistur or through a hotel). In some tourist spots (e.g. Varadero, Viñales, Cayo Largo, Trinidad) mopeds can be hired, though at a fairly high price.

For seeing the interior of the island at leisure without joining a group, one option, if somewhat expensive, is to **hire a car or camper van** (filling up with fuel is now possible without problems at the Cupet petrol stations, but remember to fill the tank in good time and always to have a functioning (!) spare tyre and wheel jack in the car). The terrain in central Cuba is flat for hundreds of miles, and rather monotonous owing to the extensive fields of sugar cane and pastures for cattle. Among the most diverse and attractive routes are the Pinar del Río area, the Valle de los Ingenios near Trinidad, the alturas near Santa Clara, the Farola hairpins at Baracoa and the coast road west of Santiago: this route, which was asphalted only a few years ago and has repeatedly been damaged by hurricanes, winds between mountain slopes and the sea, and rock falls on the road are common.

Travelling by car

Tour 1 Grand Tour of Cuba

Start and finish: From Havana to Baconao National Park
Length: approx. 1000km/620mi

Duration: 3 – 4 weeks

A 1950s showpiece
Veteran cars are a symbol of the city of Havana.

Charm of bygone days
The old colonial quarter of Camagüey reflects the prosperity of days past.

A rarity
It's easier to find the colourf of Polymita picta in the mus Holguín than on the beach.

Havana ** 6 mi/ 10 km
Cojímar
9 mi/ 15 km
San Francisco de Paula
111 mi/ 178 km
* Guamá
28 mi/ 45 km
* Cienfuegos
Topes de Collantes
59 mi/ 95 km
9 mi/ 15 km
40 mi/ 64 km * Sancti Spíritus
47 mi/ 76 km
4 mi/6 km
* Valle de los Ingenios
Ciego de Ávila
* Playa Girón
47 mi/ 75 km
3 mi/ 5 km
** Trinidad
67 mi/ 108 km
130 mi/ 209 km
* Camagüey

Scene of political events
but also a paradise for humans and other animals: the Península de Zapata

Holguín
* P. Na Gra
83 mi/ 133 km
17 mi/ 28 km
12 mi/ 20 km
* El Cobre
** Santiago de Cuba
* Parque N de Ba

Latin temperament
In Trinidad carnival is celebrated in June.

Time travel
The fort of Santiago de Cuba looks like the set of a pirate film.

This is the classic tour of Cuba, a trip across the country from the buzzing capital city Havana to sleepy colonial towns, up to lofty viewpoints in the Sierra del Escambray for a sweeping panorama of the island and down again for a true experience of the wonderful sugar-cane region around Trinidad, once the source of the country's wealth. Finally the tour reaches the east of Cuba with its Afro-Caribbean character, the main holy sites of the Santería cult (El Cobre) and many sites associated with the revolution.

Schedule at least three days in the capital city ❶ ✶ ✶ **Havana** to walk its historic trails, especially in the carefully restored old quarter, La Habana Vieja. Take plenty of time for a stroll around the Parque Céspedes, the Plaza de la Catedral and Prado. Rampa, the main street in the Vedado district, and the Malecón are also best explored on foot. Fans of art and history should take a look at the Municipal Museum, the Museum of the Revolution and the Fine Art Museum. Other important sights are the Plaza de la Revolución with its government buildings and monument to Martí, and the magnificent tombs in the Cementerio Colón. Make sure to set aside a day for the so-called Hemingway Route, too, i.e. a trip east of Havana to the fishing village of ❷ **Cojímar** (10km/6mi) and the wonderfully situated Hemingway museum Finca La Vigía in ❸ **San Francisco de Paula** (15km/9mi). Here, in the author's country residence, time seems to have stood still. A peep through the window of this colonial-style estate reveals books wherever you look, as well as whisky bottles, which may seem a little dusty but are standing there just as if Hemingway was still around to pour himself a drink. The author lived here for about 20 years, but left Cuba in 1959 shortly after the revolution, fearing he would be a »persona non grata« after the fall of the Batista regime. His residence is now an endangered monument. Round off the day in true Hemingway style in one of his favourite bars, the Bodeguita del Medio or Floridita in the old district of Havana. Allow one further day for a trip from Havana to the west of Cuba (►Tour 3).

»Queen of the Antilles«

DON'T MISS

- Habana Vieja: a stroll through the old quarter of Havana and along the Malecón is definitely a must.
- Palacio del Valle: visit an ornate palace in Cienfuegos.
- Museo Municipal in Trinidad: travel back to the age of the sugar barons
- Valle de los Ingenios: take a camera for the pretty scenery in the valley of the sugar mills.
- El Cobre: Cuba's patron saint is revered in this basilica near Santiago.

From the Cuban capital the tour goes to the south of the island, first of all to touristic ❹ ✶ **Guamá** (178km/111mi, on the motorway to the Australia sugar factory, then turn off south), where the resort on Lago del Tesoro lies in the middle of mangrove swamps. The attractions here include a hotel in pre-Columbian style and a crocodile

Mangrove swamps and fine residences

farm. Further south on the Zapata Peninsula it is another 45km/28mi to the famous Bay of Pigs, where exiled Cubans attempted an invasion in 1961. A museum in ❺ ✳ **Playa Girón** tells the story of this event. Continue for 95km/60mi via Yaguaramas and Rodas to colonial ❻ ✳ **Cienfuegos** on the Bay of Jagua. Plaza Martí and the surrounding buildings are a fine sight here. A trip to Palacio del Valle on the La Gorda Peninsula conveys an idea of the wealth of the owners of the grand mansions here. It is worth looking at the botanical garden, which has a unique collection of palm trees, cacti and species of bamboo.

Colonial jewel The route follows the coast to Trinidad, passing the mountains of the Sierra del Escambray. About 5km/3mi before reaching this colonial town, a winding road ascends to the mountains and ❼ **Topes de Collantes**, a spa known for its good air. With its uneven cobbled streets and beautiful buildings, ❽ ✳ ✳ **Trinidad** has a historic atmosphere. Recommended activities here are a visit to the museums around the Plaza Mayor and a stroll through the streets, where all kinds of craft products are on sale. Only a few miles northeast of the city discover

A wager is said to have been behind the building of this 50m/165ft-high tower in the Valle de los Ingenios.

tations once laboured to make the Trinitarios prosperous. The tower of Iznaga, once a kind of lookout point, is a reminder of those days.

⑩ ✳ **Sancti Spíritus**, 70km/45mi east of Trinidad, while often overlooked, is worth a stop for its pretty town centre, small museums, the bridge over the Yayabo and an attractive Casa de la Trova. The Zaza Reservoir is suitable for an excursion into the countryside. Camagüey, Cuba's third-largest city, is also greatly underestimated. The journey there via motorway, a distance of 184km/114mi, takes you through ⑪ **Ciego de Ávila**, a typical Cuban small town where peace and quiet reign supreme. Thanks to its location in the middle of the island, ⑫ ✳ **Camagüey** has hardly been developed for tourism, and maintains a charm of its own for precisely that reason. Taking a leisurely stroll through the quiet streets of the old quarter allows to discover hidden corners. A common and conspicuous sight on little squares and in courtyards are »tinajones«, large ceramic jars that were once used to collect rainwater and keep it fresh. Now this tour heads east on the motorway via Las Tunas and ⑬ **Holguín** (209km/130mi), a sober-looking town. However, it is worth taking a detour to the nearby Mirador de Mayabe, a beautifully situated lookout point with a rustic restaurant.

Either 135km/84mi or 153km/95mi further south (depending on whether you choose the longer scenic route via El Cobre or the shorter route on the motorway from Soriano), tread revolutionary ground in ⑭ ✳✳ **Santiago de Cuba**, the region where all Cuban liberation movements originated. Start a tour of the city on Parque Céspedes and all its historically important sights. A few interesting museums and the Casa de la Trova are close by. Be sure not to miss a visit to the Moncada Barracks: in 1953 an attack on the barracks by Fidel Castro and his comrades marked the start of the revolutionary movement on Cuba. The museum that has been installed here provides a lot of information about Cuba and the revolution. The Cementerio S. Ifigenia in the north of the city, with imposing marble graves and the mausoleum of José Martí, is also interesting.

Unofficial capital

One of the best trips around the city goes to the El Morro fortress for a superb view of the Bay of Santiago. Some 20km/12mi west of Santiago, ⑮ ✳ **El Cobre** is a place of pilgrimage where the patron saint of Cuba, the Virgen de la Caridad, is revered. The east of Santiago also holds some interesting destinations. At a distance of less than 30km/20mi, the Gran Piedra rises to a height of 1214m/3983ft in the middle of the ⑯ **Sierra Maestra National Park**. Follow the coast road a further 3km/2mi to Granjita Siboney, the rebels' hideout before their attack on the Moncada Barracks. A good 25km/16mi further east, the ⑰ ✳ **Baconao National Park** is a Unesco biosphere reserve. This area of 800 sq km/300 sq mi is home to a prehistoric valley, various museums, a zoo and wonderful lookout points.

Around Santiago

Tour 2 A Shorter Trip Around Cuba

Start and finish: Havana
Length: approx. 800km/500mi

Duration: approx. 10 days

On this tour you get a whiff of urban atmosphere in Havana, cave air near Matanzas and a fresh sea breeze in Varadero. It's also a journey back in time to the years of the revolution and the colonial period: to honour Che Guevara at a memorial site in Santa Clara and to see a display of the sugar barons' wealth in Trinidad. The tour finishes with beaches, swamps and crocodiles for nature fans.

The best beaches
From the Cuban capital ❶✱✱ **Havana** the route goes east to Varadero, the number one tourist destination on Cuba with its beautiful sandy beach, over 20km/12mi long. Only10km/6mi out of Havana you reach the fishing village ❷✱ **Cojímar**, immortalized by Ernest Hemingway in his novel *The Old Man and the Sea*.

After 82km/51mi the Puente de Bacunayagu, Cuba's longest bridge, crosses the palm-studded ❸✱✱ **Yumurí Valley**, and beyond the bridge the route soon leads into the Bay of ❹✱ **Matanzas** and the pretty colonial town of the same name. From here, it is worth taking a side trip to the impressive cave system of ❺✱✱ **Cuevas Bellamar** (5km/3mi southeast). The next stop is ❻✱✱ **Varadero** for a couple of days relaxing on the beach.

✔ **DON'T MISS**

■ Valle de Yumurí: breathtaking views of the valley of palms from the Bacunayagu Bridge
■ Che Guevara's mausoleum in Santa Clara: a place of reverent silence
■ Cienfuegos: the botanical gardens have one of the world's most comprehensive collections of palms.

Revolution in the air
Via ❼ **Cárdenas** drive on to Jovellanos and switch onto the main road to ❽✱ **Santa Clara** there. The history of this town is closely linked to the revolution, as it was here that Che Guevara fought his decisive battle. To see the landscape of the Sierra del Escambray, make sure to take a trip to the ❾✱ **Hanabanilla Reservoir** (51km/32mi from Santa Clara).

Beyond ❿✱✱ **Trinidad**, in the northeast, discover the tower of Iznaga in the ⓫✱ **Valle de los Ingenios**, whose sugar plantations made Trinidad rich. While its restored buildings, finely decorated window grilles and irregular cobblestone paving this town represents a journey back to colonial times, Playa Ancón also makes it a rewarding place for a beach holiday. ⓬✱ **Cienfuegos** with its spa atmosphere lies a further 80km/50mi away on the coast road. The municipal botanical gardens boast a unique array of plants.

Via Rodas and Yaguaramas continue to ⑬✱ **Playa Girón** (95km/ 59mi), where a museum commemorates the repulsing of the invasion at the Bay of Pigs in 1961. About 45km/28mi further north, a hotel in the style of pre-Columbian houses, a crocodile farm and the Lago del Tesoro at ⑭✱ **Guamá** can be visited. From here, drive north to return to Havana (178km/111mi) by joining the motorway at Australia.

For nature lovers

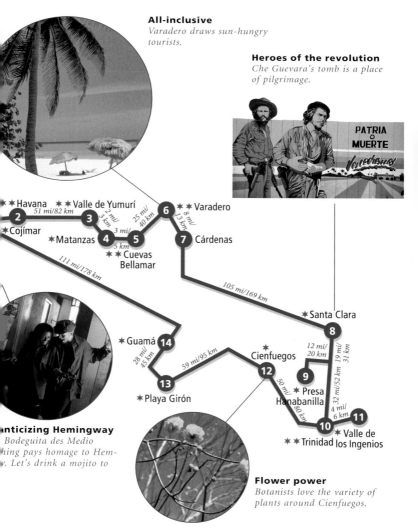

All-inclusive
Varadero draws sun-hungry tourists.

Heroes of the revolution
Che Guevara's tomb is a place of pilgrimage.

PATRIA O MUERTE

✱✱ Havana   ✱✱ Valle de Yumurí   ✱✱ Varadero
51 mi/82 km
2 mi/ 3 km
25 mi/ 40 km
8 mi/ 13 km
✱ Cojímar   ✱ Matanzas
3 mi/ 5 km
✱✱ Cuevas Bellamar
✱ Cárdenas
111 mi/178 km
105 mi/169 km
✱ Santa Clara
✱ Guamá
28 mi/ 45 km
59 mi/95 km
✱ Cienfuegos
12 mi/ 20 km
19 mi/ 31 km
✱ Presa Hanabanilla
50 mi/ 80 km
32 mi/52 km
4 mi/ 6 km
✱ Playa Girón
✱✱ Trinidad
✱ Valle de los Ingenios

Romanticizing Hemingway
La Bodeguita des Medio ...thing pays homage to Hem-...w. Let's drink a mojito to

Flower power
Botanists love the variety of plants around Cienfuegos.

Tour 3 Tobacco and Mogotes in the West of Cuba

Start and finish: From Havana to the Valle de Viñales
Length: approx. 450km/280mi

Duration: 1 – 4 days

This tour goes to Cuba's most beautiful scenery: mogotes is the name for the overgrown limestone rocks that loom up from the rust-brown tobacco fields in the Valle de Viñales. On a day trip to this valley it is best to go directly to the village of Viñales, but those who have two or three days should find time for a hike, for example near Soroa or Las Terrazas: the wonderful Sierra del Rosario mountain range is a Unesco biosphere reserve.

Starting out: centre of eco-tourism
From ❶ ✶✶ **Havana** drive west along the Sierra del Rosario; after 85km/53mi then turn north at Candelaria to visit the orchid garden of ❷ ✶ **Soroa** (►Pinar del Río) 7km/4.5mi further on, boasting over 700 kinds of orchid. A few hundred metres to the south, Salto del Arco Iris greets guests for a beach holiday in inviting, jungle-like natural surroundings. About 10km/6mi to the northeast in Las Terrazas (turn right at the barrier 3km/2mi north of Soroa) you can watch artists at work, go horse riding or hike on waymarked paths. Return to the motorway in order to continue to Pinar del Río. After 15km/9mi you reach Las Barrigonas, a small farming estate that is open to visitors.

The striking feature in the streets of ❸ ✶ **Pinar del Río** (89km/55mi from Soroa) is the columned architecture, including the Teatro Milanés. Don't miss the Francisco Donatier cigar factory and the Casa Garay, where Guayabita liqueur is made.

DON'T MISS

- El Salto: the wonderful waterfall at Soroa makes for a refreshing break.
- Las Terrazas: an overnight stay and a hike at a model ecological project on the Lago San Juan
- Viñales: get the best view of the valley of mogotes from the car park of the Hotel Los Jazmines – ideally at 6am, when the mist is still lying between the palm trees and over the tobacco fields.

Elephants' backs and tobacco fields
Only 28km/17mi to the north, in the Sierra de los Órganos, some of the most spectacular scenery on Cuba awaits: the ❹ ✶✶ **Valle de Viñales**, a fertile valley from which bare, bizarrely shaped limestone cones rise like elephants' backs. Another tourist attraction close by, in the Valle de las Dos Hermanas, is the Mural de la Prehistoria, a wall painting intended to represent the story of evolution. Those who find it too gaudy can take a break in the highly recommended Restaurant Mural, where rural dishes are served. Drive a little further

into the valley past fields of tobacco to the pretty village of ✳ **Viñales** and ✳ **Cueva del Indio** (5km/3mi from Viñales), a cave with interesting stalactites and stalagmites. The flora and fauna in the area around the cave is still intact; with a little luck it is possible to see the rare tocororo bird here, the cork palm, and the white mariposa flower.

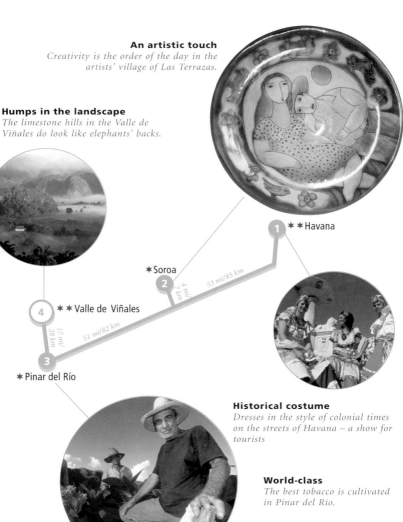

An artistic touch
Creativity is the order of the day in the artists' village of Las Terrazas.

Humps in the landscape
The limestone hills in the Valle de Viñales do look like elephants' backs.

✳✳ Havana

✳ Soroa

✳✳ Valle de Viñales

53 mi/85 km

4 mi/7 km

51 mi/82 km

17 mi/28 km

✳ Pinar del Río

Historical costume
Dresses in the style of colonial times on the streets of Havana – a show for tourists

World-class
The best tobacco is cultivated in Pinar del Río.

Tour 4 In the Footsteps of Revolutionaries

Start and finish: Guardalavaca
Length: approx. 700km/435mi

Duration: 5–6 days

Experienced riders
Many people around Holguín live off agriculture and raising cattle.

Irresistible
On the beaches at Guardalavaca, it feels like heaven.

① ✱✱ Guardalavaca

51 km

24 mi/
38 km

② Banes

Holguín **③**

34 mi/
55 km

18 mi/
29 km

9 mi/
14 km

21 mi/
34 km

44 mi/71 km

27 mi/
44 km

⑪ Dos Ríos

56 mi/90 km

⑩ Bayamo

40 mi/65 km

⑨ Manzanillo

47 mi/75 km

18 mi/
29 km

Chivirico

43 mi/70 km

✱ **Parque Nacional Gran Piedra**

17 mi/
28 km

④

17 mi/
27 km

⑤

⑥

✱✱ **Santiago de Cuba**

✱ **Parque Nacional de Baconao**

⑧

75 mi/121 km

⑦

Parque Nacional Desembarco del Granma

Rebels' refuge
The revolutionaries had their base in the Sierra Maestra.

At the foot of the Sierra Maestra
No Cuban city has more of a Caribbean vibe than Santiago.

This tour to the rebellious east of Cuba first of all follows the trail of Indians in the museum at Banes and of revolutionaries in Santiago de Cuba. Allow three extra days for a trek in the Sierra Maestra. The next stage takes the spectacular coast road from Santiago past beaches and Cuba's highest mountain, west to the sleepy coastal town of Manzanillo. Anyone who wants to stop for a swim will find plenty of sand and seawater on this round trip of 700km/435mi.

There are interesting sights to see in the immediate vicinity of ❶ ✷ ✷ **Guardalavaca**. An Indian burial place was excavated only 5km/3mi south of this seaside resort. While the Chorro de Maíta museum is a memorial to it, most of the finds are on display in the archaeological museum of ❷ **Banes** (38km/24mi southeast of Guardalavaca). About 84km/52mi southwest of Banes, ❸ **Holguín** might be a plain-looking town yet it forms an important traffic hub for Cuba. From here drive south.

On the tracks of the aboriginal inhabitants

In ❹ ✷ ✷ **Santiago de Cuba**, the »cradle of the revolution«, the rebellious history of eastern Cuba is ever-present. The main sights are the city centre around the Parque de Céspedes, the Plaza de la Revolución, the Moncada Barracks and the El Morro fort, commanding superb views across the Bay of Santiago. Some 10km/6mi outside Santiago heading east, just before Siboney, the road turns off north to the ❺ ✷ **Parque Nacional Gran Piedra**. After approximately 18km/11mi you reach the »big rock« that gives the national park its name. The ascent to the summit takes about 30 minutes and is not very difficult. Back on the coast road continue 3km/2mi to Granjita Siboney, where the attack on the Moncada Barracks was planned. 27km/17mi further on there is

Cradle of the revolution

much scenic and cultural interest in the ❻ ✷ **Parque Nacional de Baconao** (prehistoric valley, museums and other leisure facilities).

After this detour to the east of Santiago, the journey carries on west with continually stunning views of the Sierra Maestra mountains and the sea from the coast road. After 70km/44mi the little settlement of ❼ **Chivirico** with its Playa Sevilla beach is a good place to take a break. 60km/37mi further along, Cuba's highest mountain, **Pico Turquino** (1974m/6477ft) moves into view. Fidel Castro and Che Guevara's band of revolutionaries took refuge in this part of the Sierra Maestra after landing on Cuba on the yacht *Granma*. The road continues to the Gulf of Guacanayabo. Here, near the southern tip of the

Rebel country

coast at Playa Las Coloradas, after driving about 150km/95mi in the **❽Parque Nacional Desembarco del Granma**, the road reaches the place where the *Granma* landed, with a replica of the boat from which Fidel and his comrades went ashore on 2 December 1956. In **❾Manzanillo, a small port,** the route leaves the coast and turns inland towards Bayamo. Halfway there (about 25km/16mi) lies **Yara**, the starting point of the First War of Liberation, when Carlos Manuel de Céspedes freed his slaves and de-manded independence from Spanish rule. The cacique Hatuey, the first chief to rebel against Spanish, is said to have been cremated in Yara.

! Baedeker TIP

Birth of a revolutionary

No Fidel Castro heritage trail across Cuba is complete without a visit to his place of birth: the finca Las Manacas, where the revolutionary was born on 13 August 1926, lies about 3km/2mi northeast of Birán (not signposted). On the estate and in the open-air museum the graves of his parents, the Castros' residential and farm buildings, an arena for cockfights and an exhibition of photos about the life and career of the Cuban leader are on view (Mon – Sat 9am – 4.30pm, Sun 9am – 12 noon). Finca Las Manacas (also called Sitio Histórico Birán) in Birán, approx. 50km/30mi southwest of Cayo Saetía, approx. 65km/40mi southeast of Holguín.

Finally the journey leads 40km/25mi on to the capital of the province of Granma, **❿Bayamo**, whose rebellious nature is celebrated in the Cuban national anthem, *La Bayamesa*, was attested by the resistance of Indians, the revolts of slaves and struggles for liberation. Plaza del Himno and the house where Céspedes was born commemorate these times. From Bayamo drive 24km/15mi to Jiguaní, take the fork leading north (perhaps with a detour to the Loma del Yarey mountain ridge, supporting basic bungalows and a restaurant) and continue 20km/12mi across pasture land and sugar cane fields to **⓫Dos Ríos**: the most revered revolutionary hero of the 19th century, José Martí, died here in battle on 19 May 1895. A huge obelisk marks the spot. From here the route follows bumpy rural roads (incl. the 307 and the 421) on a 140km/90-mi trip back to Guardalavaca. An alternative is to leave out the detour to Dos Ríos and drive back in comfort on the country road to Holguín.

A rebellious place

← *The cathedral stands out in the cityscape of Santiago.*

Sights from A to Z

CUBA MEANS HOLIDAY HEAVEN:
THE SEA SHIMMERING TURQUOISE,
SLEEPY COLONIAL TOWNS WITH A
CARIBBEAN ATMOSPHERE, HUGE
TOBACCO PLANTATIONS AND OF COURSE THE
VIBRANT CAPITAL CITY, HAVANA, WITH ITS OLD
QUARTER LISTED AS A WORLD HERITAGE SITE.

Baracoa

L 5

Province: Guantánamo
Population: 82,000

Altitude: 0 – 20m/65ft
Distance: 1080km/670mi from Havana
286km/178mi from Santiago de Cuba

This small town with the sleepy charm of a tropical colonial village is tucked away at the extreme eastern tip of Cuba. To this day its inhabitants insist that on 28 October 1492 Columbus first set foot on the island here – and not, as the official version now has it, in Bahía de Bariay further west near Gibara (►p. 193).

Baracoa is indisputably **the oldest settlement on Cuba**, and some of the one-storey colonnaded houses with decaying tiled roofs and crumbling, pastel-shaded plaster façades seem to date back to the early days. The fertile mountain region around the town produces coconuts and cocoa, coffee and bananas.

Today Baracoa is developing into a hub for ecological tourism, thanks to treks in the Unesco-protected Alejandro de Humboldt National Park and rainforest, and boat trips on the many rivers, including picnics of roast sucking pig amidst luxuriant tropical vegetation.

History The »villa primada«, Cuba's first town, was founded in 1511 by Governor Diego Velázquez. Until 1515 it was the capital of Cuba, and three years after that the church was given the status of a cathedral. For a long period Indians lived in this area, including many who had fled from other conquered Caribbean islands. One of these was the **cacique Hatuey**, who came from Hispaniola (now Haiti) with members of his people. He resisted the Spanish conquerors, was taken prisoner and burned in public. 20 years later Indians took revenge for his death by burning down Baracoa. In the 16th and 17th centuries the town was often a **target for pirate raids**, not least because its citizens were themselves involved in smuggling. In response the **forts Seboruco, La Punta and Matachín** were built to give Baracoa better protection. However, no great wealth was to be earned here, and as other parts of the island became more attractive for settlers, the town slowly started to decline and was increasingly forgotten. After the slaves' revolts on Hispaniola new immigrants arrived. Families of French planters fled to Cuba and introduced the cultivation of coffee.

? DID YOU KNOW …?

■ … that the colourful snail Polymita picta, the »painted snail«, also known as the Cuban land snail, lives only on Cuba? It is one of the most beautiful snails, as its shell shimmers in every shade from white and yellow to orange and green. The Indian aborigines used the shells as a form of currency. The snail can still be found on the island, mainly in the east, and fine specimens can be admired in the museum in ►Holguín – or try your luck on the beaches around Baracoa …

What to See in Baracoa

Baracoa's main square has an unusual triangular shape. Cuba's oldest church, **Nuestra Señora de La Asunción**, stands on its east side. The church was built as early as 1512 when the colonization of Cuba was beginning. Today's building dates from the 19th century, as the church was destroyed by pirates several times.

Its greatest treasure is the Cross of the Vine (Cruz de Parra), which is venerated as a holy relic and was said to have been placed here by Columbus in 1492. For a long time the cross was thought to have gone missing, until in the mid-19th century it was found again on the coast. Scientific analysis has shown that it does in fact date from the 15th century and was made from the wood of the Cuban sea grape, which would confirm the theory about Columbus. Opening hours: daily 8am – 11am, 2pm – 5pm.

At the **centre of the square** stands a bust of Hatuey, a cacique from Hispaniola who fled to Baracoa with the remaining members of his tribe. Here he resisted the conquistadors, was taken prisoner and burnt at the stake.

Parque Independencia

★

◄ Cruz de Parra

◷

◄ Bust of Hatuey

First impressions are misleading: there's more than just garlic on the market at Baracoa, as the soil of the surrounding mountain region is fertile.

⏵ VISITING BARACOA

INFORMATION

Cubatur
Calle Martí 181 between Calle Ciro
Frías and Céspedes
Tel. 021/64 53 06, 453 75
cubaturbaracoa@enet.cu
This is the address of the Cubana
Aviación office: flights, twice a week to
and from Havana, are often booked
out for weeks on end during high
season; runs information desks in
hotels too.

EVENTS

Carnaval
First week of April

Foundation of the town
Each year on 15 August with street
festival, concerts and exhibitions.

WHERE TO EAT

Baracoa is not exactly a gourmet
destination. For a good meal, the best
bet is the Hotel ▶El Castillo or one of
the casas particulares: for the latter, ask
around if you have not already been
approached by someone.

▶ Moderate

La Colonial
Calle Martí 123
Tel. 021/64 31 61
Daily 10am – 10pm
This small, much-praised paladar
serves pork, shrimp and squid dishes
as well as fish in coconut milk »à la
Santa Barbara«, a Baracoa speciality, in
the living room.

Playa Maguana: Rancho Toa
Ctra. a Moa, km 20
A few miles from Playa Maguana on
the country road to Moa on the river
Toa
No phone, daily 7am – 7pm

Typical creole restaurant with a green
jungle air, a place for a trip out of
town. For ten people or more they will
roast a pig on a spit. While waiting for
this, take a kayak tour on the Toa,
which carries more water than any
other river in Cuba, or have yourself
rowed through the wild river landscape in a »cayuca« boat. The à la
carte menu lists Cuban classics such as
pork and chicken with rice, beans and yuca.

ENTERTAINMENT

**Casa de la Trova Victorino
Rodriguez**
Calle Antonio Maceo 149
Enjoy lots of atmosphere every day in
this music club next to the church,
with traditional music such as son and
boleros, or bachata and salsa for
dancing (Fri and Sun matinees from
10am with local bands, every evening
from 9pm till after midnight live
music and a show for tourists).

WHERE TO STAY

Baedeker recommendation

▶ Mid-range

El Castillo (Gaviota)
Calle Calixto García s/n Rpto. Paraíso
Tel. 021/6 45 16 45, fax 64 52 23
www.gaviota-grupo.com
This 35-room hotel stands in a small cast
on a low hill. Hiking trips are on offer fo
nature lovers.

▶ Mid-range

Hostal La Habanera (Rumbos)
Calle Maceo (on Plaza Independencia)
Tel. 021/64 52 73, 452 74
Beautifully restored colonial hotel in
the middle of town. Ten pretty rooms

Well-liked and often booked out: Porto Santo Hotel

face onto the somewhat noisy plaza, with a fantastic view from the rocking chairs on the common terrace, or onto the inner courtyard (larger, quieter rooms). Good, cheap restaurant on the ground floor. Masseur, internet, travel agency.

Porto Santo (Gaviota)
Carretera al aeropuerto s/n, Rpto. Jaitesico
Tel. 021/451 05, -6, 453 72
Fax 451 35
www.gaviota-grupo.com
36 rooms and 24 bungalows
Pretty colonial-style hotel on Bahía de Baracoa only five minutes from the airstrip. Restaurant with excellent creole cuisine.

► Mid-range/Budget
Playa Maguana: Villa Maguana
Ctra. a Moa (before reaching Playa Maguana, 22km/14mi northwest of Baracoa)
No phone
(book through Gaviota or Hotel ►El Castillo)
www.gaviota-grupo.com
Wooden cabañas (under construction) and three basic, air-conditioned rooms on the tiny beach, path to the 2km/1.25mi-long, palm-fringed Playa Maguana (daily shuttle bus from Baracoa: 10am, returning at 4pm).

► Budget
La Colina
Calle Calixto Garcia 158, Altos
Tel. 021/64 34 77, 64 26 85
ll@toa.gtm.sld.cu
Accommodation on the first floor of a small private house on the main street, with a terrace, air-conditioning, hot showers. Owner Alberto Matos Llime speaks good English and organizes tours. His wife is an outstanding cook.

Very close by, in Calle Maceo, the Casa de Chocolate is a good address for enjoying chocolate and ice cream.

Casa de Chocolate

The Matachín fortress (built 1739–1742) today houses Baracoa's **municipal museum**, with displays on regional history and culture. Opening hours: daily 8am–12 noon, 2pm–6pm.

Fuerte Matachín

🕐

In the eastern part of town, at the entrance to the little harbour, the semi-circular Fuerte La Punta today houses a restaurant. At the en-

Fuerte La Punta

! *Baedeker* TIP

In the footsteps of »Che«

Hardly anyone would stay in the renovated Hotel La Rusa for reasons of comfort, but as tiny room no. 203 of this small, cheap hotel with its worn-out mattress accommodated Che Guevara in 1960, it is in high demand ... Hotel La Rusa, Calle Máximo Gómez 161 (on the Malecón), tel. 021/430 11, fax 423 37.

trance, a wooden cross with a silver base serves as a reminder that Columbus erected the first cross on Cuban soil on this spot.

To find out more about the history of the Hotel La Rusa and its legendary proprietor »La Rusa«, an extrovert Russian artist who died in 1978, visit the **Museo de la Rusa** (Calle Ciro Frías 3, about 50m/50yd from the Hotel La Rusa): the exhibition includes faded photographs of the artist, Che Guevara and Castro, old furs and stoles, lace gloves, a vintage camera and more, as well as a small gallery showing naïve art.

Around Baracoa

✳ El Yunque

The 598m/1962ft-high table mountain El Yunque to the west of Baracoa with its anvil shape is the local landmark. It takes between four and five hours to climb to the summit.

✳ National Park Alejandro de Humboldt

The Cuchillas de Toa mountain range and the Parque Nacional Alejandro de Humboldt (700 sq km/270 sq mi, about 40km/25mi west of Baracoa) are protected by Unesco. The national park has **more species than any other park in Cuba** and more than anywhere else in the Caribbean for that matter. Researchers are constantly amazed at the variety of its flora and fauna, as again and again they discover new species here – what is claimed to be the world's smallest frog, for example, and an endemic insect-eater called the Cuban solenodon or locally the almiquí, which was thought to be extinct but was rediscovered in 2003.

The few manatees living in the Bahía de Taco, where there is a small exhibition in the visitor centre can be spotted with a good deal of luck during a boat trip (the chances are best at twilight). Subtropical rainforest, mountain cloud forest and endemic pine forest, waterfalls and river valleys can be explored on hikes covering up to 7km/4.5mi that include river crossings (take footwear for both swimming and trekking!) and often providing an opportunity to see the Cuban national bird, the **tocororo** – red, white and blue in the colours of the Cuban flag. Visits are allowed only with official guides, who can be booked through agencies in Baracoa.

Yumurí

A recommended trip starting 30km/20mi to the east in the fishing village of Yumurí follows the river of the same name through a steep-walled canyon, with opportunities to go cave-diving and angling at Playa Bariguá.

One of Cuba's most biodiverse national parks:
the Parque Nacional Alejandro de Humboldt

A day trip to the idyllic Playa Maguana, 20km/12mi northwest of Baracoa, is also rewarding.

Playa Maguana

Approximately 30km/20mi south of Baracoa, along the Playitas de Cajobabo, the upland road – La Farola – leads to Guantánamo, where in 1895 José Martí (► Famous People) landed on his return from exile.

Playitas de Cajobabo

Bayamo

J 5

Province: Granma
Population: 144,000

Altitude: 10m/33ft
Distance: 757km/470mi from Havana
127km/79mi from Santiago de Cuba

A history of rebellions has given the colonial town of Bayamo the nickname »cradle of nationalism«. Horse-drawn carriages are still a characteristic sight in the quiet capital of Granma province. Situated among wide fields of sugar cane and enormous stretches of pasture land, Bayamo with its attractive old quarter is a possible base for a tour or hiking expedition exploring the Sierra Maestra.

▶ VISITING BAYAMO

INFORMATION
In the Hotel Sierra Maestra and at Islazul, Calle General García 207
Tel./fax 023/42 32 73
Come here to book tours, for example to the old rebel headquarter Comandancia de la Plata and the ascent of Pico Turquino in the Sierra Maestra, ► p. 166.

WHERE TO EAT
► Inexpensive
Paladar Sagitario
Calle Donato Marmol 107, entre/between Calle Maceo y/and Vincente Aquilera
No phone
Daily 12 noon – 11pm
This popular little paladar serves the usual »comida criolla« on a patio.

Restaurante 1513
Calle General García 176, corner of Calle General Lora
Tel. 023/42 29 21, -39
Simple dishes and snacks.

WHERE TO STAY
► Mid-range
Hotel Sierra Maestra (Islazul)
Ctra. Central, km 7.5
Tel. 023/42 79 70, -74, 42 79 73, www.islazul.cu
The hotel is about 1km/0.5mi outside Bayamo on the road to Santiago. It has 204 air-conditioned rooms with bathrooms, a swimming pool, restaurant and a tourist office.

► Budget
Hotel Royalton (Islazul)
Calle Antonio Maceo 53, on Parque Céspedes square
Tel. 023/42 22 90/-24, fax 42 47 92
Small restored hotel with 33 basic rooms in the quiet town centre, good restaurant (7am – 10pm) and terrace bar.

Sierra Maestra: Villa Santo Domingo (Islazul)
Ctra. la Plata, km 16, Santo Domingo, Bartolomé Masó, Granma Province (about 73km/45mi southwest of Bayamo)
Tel. 023/56 53 02
vstdomingo@islazul.grm.tur.cu
20 well-furnished cottages are lined up in two rows on the river bank, and when the TV and telephone are not operating (once again), there is a fine view of the river and vegetation from the terrace. The good restaurant has a limited choice of dishes – guests eat what is available! Horseriding and swimming in the river. This is the best base for tours to the Comandancia de la Plata and Pico Turquino, which set off from here very early in the morning.

History San Salvador de Bayamo was the **second Spanish settlement on Cuba**, founded in November 1513 on a site where an Indian village had stood. It was not long before the spirit of rebellion that characterizes the history of the town made itself felt. As early as 1528 an Indian revolt broke out, and only five years later, in the nearby goldmine of Jobabo, the first rebellion by African slaves on Cuba took place. In the following years Bayamo prospered enormously as **one of the**

principal trading posts for smuggled goods and was attacked by pirates several times. In 1602 the colonial authorities arrested eight leading citizens and condemned them to death in order to put an end to the smuggling of tobacco and slaves. The townspeople reacted by taking arms, forcing the authorities to release the prisoners – the **first citizens' rebellion against the Spanish crown**.

Carlos Manuel de Céspedes (► Famous People), a member of the upper class in Bayamo, freed his slaves on 10 October 1868, an act that unleashed the First War of Independence against Spain. In a call for support (the Grito de Yara) he spoke out for the equality of all men and demanded independence from Spain »or death«. Tens of thousands joined his cause. Céspedes is today one of Cuba's great national heroes and bears the title »Father of the Fatherland«. When Spanish forces retook Bayamo in January 1869, the rebels had already burned the town down. In the **Second War of Independence** Bayamo again played a major role. **José Martí** (► Famous People) was killed in 1895 in the first days of fighting at Dos Ríos, close to Bayamo. In December 1956 Fidel Castro and his supporters landed south of Bayamo on their return from exile in Mexico. With Bayamese rebels they organized the guerrilla forces in the Sierra Maestra.

As the struggle for freedom from Spanish rule began in Bayamo, the town was immortalized in the Cuban national anthem *La Bayamesa* (woman from Bayamo). Rebel Perucho Figueredo composed the song and wrote the lyrics: »Al combate corred Bayameses ...«. The two last verses, which declare enmity to Spain, are no longer sung, owing to the close economic and political links of Cuba to its former colonial ruler.

◄ La Bayamesa (national anthem)

What to See in Bayamo

Magnificent Parque Céspedes, surrounded by the main sights of the town, is regarded as one of Cuba's loveliest squares. At statue of Carlos Manuel de Céspedes and a bust of Perucho Figueredo adorn its centre. A celebration is held here every year on 20 October, the day the anthem was written.

★ **Parque Céspedes**

The Casa Céspedes, the house in which the national hero was born, is an impressive building that survived the fire of 1869. Today it is a museum showing Céspedes memorabilia and documents from the late 19th century. The printing press on which Cuba's first free newspaper, *Cubano Libre*, was printed is also exhibited here. Opening hours: Mon – Sat 8am – 6pm, Sun 9am – 1pm.

Museo Casa Natel de Carlos Manuel de Céspedes

🕐

Directly next door, the Museo Provincial presents collections about the archaeology, natural history and culture of the region, in addition to a few remarkable exhibits such as a picture frame consisting of 13,000 small pieces of wood. Opening hours: Mon – Sat 8am – 6pm, Sun 9am – 1pm.

Museo Provincial

🕐

Poder Popular (ayuntamiento)	In front of the former town hall, now the seat of the Poder Popular, Céspedes signed a document on the abolition of slavery in 1868.
✷ **Iglesia de San Salvador**	The Iglesia de San Salvador, one of the oldest churches on the island, is very close to the square. Although part of it was consumed by flames in 1869, the Capilla La Dolorosa to the left of the altar was spared. The Virgin of Bayamo that has been placed here is dark-skinned and was supposedly modelled on a Bayamesa. In 1868 *La Bayamesa* was sung for the first time in this church, by twelve women, which is why the square in front of the building bears the name Plaza del Himno and the church itself is a protected national monument.
Casa de la Nacionalidad Cubana	To the west of the church, an archive, the Casa de la Nacionalidad Cubana, is available to those who want to pursue historical studies.
Casa de las Artistas	The southern section of Calle Céspedes no. 158 houses a gallery in the Casa de las Artistas. This building, one of the oldest in Bayamo, has a lovely patio, which is sometimes a venue for traditional concerts, and decorated ceilings. Tomás Estrada Palma, the first president of Cuba after independence, was born in this house.

Around Bayamo

Sierra Maestra	Santo Domingo (73km/45mi southwest of Bayamo) is a good base for trips into the mountains of the Sierra Maestra. This range, consisting of several chains of mountains running parallel, rises in the west to a height of 1974m/6477ft at **Pico Real de Turquino**, Cuba's highest summit, and in the east to the 1214m/3983ft of the Gran Piedra. In the past these mountains were a place of refuge for emigrants, most of them coffee planters from Hispaniola (Haiti). Apart from climbing Pico Turquino, it is possible to visit the **quarters of Castro and his comrades** from revolutionary times in the Comandancia de la Plata (only with a guide, admission fee, ► Where to Stay, Villa Santo Domingo). Approximately 28km/17mi east of Santiago, discover the **Parque Nacional de Gran Piedra**. On the road that leads through Baconao Park to ► Guantánamo, after about 10km/6mi a steep, curving road branches off to the Gran Piedra (Great Rock), to ascend through a forested mountain region. An impressive variety of plants can be seen here: the Cuban national flower, the mariposa, sunflowers, agaves, pines, bamboo, mango trees and mahogany trees. The way up from the car park involves climbing approximately 450 steps and a narrow iron ladder. Finally another ladder ascends to the summit of the Gran Piedra for an overwhelming panoramic view, weather permitting. In good visibility, the view ranges as far as Haiti and Jamaica.

Revolutionary hinterland: the Sierra del Maestra is breathtakingly beautiful.

On the south side of these Sierra Maestra foothills, **Cuba's first coffee plantations** were established by farmers fleeing from Haiti in the early 18th century. Today the plantations are a Unesco World Heritage site. The slightly weathered Finca La Isabélica (about 2km/1.25mi from Gran Piedra) is today a **museum of coffee processing**. On the grounds of the former plantation it is still possible to find coffee bushes and see where the beans were dried and ground. Opening hours: daily 8am – 2pm.

La Isabélica

🕐

About 60km/35mi west of Bayamo, Manzanillo on Guacanayabo Bay is a pretty port that was founded in the 18th century and now has an important harbour for fishing and exporting sugar.

Manzanillo

La Demajagua A further 10km/6mi south of Manzanillo, Carlos Manuel de Céspedes' sugar factory La Demajaguais now a museum. Each year on 10 October the **»Day of Cuban Culture« (Día de la Cultura Cubana)** is solemnly celebrated here to commemorate Céspedes' decision to free his slaves in 1868 and oppose Spanish colonial power. On this day men from the whole region gather, on horseback and wearing the clothing proudly worn by the mambises: a straw hat, woven trousers and sandals. Opening hours: Mon–Sat 8am–6pm, Sun until 12 noon.

Media Luna Media Luna, a sleepy town known as the birthplace of the revolutionary **Celia Sánchez**, 50km/30mi south of Manzanillo has preserved her family home as a museum.

Playa Las Coloradas A few miles from Media Luna, Las Coloradas beach is now part of the **Parque Nacional Desembarco del Granma** and enjoys the status of a protected Unesco biosphere reserve. This is where in December 1956, Castro and his supporters returning from exile in Mexico landed on the yacht *Granma*.

A **path through the mangroves** shows the way that the revolutionaries took as they came ashore.

The small **museum** retraces their route into the Sierra Maestra, and a wooden roof shelters a replica of **the *Granma* boat** (the original is kept in Havana's Museum of the Revolution). Opening hours: Mon–Sat 8am–6pm, Sun until 1pm.

The area off the coast is wonderful for diving, and the attractive surroundings of Playa Las Coloradas constitute a habitat for many kinds of endemic snails and cacti.

★ Camagüey

H 4

Province: Camagüey	**Altitude:** 50m/165ft
Population: 308,000	**Distance:** 533km/331mi from Havana 328km/204mi from Santiago de Cuba

The island's third-biggest city, still almost untouched by tourism, is situated in Cuba's largest province amongst endless expanses of pasture. Most holidaymakers only pass this pretty provincial city on their way to the dream beach of Santa Lucía in the north. This is a pity, as the old quarter of Camagüey – the biggest in Cuba! – is a huge colonial gem consisting of narrow alleyways, wonderful squares and little low houses in every pastel shade with tiled roofs and wooden balconies. In 2008 Unesco declared it a World Heritage site.

Santa María del Puerto Príncipe, one of the first Spanish settlements **History**
on Cuban soil, was founded on 2 February 1515 on the northeast
coast of the island. However, only two years later plagues of mosquitoes, poor soil and regular pirate raids required a move to the banks
of the Caonao . This, too, turned out to be a poor choice, and in
1528 the city was refounded on its present site – replacing an Indian
settlement called Camagüey, which was razed for the purpose. The
Indian name was not reintroduced until 1898, after the end of Spanish colonial rule.

A colonial gem: the buildings in Camagüey are radiant in every imaginable pastel shade.

⏵ VISITING CAMAGÜEY

INFORMATION

Infotur
Av. Agramonte (behind Iglesia de la Merced)

Cubatur
Av. Agramonte 421 entre Maceo y Independencia
Tel. 032/25 47 85, 33 62 91

EVENTS

Carnaval
In June the San Juan Carnival is celebrated with fireworks, dancing, popular orchestras, a parade and a rodeo, as well as delicious local dishes such as the ajiaco camagüeyano stew, which is cooked on the street in great cauldrons.

SHOPPING

Most souvenir shops can be found in Calle Maceo, alongside small supermarkets, bookshops, peso shops, etc.

Artex
Calle República 381
State-run shop with the usual colourful wares and a wide choice of music.

Mercado Agropecuario
The large El Río market is held on the north bank of the river Hatibonico in the mornings: fruit, vegetables and whatever else the farmers can produce in season.

WHERE TO EAT
► Moderate
① La Campana de Toledo/Parador de los Tres Reyes
Plaza San Juan de Dios 18, old quarter
Tel. 032/29 58 88
Daily 10am – 10pm
Two nice patio restaurants serving creole cooking and international dishes in a colonial building.

② El Ovejito
Calle Hermanos Agüero 280 entre Calles Honda y Carmen (on Plaza del Carmen), old quarter
Tel. 032/29 25 24
Wed – Sun 12 noon – 10pm
The name tells you what to expect: the specialities in this noble old residence are lamb dishes.

ENTERTAINMENT
① Casa de La Trova Patricio Ballagas
Calle Cisneros 171, entre Martí y Cristo (on Parque Agramonte)
Open Tue – Sun, top-quality live music such as trova and boleros.

WHERE TO STAY
► Mid-range/Budget
① Camagüey (Horizontes)
Ctra. Central km 4, Jayamá district
Tel. 032/28 72 67, -70, fax 28 71 81
?www.horizontes.cu
A concrete block some way outside the centre with 142 basic but well-kept rooms (satellite TV, phone) and six bungalows. Pool, good restaurant, open-air disco and cabaret.

② **Gran Hotel (Islazul)**
Calle Maceo 67,
entre Agramonte y General Gómez
Tel. 023/29 20 93, -94,
fax 29 39 33
www.islazul.cu
72 comfortable mid-range rooms in a
wonderful neo-Classical colonial
building in the pedestrian zone.
Small pool in the courtyard; the
elegant roof-top restaurant with a
buffet and a panoramic view over the
city comes recommended. Travel
agency, in the evenings live music in
the piano bar.

► **Budget**
③ **Colón (Islazul)**
Calle República 472
entre San José y San Martín, old
quarter
Tel. 023/28 33 46, -68
www.islazul.cu
Restored colonial hotel with 48 small
rooms (satellite TV, en suite), some
of them very basic but with lots of
charm and pretty details such as
colourful mosaic windows. Attractive lobby and courtyard, internet
service.

During the 17th and 18th centuries Puerto del Príncipe lived mainly
off smuggling and was repeatedly raided – in particular in a legendary
episode of looting by Henry Morgan in 1668. As time passed, cattle
grazing and sugar cane emerged as new sources of income, bringing
wealth to the city; alongside Havana and Santiago de Cuba, Camagüey became the **third cultural and economic centre of the island**.
During the 19th century Camagüey developed into a **centre of resistance to Spanish rule**. Ignacio Agramonte, a hero of the wars of
liberation who was born in the city, had a particularly active part in
this.

What to See in Camagüey

In response to the frequent pirate raids in the first two locations of   **Fine old quarter**
the town, the new Camagüey was laid out on a labyrinthine pattern.
The city centre is a maze of narrow, winding alleys and 21 small, ir-
regularly shaped plazas, where researchers have identified about

? DID YOU KNOW ...?

- Tinajones, huge earthen jars in which rainwater was collected and kept fresh, are the
emblem of Camagüey. As water was in short
supply in this region, the wealth of a family
was measured by the number of tinajones in
its possession. A few years ago a count was
made of the number of these jars in the city.
The result: 18,000, all dating from the 19th
century.

Camagüey Map

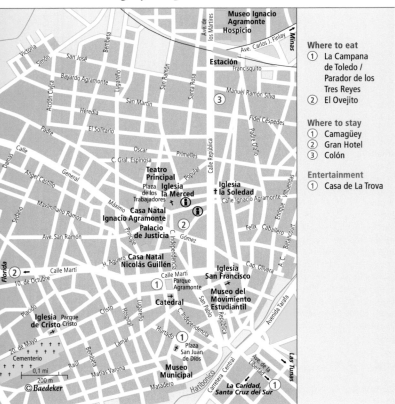

Where to eat
1. La Campana de Toledo / Parador de los Tres Reyes
2. El Ovejito

Where to stay
1. Camagüey
2. Gran Hotel
3. Colón

Entertainment
1. Casa de La Trova

©Baedeker

10,000 buildings of historical value. Most of them have a single storey and lovely tiled roofs, as the soil around Camagüey is rich in clay. Some buildings have recently been beautifully restored and fitted once more with their characteristic wooden bay windows and decorative columns.

In atheist Cuba Camagüey is thought to be the **city with the most churches**. They were allowed to fall into a sorry state, but the municipal authorities have started to restore them, putting in considerable effort and expenditure.

Plaza de los Trabajadores The centre of Camagüey is the triangular Plaza de los Trabajadores (Workers' Square), site of the house where the freedom fighter Ignacio Agramonte was born and of the fortress-like La Merced church.

The birthplace of the general and lawyer Ignacio Agramonte (1841 – 1873) was turned into a museum of the Wars of Independence in his honour. Agramonte was heavily involved in drafting the first Cuban constitution, which was proclaimed in 1873. The family's original furniture has been preserved, and many documents from the First Cuban War of Independence are on view. Opening hours: Tue – Sat 10am – 5pm.

★ **Casa Natal de Ignacio Agramonte**

Directly opposite, the oldest church in Camagüey, Nuestra Señora de la Merced, is once again resplendent. It was built in 1748, rebuilt in 1906 after a fire and recently renovated. With a little luck it will be open, permitting a glimpse into the interior and the catacombs. A small silver altar on the left bears a likeness of the Christ Child of Prague, worshipped by the faithful of Camagüey.

★ **Nuestra Señora de la Merced**

The Iglesia de la Soledad (1756) occupies the corner of Avenida Ignacio Agramonte and Avenida de los Mártires (Calle República). Its façade has recently been restored, and work is presently being done to renovate the interior. The church, a protected monument, possesses wonderful frescoes from the time when it was first built. The altar and ceiling, carved from precious kinds of wood, were painted in floral motifs.

★ **Iglesia de la Soledad**

Go three blocks northwest of Plaza de los Trabajadores to reach the Teatro Principal (1850, Calle Padre Valencia 64). This magnificent building with round arched, colourfully glazed windows was restored not long ago. Wide marble steps lead to the interior, which is used for various kinds of cultural activities.

★ **Teatro Principal**

Camagüey's museum of history, the **Museo Ignacio Agramonte**, is housed near the railway station (Avenida de los Mártires) in a former Spanish military building (1848). Alongside displays on archaeology and natural history, there is an exhibition on modern history and a well-chosen collection of Cuban painting.

> ! **Baedeker TIP**
>
> **Top-class dancing!**
> Fans of ballet should not miss a chance to see Cuba's second most important ensemble, which was founded by Fernando Alonso (ex-husband of the legendary Alicia Alonso); the performances in the Teatro Principal are famous and therefore in demand – when the dancers happen not to be on tour. A ballet festival is held in October/November every two years (2013, 2015, etc.).

One of the city's principal squares, previously called Plaza de Armas, is now named after Ignacio Agramonte. An equestrian statue of the freedom fighter (1916) has been placed in the middle of the square. He is still revered by Cubans for his bravery. Singer Silvio Rodríguez dedicated the song *El Mayor* to him. At the four corners of the square palms were planted in the mid-19th century to commemorate

★ **Parque Ignacio Agramonte**

those who were executed by the Spanish in 1851. As the colonial government of course permitted no monument, the idea with the palms was thought up instead.

Catedral ► The cathedral of Nuestra Señora de la Candelaria at the southeast corner of Parque Agramonte was first constructed in 1530, but repeatedly destroyed and rebuilt. During the War of Independence it even served as a military camp. The Virgin of Candelaria who is venerated here is also worshipped under the name Oyá, as the Afro-Cuban goddess of the dead (►Baedeker Special p. 28).

★★
Plaza San
Juan de Dios

Plaza San Juan de Dios further south has retained its colonial atmosphere more than most. Its low houses with window grilles and shingle roofs, the irregular paving stones and the Moorish-style façade of the former **hospital** reinforce this impression.

San Juan de Dios ► The plain church of San Juan de Dios was built in 1728. The Baroque interior possesses a beautiful tiled floor.

★
Municipal
museum ►
🕐

Right next to the church, the municipal museum is housed in a colonial building in the Moorish style that has accommodated in turn a hospital, a monastery and a school. The exhibition is illuminating on the theme of the development of the city and the colonial architecture of Camagüey. Opening hours: Mon – Sat 8am – 4pm.
A memorial commemorates General Ignacio Agramonte, whose body was brought to the hospital to lie in state.

Plaza del Carmen This plaza a few hundred metres further west (along Calle Hermanos Agüro) has also been nicely restored and forms an impressive ensemble consisting of a monastery church (Iglesia del Carmen) and pastel-coloured houses, palms, ceramic jars and striking bronze sculptures; look out for the »gossiping« ladies, for example.

★
Iglesia de
la Caridad

In the south of the city, the Hatibónico Bridge (1773) crosses the river of the same name to lead to the district of Caridad. The plain yellow church in this quarter is dedicated to the patron saint of the city, the Virgen de la Caridad. Dating from 1734 the church is one of the city's oldest buildings.

Around Camagüey

Minas
🕐

The little town of Minas, about 35km/22mi northeast of Camagüey, is known for its **violin factory**, which was established in 1975 in Calle Camilo Cienfuegos and is open to visitors: Mon – Sat 8am – 11am and 1pm – 5pm.

Cangilones del
Río Máximo

The Cangilones del Río Máximo, 60km/37mi north of Camagüey in the Sierra de Cubitas, are a popular daytrip excursion destination with Cubans. The river has cut into high walls of limestone, leaving natural pools that are suitable for swimming. From the village of Sola several caves can be explored.

Cayo Coco – Cayo Guillermo

G 3

Province: Ciego de Ávila
Distance: 17km/10mi off the main island's north coast

Size: Cayo Coco: 370 sq km/143 sq mi
Cayo Guillermo: 13 sq km/5 sq mi

A causeway 17km/10mi long and a checkpoint separate Cuba (and most Cubans) from the all-inclusive holiday paradise on the offshore islands of Jardines del Rey (www.jardinesdelrey.cu), with its rippling turquoise sea, shining white beaches and coral reefs.
The little islands of this archipelago are booming, with gigantic hotel villages, some of them built in the colonial style. Ernest Hemingway once dropped anchor at the enchanting little Cayo Guillermo and immortalized the beauty of the scene in *Islands in the Stream*.

A world away from everyday cares: Cayo Coco's dream beaches of powdered white coral

▶ VISITING CAYO COCO

INFORMATION
In the hotels and Infotur office, and at the airport.

GETTING THERE
17km/11mi causeway (toll; passport required!), about 20km/12mi beyond Morón.

WHERE TO EAT
► Moderate
① *Cayo Coco: La Cueva del Jabalí*
Tel. 033/30 12 06
Restaurant and bar in a cave labyrinth. For tourist groups suckling pig is roasted on a spit in the evenings and a cabaret ensemble performs dances.

② *Cayo Coco: Parador La Silla*
On the last third of the causeway to Cayo Coco, km 18
Tel. 033/30 21 37
A simple cafeteria with a grill and bar. Guests can go up to the mirador to try and spot flamingos in the distance. Sometimes the graceful birds can also be seen close to the causeway, usually early in the morning or at dusk.

Baedeker recommendation

► Moderate/Inexpensive
③ *Cayo Coco: Sítio la Güira (also Ranch Los Márquez)*
Ctra. a Cayo Guillermo
Tel. 033/30 12 08
Daily 9am – 10pm
A »ranch« for trippers, part of the Rumbo chain. Farm animals and hacks for riders, snacks and Cuban meals, a few basic cabañas to rent.

WHERE TO STAY
► Luxury
① *Cayo Coco: Melía Cayo Coco*
Playa Las Coloradas
Tel. 033/30 11 80, fax 30 11 95
www.melia-cayococo.com, www.sol-meliacuba.com
The island's top hotel for originality and quality: this large all-inclusive resort (for guests aged 18 and over) at the eastern end lies between the sea, beach and lagoon. Two-storey chalets, some on the lagoon and connected by walkways, two pools, entertainment programme.

② *Cayo Guillermo. Melía Cayo Guillermo (Gran Caribe)*
Tel. 033/30 16 80, fax 30 16 85
melia.cayo.guillermosolmeliacuba.com
www.solmeliacuba.com
309 lovely four-star rooms in all available pastel colours in two-storey cottages spread across a large tropical garden, some featuring a terrace or balcony with a sea view. Pool area, water sports, disco.

Holiday beneath palm trees at Club Melía, where the bungalows are scattered around a tropical garden

► Mid-range

③ *Cayo Coco: Hotel & Club Tryp Cayo Coco (Meliá and Cubanacán)*
Playa las Conchas
Tel. 033/30 13 00, fax 30 13 86
tryp.cayo.coco@solmeliacuba.com
www.solmeliacuba.com
A resort like a colonial village: somewhat overpriced and no longer new: a hotel with an interesting pool landscape around a fountain, pavilions in an extensive garden, about 500 rooms and bungalows. The 3km/2-mi beach is not always well kept.

④ *Cayo Coco: Villa Gaviota Cayo Coco (Gaviota)*
Ctra. a Cayo Guillermo
Tel. 033/30 21 80,
fax 30 21 90
www.gaviota-grupo.com
Situated a little distance from the gigantic resorts, this complex appears tiny by comparison: only 48 rooms in three-star bungalows by the sea, for all-inclusive package stays. Pool, internet.

Mangrove forests and swamps are the dominant features of the island. So far only a small area has been developed for tourism, but ambitious plans have been made for this holiday paradise: infrastructure for some 16,000 tourists with low environmental impact, which will supposedly not endanger the flamingos, pelicans and other marine birds living here. A tunnel beneath the Piedraplén land bridge will regulate the flow of water, but it remains to be seen what effects the expansion of the international airport will have on Cayo Coco.

Cayo Coco: holiday heaven

? DID YOU KNOW ...?

■ ... that Cayo Coco got its name not from coconut palms but from the little white herons that can often be spotted here?

Cayo Coco is a **little world of its own**. It has its own post office and hospital, an environmental research station (Centro de Investigaciones de Ecosistemas Costeros) and an airport. It is governed from a »town hall« on the main square on Cayo Coco. Rooms and suites for guests, restaurants, etc. are accommodated in the neighbouring buildings.

The scientists based on Cayo Coco have recorded 300 species of birds on the island, including many pelicans and herons, which can often be spotted. The flamingo population alone is said to number 25,000 birds, but it is questionable how long the fauna will remain in view of new hotels being constructed. On a trip to the **Parque Natural El Bagá nature reserve** (in the west of Cayo Coco, opening hours daily 9am – 5pm, approx. 7.6 sq km/2.9 sq mi with restaurants) visitors can watch the wildlife in lagoons and mangrove channels or on walking trails, and climb a lookout tower. The attractions in the leisure park are dolphins, crocodiles, sea turtles, iguanas and flamingos. Shows are staged, and bikes can be hired. For those who like things less touristy there is the 2km/1.25mi-long **Las Dolinas »environmental trail«** (next to the Cueva del Jabalí restaurant): a guide provides

◄ Animal haven: El Bagá

Cayo Coco Map

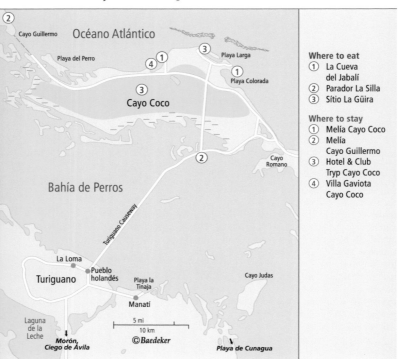

Océano Atlántico

Cayo Guillermo
Playa del Perro
② ④ ① Playa Larga
③
① Playa Colorada
③ Cayo Coco
Cayo Romano
②
Bahía de Perros
Turiguano Causeway
La Loma
Pueblo holandés
Turiguano
Playa la Tinaja
Cayo Judas
Manatí
Laguna de la Leche
Morón, Ciego de Ávila
5 mi
10 km
©Baedeker
Playa de Cunagua

Where to eat
① La Cueva del Jabalí
② Parador La Silla
③ Sítio La Güira

Where to stay
① Melía Cayo Coco
② Melía Cayo Guillermo
③ Hotel & Club Tryp Cayo Coco
④ Villa Gaviota Cayo Coco

explanations about the island vegetation (for example mangroves and the common, red-trunked almácigo tree) and the use of plants and wood in Cuban everyday life, including for coffins and musical instruments.

Cayo Guillermo ★ A second causeway connects Cayo Coco with Cayo Guillermo (13 sq km/5 sq mi). This small island, surrounded by a palm-fringed sandy beach 5km/3mi long, was only recently discovered for tourism. The hotel bungalows, low-built using natural materials, blend into the landscape. A conspicuous feature are dunes up to 15m/50ft high on Playa Pilar, which was named after Hemingway's boat.

The coral reef off the north coast is a magnet for divers and snorkellers, and bird-watchers too are happy here.

Around Cayo Coco and Cayo Guillermo

Ciego de Ávila Probably the Cuban city least touched by tourism: holidaymakers know the name of Ciego de Ávila (population 104,000) only as a destination on their flight ticket if they have booked a package holiday to Cayo Coco and Cayo Guillermo, which are about 100km/60mi to the north. A trip to this city from islands that are entirely devoted to tourism gives an authentic glimpse of everyday provincial life in Cuba – including queues at restaurants and peso stores, and slow transport by horse-drawn carriage, as petrol is in short supply.

Ciego de Ávila has kept the charm of a small Cuban provincial town. It boasts no special highlights, but the **Parque José Martí** conveys a particularly good impression of life in a place like this. Decorative 19th-century buildings surround the square.

Morón, the second-largest town in the province, is situated about 65km/40mi south of Cayo Coco. Its name derives from a Spanish immigrant who came from Morón de la Sevilla. In the 18th century there is said to have been a mayor there who took advantage of the citizens in such a disgraceful way that one day they attacked him and took away all his clothes. To this day someone who has lost everything is described in Cuba as being like the cock of Morón – crowing and without feathers. The cock is thus the emblem of the town, which was founded in 1750. In commemoration a monument by the Cuban sculptor Rita Longa was erected on the main street, the rooster crowing every day at 6am and 6pm.

Morón attracts hunters and anglers, who can pursue their hobbies in the surrounding forests and swamps. There are two lakes close to the town: the **Laguna de la Leche**, which has milky water due to the lime and magnesium in the soil, and the almost circular **La Redonda** 18km/11mi north of Morón, which is full of trout.

Small-town atmosphere: horse-drawn carriages are part of the scene in Morón.

★ ★ Cayo Largo

Archipiélago de los Canarreos
Distance: Approx. 80km/50mi from the
southwest coast of the main island

Size: 38 sq km/15 sq mi

Landing on Cayo Largo is a wonderful experience: the sea glitters in every imaginable shade of blue, while yachts and catamarans bob up and down in the marina. The 25km/16mi-long todo-incluído islet to the south of the main island of Cuba, part of the Canarreos Archipelago, attracts holidaymakers and daytrippers from Havana thanks to its endlessly long, blindingly white sandy beach, where there is usually no shade however.

Professional divers compare the coral reef here to the best spots in the world, including the Maldives. Iguanas, sea turtles and dolphins are also in their element here. In recent years the island has been hit

Snorkelling in paradise: the sea shimmers in shades of blue and turquoise.

by severe hurricanes and suffered great damage. Tourists have had to be evacuated repeatedly, so it is better not to come here in September and October.

The village of Isla del Sol in the west of the island is home to the thousands of Cubans who work in the holiday resorts. At the edge of the village near the Marina Gran Caribe are a restaurant, an open-air bar, a dance club, a bank, a local museum, an international mini-clinic with a dentist, and the small Granja de las Tortugas turtle farm, which is worth seeing.

Isla de Sol

The little local museum at the edge of the village presents historical information from the days of seafaring and the 1960s, when the island was still a fishermen's collective and the first hotels were built.

◄ Casa Museo

Die Playa Sirena on the west coast has a reputation as one of the finest beaches in the Caribbean, and its **unusually fine sand** is famous. The locals even claim that its powder-like structure means it stays pleasantly warm without getting too hot quickly.

**★ ★
Playa Sirena**

The section of beach on the peninsula is over 2km/1.25mi long and can be reached on a shuttle boat from the marina. All kinds of water sports are on offer here – from windsurfing, sailing, jet skis and kayaking to snorkelling and diving trips. A restaurant, bar and changing cabins are on site.

From Playa Sirena it is possible to walk for miles along the beach to **Playa Lindamar**, where most of the hotels are situated, and on to

Cayo Largo *Map*

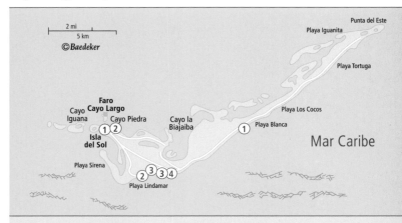

Where to eat	Where to stay
① Taberna del Pirata	① Barceló Cayo Largo Beach Resort
② El Marino	② Sol Club Cayo Largo
③ Rachón El Espigón	③ Sol Pelícano
	④ Veraclub Lindamar

⏵ VISITING CAYO LARGO

INFORMATION

Cubatur
Tel. 045/24 82 46, fax 24 82 18
representantes@cubaturcayo.cubcls.-
co.cu

Cubanacán
Tel./fax 045/24 82 80
In the Melía Sol Pelícano Hotel
www.cayolargodelsur.cu, www.cayo-
largo.net (Canadian »fan page«).

WHERE TO EAT

▶ Inexpensive

① Taberna del Pirata
Marina Gran Caribe
Open-air bar by the marina, with
bocaditos (sandwiches), beer and
cocktails.

② El Marino
Marina Gran Caribe
Tel. 045/24 81 37
A high-class little restaurant with
delicious seafood, fish and meat
dishes.

③ Rachón El Espigón
Veraclub Lindamar (▶below)
Tel. 045/248 11 16
Open-air restaurant on the beach with
a sea view and international cuisine.

WHERE TO STAY

▶ Luxury

① Barceló Cayo Largo Beach Resort
Playa Blanca
Tel. 045/24 80 80, fax 66 87 98

www.barcelo.com
Colourful houses, each containing
several apartments, with every imaginable four-star all-inclusive comfort
and a big pool.

Baedeker recommendation

▶ Luxury
② Sol Club Cayo Largo (Melía)
Tel. 045/24 82 60, fax 24 82 65
sol.cayo.largo@solmeliacuba.com
www.solmeliacuba.com
A pretty luxury resort with two-storey,
creole-style cottages around the big pool a.
in the dunes, some with a sea view. Four
restaurants, five bars, sauna and massage,
water sports.

▶ Mid-range
③ Sol Pelícano
Cayo Largo del Sur
Tel. 045/24 83 33, fax 24 81 67
sol.pelicano@solmeliacuba.com
www.solmeliacuba.com
This resort with colonial-style architecture has 300 rooms (including eight
suites) right by the sea and its own
beach, a swimming pool, tennis and
volleyball courts, aerobics, dance
courses and Spanish lessons.

④ Veraclub Lindamar (Gran Caribe)
Playa Lindamar
Tel. 045/248 11 18 (Complejo Isla del
Sur), fax 24 81 60
www.gran-caribe.com
Spacious and comfortable wooden
cabanas on stilts with palm-leaf roofs
on the beach and a stunning sea view
from the hammocks, much favoured
by Italian guests.

Playa Blanca, **Los Cocos** and **Tortuga** on the south coast, where things are a little quieter than on the other sections of coast.

Excursions

From Marina Isla del Sur, trips are run to the islands west of Cayo Largo, including Cayo Rico, an idyllic little island with a lobster restaurant, or Cayo Cantiles, to visit its colony of monkeys.

Cayo Rico

Cayo Iguana is another destination for an interesting excursion. The iguanas that live here are not afraid of humans. **Day trips** to Havana, Pinar del Río, Trinidad, Isla de la Juventud, Guamá, Cienfuegos, Camagüey, Varadero, Santiago de Cuba and the British Grand Cayman island can be booked.

★
Cayo Iguana

★ Cienfuegos

E 3

Province: Cienfuegos
Population: 139,000

Altitude: 5m/16ft
Distance: 256km/159mi from Havana
658km/409mi from Santiago de Cuba

Cienfuegos is a delightful little town with palm-shaded squares, a fairy-tale architectural mixture of neo-Classical and Arabian Nights, a modern marina and beach hotels close by on the south coast. The »pearl of the south« did not escape the eyes of Unesco: since 2005 the historic core of the town has been a World Heritage site. Cienfuegos greets visitors with plenty of charm and music – the great Cuban sonero Benny Moré was born in this province.

Cienfuegos is situated on the edge of the plain of Las Villas on the south coast of Cuba. A unique natural harbour on a 20km/12mi-long bay and a fertile hinterland greatly benefited the growth of the town. Thanks to the construction of an enormous sugar-loading facility in the 1960s (on the initiative of Che Guevara), oil refineries and a fertilizer factory, Cienfuegos became an important industrial city.

»City of 100 Fires«

After the discovery of the island by Columbus at the end of the 15th century, pirates made a base in this bay and raided Spanish ships. In order to combat these activities, the Spanish built the fort of Castillo de Nuestra Señora de los Ángeles de Jagua here in 1745. In 1819 French settlers founded the town, which was first called Fernandina de Jagua. In 1829 it was named after the governor of the time, José Cienfuegos.
Soon the town became a centre of the sugar industry – in the late 19th century there were already 100 sugar mills here. The plantations

History

▶ VISITING CIENFUEGOS

INFORMATION

Cubatur

In the Hotel Jagua and at Calle 37 (also: Paseo del Prado; halfway along, this street is called the Malecón) entre Av. 54 y 56
Tel. 043/55 12 42
cubaturcfg@enet.cu
Various excursions and tours, e.g. »A todo vapor« trips to a sugar mill in old steam trains.

SHOPPING

At *Artex Topacio*, Av. 54 (Bulevar), entre Calles 35 y 37 in the old quarter you can find all sorts of souvenirs: cigars, rum, books, music ... (also in the Artex shop in Teatro Terry). At *El Embajador*, Av. 54 (Bulevar) and corner of Calle 33, connoisseurs will find excellent cigars and rum, as well as Cuban coffee, all of which can be tried in the adjoining café.

EVENTS

Benny Moré International Festival

In honour of the famous musician who came from this region, the founder of son, Cienfuegos holds a festival every other September with lots of son events.

WHERE TO EAT

▶ Moderate

① *La Cueva del Camarón*
Calle 37 no. 4 entre 0 y 2
Tel. 043/55 11 28
Restaurant near the Palacio del Valle specializing in fish and seafood. Nice atmosphere and a large selection of wine.

② *Palacio del Valle*
Calle 37, corner of Av. 0, Punta Gorda
Tel. 043/55 12 26
Daily 10am – 10pm
This restaurant in the ornate Palacio

It's a question of taste: Gothic, Moorish and neo-Classical features are all present on the Palacio del Valle.

del Valle provides a fine ambience for enjoying Cuban specialities, especially fish and seafood, to the accompaniment of piano music.

► Inexpensive

③ **La Verja**
Avenida 54 (also called Bulevar) entre Calles 33 y 35, old quarter
Tel. 043/51 63 11
Daily 12 noon – 11pm
An oasis in the bustling pedestrian zone: typical Cuban and other simple meals (hamburgers), bags of colonial atmosphere in the dining room beneath a stucco ceiling and chandeliers, as well as in the lovely courtyard.

ENTERTAINMENT

① **Casa de la Música**
Calle 37 (Prado), entre Av. 4 y 6
Fri, Sat from 10pm, Sun afternoon matinees from 5pm
The best-known salsa bands perform in this music club.

② **Club Cienfuegos**
Paseo del Prado (Calle 37) entre Av. 10 y 12 (next to the marina), Punta Gorda
Tel. 043/51 28 91
Daily 9am – 1am
In the beautifully restored former yacht club (1920) you can play pool or tennis, drive a go-kart and dine in an upmarket à la carte restaurant (La Lobera) or at a low price on the terrace (El Marinero); pool, shops. At night dancing on the waterfront terrace to the sounds of salsa and trova from live bands or DJs.

WHERE TO STAY

► Luxury/Mid-range

② **Jagua (Gran Caribe)**
Calle 37 no. 1, entre 0 y 2, Punta Gorda
Tel. 043/55 10 03, fax 55 10 45

www.gran-caribe.com
Batista's brother built this hotel in the late 1950s right on the Bay of Cienfuegos. 144 rooms and suites with a balcony for fantastic sea views.

► Mid-range

③ **Carrusel Club Amigo Faro Luna (Cubanacán)**
Playa Rancho Luna: Ctra. de Pascaballos km 18
Tel. 043/54 80 30, fax 54 80 62
www.cubanacan.cu
Quiet little beach hotel near Playa Rancho Luna, 14 rooms with air conditioning and radio. Good for water sports, diving base.

④ **Rancho Luna (Horizontes)**
Playa Rancho Luna: Ctra. Rancho Luna, km 16
Tel. 043/54 80 12
Fax 54 81 31
www.horizontes.cu
Situated directly on the beach of Rancho Luna, with 255 rooms and everything you'd expected from a beach hotel (good facilities for diving and snorkelling).

Baedeker recommendation

► Luxury

① **La Union (Cubanacán)**
Calle 31, corner of Av. 54 (Bulevar), old quarter
Tel./fax 043/55 10 20, 55 16 85
comercial@union.cyt.cu
www.cubanacan.cu
Chandeliers and Moorish-style interior, wicker chairs and columns, a patio in antique design: this restored colonial building in the 3 to 4-star category is a sight for sore eyes! It has a small pool in the patio and rooms with antique furnishings that are reasonably priced by Cuban standards. Bar on the roof terrace, gym, massage.

were continually supplied with new labour by a flourishing slave trade. In this way the sugar barons made their fortunes, as can be seen to this day in the magnificent architecture of the town centre. Cienfuegos was also spared damage in the War of Independence.

What to See in Cienfuegos

★★
Parque Martí

The town is laid out on regular right-angled grid pattern.Its main square, Parque Martí, is dominated by a large monument to the eponymous hero of liberation, erected in 1902 when the Republic of Cuba was founded. The fine Glorieta, pretty gardens and wonderful architecture give Parque Martí the atmosphere of a spa town.

Catedral ►

On the east side of Parque Martí, the rather plain Catedral de Nuestra Señora de la Purísima Concepción (1831–1869) became a cathedral in 1904.

Colegio
San Lorenzo ►

The rebels of 5 September 1957 took refuge in the Colegio San Lorenzo on the north side, a building that now houses a school.

★
Teatro
Tomás Terry ►

The most impressive building on Parque Martí is the Teatro Tomás Terry (900 seats), built by a citizen of Cienfuegos in honour of his father, who had come to Cuba from Venezuela to make his fortune in the slave trade and sugar cultivation. The theatre was inaugurated in 1895 with a performance of Verdi's *Aida*; stars such as Enrico Caruso and Sarah Bernhardt were fêted here.

Terry is commemorated by a marble statue in the vestibule. The opulent interior is adorned with marble, expensive wood and mural paintings. The stage and stalls seating can be adjusted to the same height in order to hold balls. From the roof there is a fine view of the town and the Bay of Jagua. Opening hours: Mon–Sat 9am–6pm, Sun 9am–12 noon.

On the southwest side of the square note the villa of sugar baron Don José Ferrer with its turrets. It now houses the arts centre (**Casa de Cultura**). Caruso stayed here in 1920. It is possible to go up to the top for a view of the park. To the west of the Casa de Cultura lie the port and what used to be the Chinese quarter.

The neo-Classical town hall has been restored to its former splendour.

Cienfuegos Map

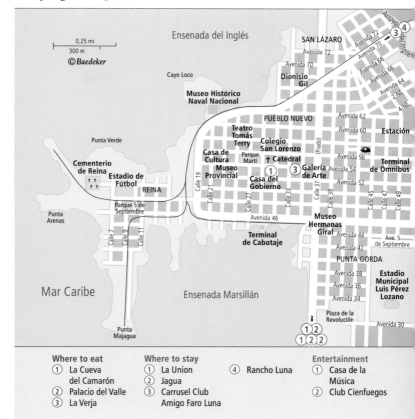

0,25 mi
300 m
©Baedeker

Ensenada del Inglés

SAN LÁZARO

Avenida 72
Avenida 70
Avenida 72
Avenida 70
Avenida 68
Avenida 66
Avenida 64
2-NE
4-NE

Cayo Loco

Dionisio
Gil

Avenida 62

Estación

Museo Histórico
Naval Nacional

PUEBLO NUEVO

Avenida 60

Punta Verde

Teatro
Tomás
Terry

Colegio
San Lorenzo

Casa de
Cultura

Parque
Martí

+ Catedral

Museo
Provincial

Casa del
Gobierno

Galería
de Arte

Avenida 56

Terminal
de Omnibus

Avenida 54

Avenida 52

Cementerio
de Reina

Estadio de
Fútbol

Calle 19

Calle 21

Calle 27

Calle 33

Calle 37

Calle 39

Calle 45

Calle 47

Calle 49

Punta Verde

REINA

Punta
Arenas

Parque 5 de
Septiembre

Avenida 46

Museo
Hermanas
Giral

Calle 7

Calle 9

Calle 11

Terminal
de Cabotaje

Avenida 44

Ave. 5
de Septiembre

Avenida 42

PUNTA GORDA

Mar Caribe

Ensenada Marsillán

Avenida 38

Avenida 36

Estadio
Municipal
Luis Pérez
Lozano

Avenida 34

Punta
Majagua

Plaza de la
Revolución

Avenida 30

Where to eat
① La Cueva
   del Camarón
② Palacio del Valle
③ La Verja

Where to stay
① La Union
② Jagua
③ Carrusel Club
   Amigo Faro Luna
④ Rancho Luna

Entertainment
① Casa de la
   Música
② Club Cienfuegos

The **Museo Histórico** of Cienfuegos on the south side of Parque Martí displays archaeological finds, documents and weapons from the era of the War of Independence, as well as personal items that belonged to the great sonero Benny Moré, who was born here. Opening hours: Tue – Sun 9am – 5pm.

From the town centre , the avenue Calle 37 (Prado) leads to the Punta Gorda peninsula, where a few fine residences attest to fin de siècle prosperity.
The building right next to the Hotel Jagua is the Palacio del Valle (► Where to Eat), built between 1913 and 1917 in a highly ornate style combining Gothic, Moorish and neo-Classical features. The

Punta Gorda

★
◄ Palacio del Valle

owner, a Spanish businessman, spent 1.5 million US dollars on the design. Before the revolution, the son of President Batista bought the estate and opened a casino there.

Castillo de Jagua

The Castillo de Jagua (Fort Jagua) guards the 300m/330yd-wide harbour entrance on the east side of the bay. This small fort, built in 1745 with strong outworks, was once the site of heavy fighting. Inside, the fort houses a bar and restaurant; opening hours: Tue – Sun 9am – 6pm.

Around Cienfuegos

Jardín Botánico Soledad

The Jardín Botánico Soledad (15km/9mi southeast of Cienfuegos), covers an area of 1 sq km/0.4 sq mi on a site that was once used as a research station for crops, founded in 1901 by Edwin Atkins, who owned the sugar mill now called Pepito Tey. Initially cultivating sugar cane on 4.5 hectares/11 acres of his plantation for research purposes, Atkins later added other plants with commercial uses such as trees yielding fruit and valuable wood. In 1919 the estate was made into a

The Botanical Garden is full of treasures.

botanical garden, which is now under the care of the Cuban Academy of Sciences.

2300 plants from all continents can be admired in the park, including 28 kinds of bamboo, 305 different species of palms (60 of them growing on Cuba) and 89 types of ficus. The collections of pulses, cacti, orchids and fresh-water algae are also unique. Unfortunately the park was severely hit by Hurricane Lilly in summer 1996; 80% of the area was damaged and 20% of the plants destroyed. A small exhibition presents the history of the garden. Opening hours: daily 8am – 4pm.

! Baedeker TIP

A popular cascade
In the middle of the forest at the foot of Pico San Juan (1156m/3793ft) in the Sierra del Escambray (approx. 40km/25mi east of Cienfuegos), »El Nicho« offers a swim in little pools or an exploration of the mountainous surroundings and the Hanabanilla Reservoir on horseback (bookings through the hotels).

About 20km/12mi south of Cienfuegos on the east side of the bay, Playa Rancho Luna is a wonderful beach with hotels and outstanding diving grounds.   **★ Rancho Luna**

Guantánamo

K 5

Province: Guantánamo
Population: 209,000

Altitude: 0 – 5m/16ft
Distance: 910km/565mi from Havana, 86km/53mi from Santiago de Cuba

Anyone who travels to Cuba knows the song celebrating a beautiful peasant girl from Guantánamo (»Guantanamera«), and everybody, too, knows about the infamous American internment camp on a naval base in the far southeast of Cuba on Guantánamo Bay. Despite this fame, the provincial capital sees few tourists.

What to See in Guantánamo

Guantánamo's main square – and until the revolution the favourite hangout of American sailors – is Parque Martí, lined by pretty 19th-century buildings rather than any important sights.   **Parque Martí**

However, the **cacti on roofs** of the houses around the square are conspicuous. Cacti are said to ward off the evil eye. If the cactus dies, its owner can expect a bad year.

Outside the town, a somewhat neglected rock garden with sculptures of animals by local artist Angel Iñigo Blanco can be visited. The stone zoo consists of 318 figures, including a giant snake fighting with a zebra and smaller animals such as rabbits, frogs and guinea fowl.   **Rock garden**

Around Guantánamo

Caimanera

Caimanera, 20km/12mi south of Guantánamo (on the western shore of Guantánamo Bay and on the border to the American naval base), lives off fishing and salt production. As this is the start of the closed military area, two checkpoints have to be passed to enter the town. Tourists may enter only if they have a hotel reservation and present their passport.

To the south is the fence that surrounds the base. In order to reduce the danger of border conflicts, the watchtowers of the US forces were set back from the fence. It is unsettling to think that the biggest minefield in the western hemisphere is in front of you.

Guantánamo Bay

The **American naval base** (116 sq km/45 sq mi) is situated about 25km/16mi south of Guantánamo. Before Cuba became independent, the United States took care to secure influence.

A right to intervention conceded in 1901 was incorporated in the constitution in the Platt Amendment. As a result Cuba had to cede an area on Guantánamo Bay to the United States government. Initially this was only a small military camp, but after the Second World War it was expanded to include a big harbour and an air force base.

Until the 1959 revolution the Guantánamo base was one of Cuba's main employers and important for the economy of the region. Since the attacks of September 2001, the USA has used the base as an internment camp for suspected Al Qaida and Taliban terrorists.

What will happen in the future is an open question. The Cuban state is entitled to the sum of US$ 2000 per year according to the lease agreement – money that is paid but has not been accepted since 1960. The agreement was made for a period of 100 years, but as termination is possible only by mutual consent, changes cannot be expected soon.

Altos de Malones

A trip to the nature reserve Altos de Malones on the east side of the bay, from where the military base can be overlooked, is one of the tourist attractions of this area. However, the tour has to be booked at least 24 hours in advance in Santiago de Cuba, Baracoa or Guantánamo. Many rare plants grow in the closed military zone, especially cacti, which were probably planted as a kind of natural security fence.

The programme includes visiting a bunker that is intended to be a command post if the worst happens. A large model of the base – built to scale with details true to the original – helps visitors get their bearings. From there steps lead up to a platform where powerful telescopes make it easier to spy on the base. There is also a restaurant at the viewpoint (► Where to Stay), but don't expect too much of this trip, as the view of the US military base is unclear; the bay panorama is the more impressive sight.

VISITING GUANTÁNAMO

EVENTS
Fiesta de la Guantanamera
The annual festival that takes place in early December is all about concerts and folklore, French tumba and Franco-Haitian traditions. Every Saturday the »Noches Guantanameras« are held with a street festival on Calle Pedro A. Pérez.

WHERE TO EAT
► Moderate
Mirador de Malones
This restaurant with a view stands in an elevated position and overlooks the American naval base. Creole cooking. The trip here has to be booked via Gaviota (passport required).

► Inexpensive
La Cubanita
Calle José Martí, corner of Calle Flor Crombet
No phone
Basic eatery near Parque Martí: typical Cuban menu with lots of pork and chicken, served with rice and beans.

ENTERTAINMENT
Casa de la Trova
Calle Maxímo Gómez entre Calle Donato Marmol y Bernabe Varona
Daily from 8pm
Traditional music club, where you might bump into the »Guantanamera«.

WHERE TO STAY
► Mid-range
Caimanera: Hotel Caimanera (Islazul)
Loma Norte
Tel. 021/994 14
www.islazul.cu
Small hotel (17 rooms) with a view of

The people of Guantánamo are always ready to celebrate a fiesta.

the Guantánamo naval base. Only for groups, pre-book via Islazul, take passport.

► Budget
Hotel Guantánamo (Islazul)
Calle 13 Norte, entre Calle Ahogados y 2 de Octubre (on Plaza Mariana Grajales)
Tel. 021/38 10 15
The best hotel in town offers 124 basic rooms a little outside the centre in a modern four-storey building. Pool. Here you can book guided tours to the ►Mirador de Malones quickly without a lot of red tape.

★★ Guardalavaca

K 4

Province: Holguín
Distance: approx. 800km/500mi from Havana
54km/34mi northeast of Holguín

Altitude: 0–30m/100ft

Several bays with turquoise water and beaches of fine sand, shaded by sea grapes and palm trees: this is the pristine scene on the north coast of Cuba, about which Columbus enthused in 1492: »This is the most beautiful land human eyes have ever seen.« Today it is a mecca for holidaymakers, with luxury hotels in a remote place whose name means »watch over the cow« ...

The gentle hills of Guardalavaca's back country are a chance to see Cuba at its most unspoiled. Here you still find **many small private estates** with bohíos, fences of euphorbia, palm groves and banana plantations. An excursion to Banes, Bariay or Cayo Saetía gives a glimpse of Cuban rural life.

Around Guardalavaca

★
Chorro de Maíta

On the road to Banes, a turn-off leads to the **Museo Arqueológico Chorro de Maíta** (5km/3mi east of Guardalavaca) where a large **Indian cemetery** (1490–1540) with 108 skeletons, including one of a European monk, was found. Researchers concluded that they all died a natural death. The different forms of burial and the great variety of grave goods (gold, corals, copper and shells) indicate a diversity of funeral rites. A small photographic documentation describes the excavation and research work before the museum was opened in 1990. It is possible to visit the **reconstructed site of the finds**: Tue–Sat 9am–5pm, Sun 9am–1pm. Opposite the museum it is worth paying a visit to a reconstruction of a **Taíno village** (Aldea Taína) with an open-air restaurant and an »Indian« show.

! *Baedeker* TIP

Swim with dolphins and seals
On Cayo Jutía, a small island in the Bahía de Naranjo (about 8km/5mi from Playa Guardalavaca), dolphins and the seals Fernanda, Bonny and Vito perform tricks for visitors, who can swim with them and touch them. Parque Natural Bahía de Naranjo; opening hours: daily 9am–9pm.

Banes

The small town of Banes (32km/20mi southeast of Guardalavaca) with its colourful houses and pretty verandas is not very old, having been founded at the end of the 19th century.
Apart from being the birthplace of the dictator Batista, Banes is known for pre-Columbian finds that have been collected and investi-

Even Columbus was overjoyed at the sight of the beaches of Guardalavaca.

gated here. From about 100 excavations in the area it is known that the region was settled 6000 years ago by one of the oldest Indian cultures in the Caribbean.

The Museum of Indo-Cuban culture has one of Cuba's best archaeological collections – named after the powerful cacique Bani. The carefully presented exhibitions uses ceramics, tools, grave foods and jewellery to cast light on the everyday life of the Taínos.

Of approximately 14,000 objects – finds from the nearby Indian cemetery Chorro de Maíta and other excavation sites – only about 1000 are on display. The most important item in the collection is a golden amulet in the form of a woman. Opening hours: Tue–Sat 9am–5pm, Sun 8am–12 noon.

★
◀ Museo Bani-Indocubano
🕐

It is easy to understand the enthusiasm in the letters of Christopher Columbus, describing first impressions of Cuba at the sight of the broad bay, the turquoise sea, gently swaying palm trees and the gentle, green ranges of hills along the Bay of Bariay.

★ ★
Bahía de Bariay

The great explorer landed here (40km/25mi west of Guardalavaca) on 28 October 1492. Searching for gold, he left Cuba again on 12 November, taking with him 13 Indians whom he presented at the Spanish court.

Confusingly, there are several places on the Bahía de Bariay with **monuments and memorials to the arrival of Columbus** marking the spot where he is thought to have landed. At the place that is probably the most historically accurate site, in the bay on Cayo Bariay (Punto del Gato on the west side of the bay), a small **Taíno village** has been reconstructed, with several bohíos and Indian items of everyday use from that period. A little north on Cayo Bariay, an **imposing monument** was erected in 1992 for the 500th anniversary of the dis-

★
◀ Parque Monumento Nacional

⏵ VISITING GUARDALAVACA

WHERE TO EAT
▶ Moderate
Conuco Mongo Viña
Playa Estero Ciego
Tel. 024/309 15
Daily 9am – 4pm
A few miles from Playa Esmeralda, a restaurant with terrace and a nice view of the lagoon and Cayo Jutía. Mainly Cuban dishes.

El Ancla
Playa Guardalavaca
Tel. 024/303 81
Daily 11am – 10.30pm
This restaurant at the western end of the beach specializes in seafood and creole dishes.

El Cayuelo
Playa Guardalavaca
Tel. 024/307 36
Daily 9am – 11pm
Restaurant on Guardalavaca's east beach; sea views, fresh fish and seafood, astonishingly cheap lobster.

WHERE TO STAY
▶ Luxury
Occidental Grand Playa Turquesa (Occidental and Gaviota)
Playa Turquesa, Yuraguanal, Rafael Freyre
Tel. 024/305 40, fax 305 45
www.gaviota-grupo.com
www.occidental-hoteles.com
Prize-winning four-star accommoda-

Lobster is not expensive at El Cayuelo.

tion with two-storey houses (500 rooms) in bright Lego colours, an Italian and an Asian restaurant, and no fewer than seven pools, some of which are connected by little cascades.

Baedeker recommendation

▶ Luxury
Paradisus Río de Oro (Melía and Gaviota
Playa Esmeralda
Tel. 024/300 90, fax 300 95
paradisus.rio.de.oro@solmeliacuba.com
jefe.ventas.pro@solmeliacuba.com
www.solmeliacuba.com
Top-class beach resort, ultra all-inclusive and one of the best in Cuba: the complex extends across a tropical garden along a relatively small beach with hammocks. Italian and Cuban food, even a Japanese restaurant! The spa too is Asian-style, and has a Turkish bath and a »Bali shower«.

Playa Pesquero (Gaviota)
Playa Pesquero, Rafael Freyre
Tel. 024/305 30
fax 305 35
jefe.ventas@ppesquero.tur.cu
www.gaviota-grupo.com
Cuba's largest hotel with almost 1000 rooms is a little town of its own, with street names and a »boulevard« for strolling, shopping and dancing. It is actually possible to get lost in the pool zone. Two-storey buildings with every amenity, eight restaurants and bars.

Sol Río de Luna y Mares Resort (Melía and Gaviota)
Playa Esmeralda
Tel. 024/300 30, 300 60, fax 300 65
sol.rio.luna.mares@solmeliacuba.com
www.solmeliacuba.com
Two pleasant complexes with accom-

modation in two- and three-storey houses share a bay on Playa Esmeralda. Río de Mares (tel. 024/300 60) is closer to the sea. Gigantic pool, rooms suitable for disabled travellers.

► **Mid-range**
Brisas Guardalavaca (Cubanacán)
Calle 2, Playa Guardalavaca
Tel. 024/30 21 89
fax 301 62, 304 18

www.cubanacan.cu
Two family-friendly all-inclusive hotels at the extremely beautiful east end of the palm-fringed beach. The 437 large rooms are spread over a four-storey building (balconies have sea or mountain views) and two-storey houses. 2 pools, tennis court, disco, children's club, several Italian eateries.

covery of America (with a Columbus Restaurant). Here the Cuban artist Caridad Ramos Mosquera designed an ensemble in several parts, a symbol of the invasion of the New World from Europe: in the middle of a palm grove, 16 Indian idols (images of gods and humans) stand in an arc, which is penetrated by a wedge-shaped formation of Greek columns. Loudspeakers emit the sounds that the conquistadors would have heard when they arrived: the sea, wind, animals, etc. Opening hours: daily 9am – 5pm.
The road to the Bay of Bariay branching off at the village of **Fray Benito** is undergoing much-needed repairs at present.

While in the area, consider a trip to the **limestone caves** of Mayarí (70km/45mi south of Guardalavaca). Many of the pre-Columbian tools (8th – 11th century) found on Cuba were discovered here.

Mayarí

A safari in Cuba? Yes, this too is an option. Visitors to Cayo Saetía share the islet with zebras, antelopes, water buffalo and other exotic animals and birds. Not only cameras are used for shooting them: this island southeast of Guardalavaca, 120km/75mi from Holguín is a hunting ground. Only a narrow channel separates it from the main island. A lifting bridge leads across the channel to an area of 42 sq km/16 sq mi that until not long ago was reserved for the hunting and ocean-fishing trips of high-ranking party cadres. This is why even animals such as zebras, antelopes, ostriches and red deer live there. They were brought in to recreate a kind of African hunting environment.

✸
Cayo Saetía

However, it is not only the **safari wildlife** that makes this relaxing place so attractive. Sheltered little coves with fine-grained white sand are inviting places for swimming and lazing around, and riders can explore the terrain on horseback in search of zebras and ostriches.
Options include sailing and angling, and for divers the coral reef off the north coast holds a colourful world of marine flora and fauna in store. Trips are run from Santiago de Cuba, Holguín, Santa Lucía and Guardalavaca, some by helicopter.

LA BODEGUITA
DEL MEDIO

★ Havana (La Habana)

C 2

Province: Havana
Population: 2.19 million
(greater Havana approx. 3 million)

Altitude: 0 – 10m/30ft
Distance: 860km/535mi von Santiago
de Cuba

La Habana, as the Cubans call it, gives most people a tingling feeling, turns almost everyone's head, and in some cases causes the senses to run amok. »The old lady of the Caribbean« has captivated pirates and guerrilleros, dictators and mafiosi, and authors such as Ernest Hemingway and Graham Greene.

Since she got a facelift from Unesco in the 1990s, the 500-year-old diva has looked good in her new finery, especially in the old quarter with its cobbled alleyways: medieval forts at the harbour entrance, endless colonnades and arcades around the squares, aristocratic pala-

Highlights Havana

»Viva la Revolución!«
A dose of revolutionary education is part of the Cuba experience – in the Museo de la Revolución in the former presidential palace. Perfect for would-be revolutionaries and all those who want to demonstrate solidarity with Che Guevara.
▶ page 221

Malecón
Five miles for walking up and down, being splashed by waves and serenaded by musicians – on the world's most beautiful and vibrant waterfront promenade.
▶ page 226

Fortaleza de San Carlos de la Cabaña
Walk in the footsteps of pirates through a large castle (much more attractive than its counterpart El Morro, which draws many visitors!) and enjoy the Cañonazo ceremony every evening.
▶ page 232

Panoramic dining, a mojíto at sunset
A view to die for on the 36th floor of the FOCSA skyscraper: in the French restau-

← *Mojito and more in the bar where Hemingway was a regular*

rant La Torre for a view of the Malecón, in the bar to admire the sunset.
▶ page 203

Tropicana
Feather boas and chandeliers, long, long legs, dancing and erotic performances, folklore and circus-style artistry – no-one should miss this world-famous cabaret!
▶ page 205

Veteran car tour
A rattling, jolting 50s ride through Havana.
▶ page 202

1950s cars – a great way to tour the city

Casa de la Música
A must for salseros and salseras – swing your hips to the sound of the leading salsa bands.
▶ page 205

ces with enchanting, luxuriantly planted patio courtyards, colourful mosaic windows and marble wherever you look.

Havana has hundreds of marvellously ornate palacios and colonial buildings, many of which have had new life breathed into them as splendid hotels. However, many Habaneros have had to make way for this – and move out to the new concrete housing blocks at the edge of the city. The further you get from the **restored chocolate-box old quarter** – which involves no more than crossing the elegant **Boulevard Paseo del Prado** – the more the façades crumble, and in the **Centro** district it is not unusual for a balcony or even a whole house to collapse. Time and especially the sea air takes its toll on the façades. The most exposed are those on **the famous Malecón waterfront road**.

Despite this, music is in the air everywhere, mercilessly schmaltzy Latino hits booming day and night from the door of every rickety-looking house. The Malecón leads to **Vedado, a modern commercial quarter** with Art Deco houses and high-rises, including the most famous hotels from the 1950s, when Havana's casinos and raunchy nightclubs made it the sin city of the Caribbean.

history

1519	Havana is founded on its present site, a bay on the north coast (first settlement on the south coast in 1514).
1553	The seat of the governor is transferred from Santiago to Havana.
1762	British forces occupy the city for a year.
1982	Unesco declares the old Habana Vieja quarter a World Heritage site.

In all probability Havana was first founded in 1514 as San Cristóbal de la Habana on Cuba's southwest coast. The unfavourable conditions there caused the settlement to be moved three times; the present site on the north coast was not occupied until 1519 and turned out to be a perfect choice, as the **harbour of Havana** became an important hub of trade in the New World. The first expeditions to the mainland started out from here. Havana became the base for the conquistadors to colonize the island, and the principal port for the slave trade in Central America and the Caribbean. Moreover, it was the place where heavily laden fleets assembled for the voyage back to Spain.

In 1538 French pirates burned the city down with the help of discontented slaves, and in July 1555 Havana was plundered by the French privateer Jacques de Sores. After this raid King Philip II of Spain gave orders for the harbour to be better protected. First of all the **La Fuerza fort** (1558 – 1577) was built, then the **fortress of El Morro at the harbour entrance with its twin bastion La Punta** (1589 – 1630) on

El Morro fortress was unable to resist British forces, who took the city in 1762.

the opposite side, so that attacking ships would be caught in cross-fire. Despite all these measures, British ships found a gap in the defences, landing east of El Morro in July 1762 and capturing the city from there. However, only a year later Cuba was returned to the Spanish Crown in exchange for Florida at the peace of Fontainebleau. Now that Spain was again in control, the colonial power immediately built **La Cabaña fort** to provide extra protection.

In the following period a good deal was invested in the **architectural embellishment of the Cuban capital**: splendid buildings were erected, beautiful squares and avenues laid out. There was no shortage of money, as great profits were being made in the slave and sugar trade. Under Governor Tacón Havana grew constantly from the 1830s, and the city walls were torn down.

Even before the construction of a water pipeline in 1893 for the expanding urban area, **Havana was**

? DID YOU KNOW ...?

- ... that Havana was the world's third capital city to have gas lighting (1848), and the fourth to be connected to a railway (1837)?

Havana Historic colonial quarter

300 ft
100 m
©Baedeker

Where to stay
⑤ Palacio O'Farrill
⑧ Santa Isabel
⑨ Ambos Mundos
⑩ Hostal
El Comendador
⑬ El Mesón
de la Flota

1 Palacio de los
Condes de
Santovenia
2 Palacio del
Segundo Cabo
3 Ministerio de
Educación
4 La Bodeguita
del Medio

Map labels: Tacón · Catedral de la Habana · Plaza de la Catedral · Empedrado · Avenue Carlos M. de Céspedes · Palacio de los Condes de Lombillo · Mercaderes · Castillo de la Real Fuerza · El Templete · San Ignacio · Museo de Arte Colonial · O'Reilly · Plaza de Armas · Baratillo · Narciso López · Palacio de los Capitanes Generales · Obispo · Taberna del Galón Casa del Café · Oficios · Casa del Obispo · Jústiz · Casa de Africa · Casa del Arabe

regarded as Latin America's most progressive city. In 1898 the US cruiser *Maine* exploded in Havana harbour, an event that has never been explained. This triggered off a **naval battle at Santiago** with the Americans, after which Spain was forced to give up its last remaining colony. In the following decades the **influence of the United States** increased immensely in Cuba. Havana became something akin to a Caribbean suburb of Miami and New York – an enormous entertainment quarter with new hotels, fashionable clubs, casinos and brothels.

This all changed very quickly after the triumph of the revolution in 1959. From now on investments were made in education, the health system and urban development. Instead of slums, giant »micros« (housing blocks, ►p. 61) were built to provide decent accommodation for the people. Economic aid from several states of the eastern bloc under the leadership of the Soviet Union made it possible for the city to develop continually. By the time of the »período especial« from 1990 at the latest, building materials and money were in short supply, and the city gradually started to decay. This process has been halted so far only in Habana Vieja. Thanks to restoration with the support of Unesco and under management of the state city historian Eusebio Leal Spengler, in the last decades Havana's old quarter has become a veritable open-air museum with lots of atmosphere and exemplary restoration of palacios (many of them Habaguanex hotels) and alleys thronged which strolling tourists and Habaneros.

✶ ✶ La Habana Vieja (old quarter)

The glamour is back

La Habana Vieja is the name of the historic quarter on the western side of the harbour entrance. This is the most beautiful and of course

the most visited district in Havana. Some of the splendid old buildings are in a bad state, but since the early 1990s many of them have
been restored with aid from Unesco. It is already evident that Habana Vieja will soon be a jewel again.

The main sights of the old quarter are close to Plaza de Armas and
Plaza de la Catedral. The section below entitled »colonial city centre«
describes a **walk (blue)** to all the highlights. This short route can of
course be extended as required. To get to know the less spectacular
and so far not wholly restored corners of Habana Vieja, add on the
»southern old quarter« (green) route) starting from Plaza de Armas.
It's also worth considering a detour to the Prado showcase boulevard, best reached via Calle Obispo. The following walk starts off
where it all began.

Colonial City Centre (Walk)

The old parade ground Plaza de Armas, also known as Parque Céspedes after the national hero **Carlos Manuel de Céspedes** (►Famous
People), to whom a monument was erected in a small, palm-shaded
park, is one of Havana's most beautiful squares. The plaza became
Havana's most popular rendezvous for fine society and remains to
this day the place to see and be seen. Bookworms will find Latin
American literature (especially second-hand) at many stalls, and bib-
liophiles come here in search of literary treats and rarities.

★ ★
**Plaza de Armas –
Parque Céspedes**

A small neo-Classical temple on the east side of the square commemorates the foundation of Havana in 1519. In the little courtyard
of the Templete stands a cutting from the original ceiba tree beneath
which the first holy Mass was celebrated. On **16 November, the foundation day of the city**, Habaneros still honour an old custom by
walking around the tree three times and touching its trunk, which is
said to make a wish come true. Inside, three paintings by the French
artist Jean-Baptiste Vermay (1786 – 1833) depict the first Mass and
first assembly of citizens in Havana as well as the consecration of the
temple in 1828.

★
El Templete

! *Baedeker* TIP

Un, dos, tres – learn salsa!

Dancing salsa is extremely easy in principle, but
it is better to let real professionals show you how
to move your hips. There are now several good
dance schools with professionals as instructors
and partners, especially in Havana. The Conjunto
Folklórico Nacional and the Teatro Nacional also
offer salsa courses.

▶ VISITING HAVANA

INFORMATION

Asistur
Paseo del Prado 208, entre Calles
Colón y Trocadero (in the Casa del
Científico), Centro
Tel. 07/866 44 99
fax 866 80 87
www.asistur.cu

Cubatur
Oficina Central Cubatur, Calle 15 no.
410 entre F y G, Plaza
Tel. 07/836 20 76
dcomercial@cmatriz.cbt.tur.cu
www.cubatur.cu

Infotur
e.g. Calle Obispo, corner of San
Ignacio, Habana Vieja
Tel. 07/863 68 84
www.infotur.cu

TRANSPORT

Explore the old quarter on foot, or
take **bicycle taxis** (bici taxis) for short
distances in this district (max. CUC 1,
be ready to bargain). **Cocotaxis**: this is
the name of the noisy, yellow three-
wheeled old-timers (fixed prices).
Taxis: e.g. Panataxi (tel. 07/55 55 55).
Trips at night and outside the old
quarter and Centro are more
expensive. **Taxis particulares** (old La-
das, do bargain!) and »colectivos« (old
cars that run on a fixed route as pool
taxis) are cheaper. **Cycle hire**: for
example from the Cuban-Canadian
joint venture Bicicletas Cruzando
Fronteras (Calle Monserrate, corner of
Calle Neptuno, Habana Vieja, tel. 07/
860 26 17). Metro buses or **Camellos**:
it's best to have no bag and no great
sums in cash when you squeeze in, and
note that the Cubans form an orderly
queue at bus stops, asking who is »el
ultimo?«; the fare is a few centavos in
moneda nacional, not CUC. **Carriage
rides** through the city (book at Infotur) start from Plaza de San Francisco de Asís. **Chauffeur-driven
veteran cars** e.g. a 1949 Dodge or 1956
Chevrolet (e.g. along Gran Car). Of
course you can also approach the
owners and drivers of these old
beauties in front of the Capitolio. **Hire
cars** ►Practicalities.

EVENTS

Carnival, the biennial art show, international jazz or film festivals – see
what's on in Havana under the heading Festivals, Holidays and Events
(► p. 93). The weekly listings
magazine *Cartelera* has tips
(www.cartelera.com).

SHOPPING

Mon – Sat: the **Tacón market**, a huge
maze of a crafts market (cramped and
crowded – be sure to haggle!) in Calle
Empedrado at the end of Calle Mercaderes, on the right next to the
cathedral. Everything that tourists love
is for sale in the **Palacio de Artesanía**, a
fine old residence with a lovely patio:
rum and cigars, a picture of Che on t-
shirts and mugs, maracas, costume
jewellery... (Calle Cuba, corner of
Tacón 64, Habana Vieja). Don't buy

*It's better not to buy cigars from the illegal
rollers who work in Havana's back rooms.*

cigars at the street corner (Baedeker Tip p. 212), but from the *Casa del Habano* – the best address for cigar smokers; the attached restaurant serves Cuban and international cuisine (Av. 5, corner of Calle 16, Miramar). In the large modern department store *Plaza Carlos III* you can gape at all the things available for Cubans to buy – if they have pesos convertibles or foreign currency (Calle Salvador Allende/at Calle Aramburu, Centro) The mirror-glass *Galerías de Paseo* (Paseo, on the Malecón opposite Hotel Melía Cohíba in Vedado, open daily) is an expensive place with boutiques, cafeterias and the city's best jazz club. There are lots more shops in Calle Obispo (Habana Vieja) and the Centro district in Calle *San Raffael* (also »Bulevar« San Rafael), *Calle Neptuno* and *Avenida de Italia*: more socialist than chic, goods priced in pesos, hairdressers, cheap cafeterias.

WHERE TO EAT

► Expensive/Moderate

① *La Cecilia*
Av. 5ta., entre Calles 110 y 112
Miramar
Tel. 07/204 15 62
Daily 12 noon – midnight
Sit on the terrace among twittering birds and exotic plants to enjoy genuine Cuban food. Cuban musicians perform Thu – Sat.

⑨ *La Torre*
Edificio Focsa, Calle 17, near Calles M y N, Vedado
Tel. 07/07/838 30 88, -89
Daily 12 noon – midnight
Bar and French restaurant in Cuba's tallest building (Edificio FOCSA, ► p. 228, separate entrance). On the 36th floor they serve one of the city's most expensive mojítos, with the best view

(towards the Malecón from the restaurant, a sunset view from the bar).

⑪ *Paladar Los Cactus de 33*
Av. 33 no. 3405, entre Calle 34 y 36
Playa
Tel. 07/203 51 39
Daily 12 noon – midnight
Pleasant ambience, a backdrop favoured by magazines and TV. Typical Cuban dishes (try the chicken breast with olives and mushrooms!) and attentive, friendly service.

Baedeker recommendation

► Moderate

④ *Restaurant 1830*
Malecón, near Calle 20, Vedado
Tel. 07/838 30 90
Daily 12 noon – midnight
(on Saturdays show on the seafront terrace with salsa music and dancing, bar and night club until 4am). High-class restaurant, one of the best in Cuba, with outstanding service and excellent international cuisine. A violinist plays classics on request.

► Moderate

② *Dos Gardenias*
Av. 7ma, corner of Calle 26
Miramar, Playa, Tel. 07/204 81 88, 204 95 17
Daily 12 noon – midnight
In addition to creole dishes, Chinese specialities and pizza are served in this modern restaurant. Bar with dancing, live music.

③ *El Aljibe*
Av. 7ma, entre Calles 24 y 26, Miramar
Tel. 07/204 15 83
Daily 12 noon – midnight
Why not sample what is said to be the best chicken in town on a wooden terrace beneath whirling fans?

⑥ *La Divina Pastora*

Fortaleza de San Carlos de la Cabaña
Tel. 07/860 83 41
Daily 12 noon – 11pm
Fish dishes are the speciality here.
From the restaurant diners have a
great view of Habana Vieja.

⑩ *La Guarida*

Calle Concordia 418 entre Gervasio
and Escobar, Centro
Tel. 07/866 90 47
www.laguarida.com
Mon – Fri 12 noon – 3pm, 7pm – 4am,
Sat – Sun 7pm – midnight
Privately run, fairly expensive restaurant known from the *Strawberry and Chocolate* film, since when an international crowd has been coming here
(so book in advance to avoid queuing
on the flight of curved marble steps):
fish, pork, lamb, chicken and rabbit,
all cooked to unusual recipes with
imaginative sauces.

⑤ *Cojímar: La Terraza de Cojímar*

Calle Real y Candelaria
Tel. 07/763 94 86, 763 92 82
daily 11am – 11pm
Hemingway enjoyed the stunning sea
view from »La Terraza«. His boatman
Gregorio Fuentes (died in 2002) used
to come here while in his nineties and
tell stories of the old days. The seafood
and fish dishes here are also good, and
the barman mixes an excellent mojíto.

▶ Moderate/Inexpensive

⑧ *Parillada La Casona de 17*

Calle 17, entre Calles M y N (opposite
the FOCSA skyscraper)
Vedado
Tel. 07/835 31 17, 838 31 36
Grill and bar on two storeys, posher
upstairs. Huge portions, spilling over
the rims of the plates, include pollo à
la casa (chicken), and even the lobster
won't break the bank.

▶ Inexpensive

⑦ *Paladar Torresson*

Malecón 27, entre Prado y Cárcel,
Centro
Tel. 07/861 74 76
Daily 12 noon – midnight
Wonderful location, the balcony of
this paladar providing a view of the sea
and the comings and goings on the
waterfront promenade. Delicious Cuban home cooking from a juicy chop
(chuleta) to shrimps (camarones), all
as a fixed menu including soup,
vegetables and salad.

ENTERTAINMENT

At matinees the Cubans usually pay for
admission in pesos, foreigners a few
CUC; in the evening all pay in pesos
convertibles, or the tourist pays for
everyone ...

Beautiful women in stunning costumes at the Cabaret Tropicana

④ *Cabaret Tropicana*
Línea del Ferrocarill y Calle 72
Marianao
Tel. 07/267 17 17, -19, show daily
from 10pm (unless it rains)
This world-famous cabaret has 60
years of show experience: ballet,
acrobats and a pot pourri of Cuban
music – not only long legs and bare
breasts, but also genuine veteran
Cuban stars (book through the hotels
or a travel agency, incl. transport and
drinks). The best alternative – and
good value for money – is the *Cabaret
Parisién* (Hotel Nacional, tel. 07/
83 80 294, Fri – Wed 9pm – 2.30am) or
the smaller *Cabaret Nacional* (Calle
San Rafael in the basement, next to
the Hotel Inglaterra): not quite a
perfect show, but a likeable ensemble
with professional dancers who dance
with the audience afterwards (from
9pm).

① *Conjunto Folklórico Nacional
(Patio de la Rumba)*
Calle 4 no. 103, entre Calzada y Calle
5 (Quinta Avenida), Vedado
No phone, Sat 3pm – 5pm
Afro-Cuban show: this well-known
folklore troupe with genuine Santeros
(priests) makes the batá drums talk
and the gods dance.

③ *Ballet Nacional de Cuba*
Gran Teatro, Prado am Parque Nacional, Centro
Tel. 07/86 13 07 78, 861 30 96
Alicia Alonso is a legend in Cuba and
famous far beyond its shores. If you
prefer violins to salsa and rumba for
once, and want to see Cuba's best
classical dancers, don't miss a performance here (programme in the
weekly listings magazine *Cartelera*).

② *Bar Monserrate*
Calle Monserrate (Av. de Bélgica),

corner of Obrapía, Habana Vieja
Tel. 07/860 97 51, daily 11am – 3am
Cuban and foreign clientele, the
drinks and live music are good, the
food much less so!

*The bar is still empty, but later excellent
cocktails are served here.*

⑦ *Delirio Habanero*
Calle 39 y Paseo (in the Teatro
Nacional near Plaza de la Revolución), Vedado
Tel. 07/873 57 13, Tue – Sat 12 noon –
3am (matinees too)
Piano bar with live music and a view
of the Plaza de la Revolución: boleros,
salsa, rock and classical music to go
with snacks, rum and cocktails.

⑤ *Casa de la Música*
Calle 20 entre Calles 35 y 33
Miramar, Playa
Tel. 07/204 04 47, daily from 10pm
(Tue – Sun afternoon concerts too)
Sometimes the bands don't start
playing until 1am, but it's worth the
wait: Habaneros say the atmosphere is

Havana Map

0,25 mi
500 m
©Baedeker

Estrecho de la Flórida

Caleta de San Lázaro

Santa Fé

Malecón

Calzada (Calle 7)

CVD
José Martí (Calle 7)

Embajada
Suiza

Monumento
USS Maine

Calzada

Calle K

Línea

Calle 17

Calle 13

Hospital

Línea

Calle 15

Calle 19

Calle 21

Calle I

Calle H

Calle 17

Calle 21

(Calle 23)

Calle 25

Casa de A.
Santamaria

Monumento
A. Maceo

Humboldt

Malecón

Príncipe

Torreón de
San Lázaro

Hospital
Hermanos
Ameijeiras

Avenida de los Presidentes

VEDADO

Calle F

Calle 15

Heladería
Coppelia

Rampa

Calle 27

Vapor

San Lázaro

Animas

Virtudes

Miramar

Museo
Artes
Decorativas

Calle 19

Calle 21

(Avenida G)

Calle 25

Universidad
de La Habana

Julio A.
Mella

Concordia

Neptuno

San Miguel

Oquendo

Lucena

Marqués González

Belascoaín (Padre Varela)

(Avenida G)

Museo
Antropológico

Museo
Napoleónico

Calzada Infanta (Avenida Menocal)

San Francisco

San Martín (San José)

Espada

Aramburu

Soledad

Calle D

Calle 21

Calle 23

Hospital
General Calixto
García

Calle Ronda

Estadio
Juan Abrahantes

Zanja

Salud

Jesús

Oquendo

Rampa

Hospital

Calle C

Calle 27

Hospital
Hospital

Castillo
del Príncipe

Avenida Carlos III

Hospital
(Salvador Allende)

Enrique Barnet (Estrella)

Maloja

Peñalver

Subirana

Marqués González

Calle B

Calle A

Hospital

Calzada de Zapata

Feria
de la
Juventud

Lugareño

Bruzón

Pozos Dulces

Almendares

Calzada de Ayestarán

Calzada de Infanta (Menocal)

Desagüe

Benjumeda

Árbol Seco

Santo Tomás

Estadio
José M. Pérez

Paseo

Cementerio
de Cristóbal
Colón

Calle 37

Calle 2

Teatro
Nacional

Avenida Carlos M. de Céspedes

Museo
Filatélico

Avenida Rancho Boyeros

19. de Mayo

Factor

Hospital

Clavel

Santa Marta

Retiro

Avenida Manglar (Arroyo)

Calle 39

Paseo

Plaza de la
Revolución

José Martí

Biblioteca
Nacional

Aranguren (Zaldo)

San Martín

Avenida D

Universidad
Esteves

Calle 41

Avenida de Colón

Aeropuerto

Pedro Pérez

Calzada de Ayestarán

Avenida 20 de Mayo

CERRO

Masó

Estadio Latinoamericano

Where to eat

1. La Cecilia
2. Dos Gardenias
3. El Aljibe
4. Restaurant 1830
5. La Terraza de Cojímar
6. La Divina Pastora
7. Paladar Torresson
8. Parillada
   La Casona de 17
9. La Torre
10. La Guarida
11. Paladar Los Cactus

Where to stay

1. Habana Riviera
2. Melía Cohiba
3. Residencial Marina
   Hemingway
4. Nacional de Cuba
5. Palacio O'Farrill
6. Casa del Científico
7. Tryp Habana Libre
8. Santa Isabel
9. Ambos Mundos
10. Hostal
    El Comendador

1 Palacio de los Capitanes Generales
2 Museo de Arte Colonial
3 Bodeguita del Medio
4 Casa de Puerto Rico
5 Casa de la Obra Pía
6 Casa de Africa
7 Casa Benito Juarez
8 Casa del Arabe
9 Museo Numismático
10 Museo de Finanzas
11 Drugeria Johnson

Entertainment
① Conjunto Folklórico Nacional
② Bar Monserrate
③ Ballet Nacional de Cuba
④ Cabaret Tropicana
⑤ Casa de la Música
⑥ Casa de la Amistad
⑦ Delirio Habanero
⑧ Café Cantante Mi Habana

Telégrafo
Inglaterra
El Mesón de la Flota
Villa Babi

better here than in the new Casa de la Música in Centro (Calle Galiano), where the leading salsa and hip-hop bands also play. Before the performance starts, guests can enjoy the typically Cuban comedy warm-up shows, browse the CDs in the shop (daily 10am–00.30am) or chill out on the second floor in the El Diablo Tun Tun piano bar.

⑧ Café Cantante Mi Habana
Just around the corner from the Teatro Nacional, Paseo, at the corner of Calle 39 on Plaza de la Revolución, Vedado
Tel. 07/87 84 27 3
Daily 10.30pm – 6am
Good live salsa music if you can get past the bouncers (officially couples only in order to keep out prostitutes; women and female couples, including women tourists accompanied by Cuban women, simply pay (have the right change ready) and walk in).

⑥ Casa de la Amistad
Avenida Paseo 406, entre Calles 17 y 19, Vedado

Tel. 07/830 31 14, -15, from 9pm
Arts centre with restaurant in an old villa with a big garden, venue for a »Noche Cubana« on Saturdays with live bands and a dance show where guests join in (salsa, bolero). Every Tuesday: »Chan Chan« with música tradicional (son, La Guaracha etc.). Sometimes the Cubans dance a polonaise, and tourists just have to try and keep up…

WHERE TO STAY
▶ Luxury
⑨ Ambos Mundos
Calle Obispo 110, corner of Mercaderes-Cabaret Vieja
Tel. 07/86 71 03 9, fax 860 97 61
www.habaguanex.ohc.cu
Reopened in 1997 after renovation. The room in which Hemingway wrote *For Whom the Bell Tolls* can be visited. 54 rooms.

① Habana Riviera
Paseo y Malecón, Vedado
Tel. 07/833 40 51, fax 833 37 39
www.hotelhabanariviera.com
The Hotel Riviera was built in 1956–57 under Batista, using the money of his American friend, the criminal Meyer-Lansky. Ginger Rogers is said to have inaugurated the cabaret by chance and Johnny Weissmuller to have been one of the first guests. Meyer-Lansky's casino was even competition for Las Vegas; gaming and prostitution were the main business here until the revolution. Today this is one of the best hotels in town. The adjoining Copa Room (formerly Palacio de la Salsa), a gigantic palace of music where Cuban bands play for dancers, is known all over the island.

② Melía Cohiba
Calle Paseo e/1ra y 3ra, Vedado

Modern luxury, Cuban-style: Melía Cohiba

Tel. 07/833 36 36, fax 834 45 55
melia.cohiba@meliacuba.com
www.meliacuba.com
One of Havana's most modern luxury
hotels, with its tall towers visible from
far away on the Malecón. The grand
lobby is marble-clad, and the 462
rooms are popular with business
guests as well as tourists.

⑤ *Palacio O´Farrill (Habaguanex)*
Calle Cuba, corner of Chacón,
Habana Vieja
Tel. 07/860 50 80, fax 860 50 83
jrecepcion@ofarrill.co.cu,
www.habaguanex.ohc.cu
Wonderfully restored colonial palace
whose 38 luxurious rooms show off
200 years of Cuban-Spanish architectural history: tall double doors, an
arcaded patio courtyard, glass mosaics
and a domed glass roof.

④ *Nacional de Cuba (Gran Caribe)*
Calle O, corner of 21, Vedado
Tel. 07/83 80 294, fax 83 65 171
www.hotelnacionaldecuba.com
This elegant and proud building
(1930) with its two towers rises on a
small eminence in the Vedado district,
not far from the Malecón. The garden
is a paradise with a superb view of the
sea and the city. 461 rooms with every
amenity, though some of them small,
15 suites and a presidential suite make
this hotel a fine place to relax.

⑧ *Santa Isabel*
Calle Baratillo no. 9, entre O'Reilly y
Narciso López, Habana Vieja
Tel. 07/860 82 01, fax 860 83 91
www.habaguanex.ohc.cu
This hotel in the palace of the Conde
Santovenia dating from the late 18th
century, a magnificent building where
splendid festivities once took place,
was completely restored and reopened
in 1997.

Baedeker recommendation

► **Luxury**
⑪ *Telégrafo*
Prado, corner of Neptuno (at Parque
Central), Centro
Tel. 07/861 10 10, fax 861 47 41
subgerente@telegrafo.co.cu
www.habaguanex.ohc.cu
reserva@telegrafo.co.cu
www.habaguanex.com
A perfect combination of old and new, a
ruined look with modern steel-and-glass
design: the façade of a hotel dating from
1888 conceals surprisingly chic and stylish
rooms with four-star luxury.

► **Mid-range**
⑩ *Hostal El Comendador*
Calle Obrapía, corner of Baratillo (the
same entrance and reception as the
Hostal Valencia in Calle Oficios,
which is better known to bus and taxi
drivers), Habana Vieja
Tel. 07/867 10 37, fax 860 56 28
reserva@habaguanexhvalencia.co.cu
www.habaguanex.ohc.cu
Travellers must have lived like this in
Havana 200 years ago! Duck when
you enter the room: low wooden
beams, a bath-tub supported on
curved bronze lion's paws, a view of
the harbour beyond the wrought-iron
grille. Lots of original charm, if
somewhat overpriced.

⑫ *Inglaterra*
Prado, no. 416, corner of San Rafael
Habana Vieja
Tel. 07/86 08 59 3, fax 860 82 54
www.gran-caribe.com
Azulejos (tiles) on the walls, stucco
ceilings and a Sevillian patio transport
guests to Moorish Spain. 83 comfortably furnished rooms (some
without windows), three of them with

Inglaterra Hotel in the Spanish and Moorish style

a terrific panoramic view from the balcony. Souvenir shop, crafts on sale, tourist office, bureau de change.

③ **Marina Hemingway: Residencial Marina Hemingway/El Viejo y el Mar**
Calle 48 y 5ta. Ave., Santa Fé, Playa
Tel. 07/204 16 89, fax 204 66 53
www.hemingwayyachtclub.org
Sailors and yacht owners appreciate accommodation in the Marina Hemingway, 10km/6mi from the centre, with the hotels El Viejo y El Mar (186 rooms) and Jardín del Edén (88 rooms). Between the four water channels there are also 42 houses and 36 bungalows, restaurants, two swimming pools, a dance club and well-stocked shops for groceries and souvenirs.

⑦ **Tryp Habana Libre**
Calle L entre 23 y 25, Vedado
Tel. 07/834 61 00, fax 834 63 65

tryp.habana.libre@meliacuba.com
www.meliacuba.com
In what was previously the Hilton Hotel, which looks like a big box from outside and is undergoing renovation, are a bureau de change (cash drawn on credit card), offices of airlines and a tourist office. Guerrilleros stayed in the hotel in the revolutionary years.

► **Mid-range/Budget**
⑬ **El Mesón de la Flota**
Calle Mercaderes, no. 257,
near Plaza Vieja
Habana Vieja
Tel. 07/863 38 38, fax 862 92 81
www.habaguanex.com
A colonial gem and former tavern for Spanish seamen that still has maritime charm. Only five large rooms, a noisy flamenco show in the afternoons and evenings.

► **Budget**
⑥ **Casa del Científico**
Prado, no. 212, corner of
Calle Trocadero, Centro
Tel. 07/862 16 07, tel./fax 862 16 08
www.casadelcientifico.com
A fine palacio with rather basic rooms, some without window, some without en-suite bathroom. Service on the terrace restaurant is patchy.

⑭ **Villa Babi**
Calle 27 Nr. 965, entre Calles 6 y 8
Vedado
Tel. 07/830 63 73, tel./fax 830 20 94
www.villababi.com
The widow of Tomás Gutiérrez Alea (director of *Strawberry and Chocolate*), a film producer, lets a few rooms, some with en-suite bathroom, in an attractive house full of photos, messages scribbled by her guests, art and kitsch. Garden with papaya tree and palms.

This is the start of Calle Baratillo, where coffee and rum can be tasted and souvenirs are sold in the **Casa del Café**, Casa del Rón and **Taberna del Galeón**, and a handful of other places.

Calle Baratillo

On the other side of the square, the imposing Castillo de la Real Fuerza, the **is the oldest fort in the city** and the second oldest in the New World. Construction began in 1558 and was completed in 1577. A small drawbridge leads from the hills opposite to the massive structure. The castle's location made it an easy target, and before long it was taken by French pirates. From the battlements there is a fine view across to the Fortaleza de San Carlos de la Cabaña (►Around Havana: The East), a statue of Christ by Cuban artist Jilma Madera, and towards the harbour. The fort itself is now home to a ceramics museum, a gallery, a bar and various souvenir shops (cigars).

Look up to the tower to see the emblem of Havana, La Giraldilla (weather vane). The bronze figure represents Inés de Bobadilla, the wife of Governor Hernán de Soto. She is said to have stood here and waited for her husband after his departure for Florida – in vain, as he never returned. In one hand she holds the Spanish Order of Calatrava, which de Soto wore, and in the other the Cuban national tree, the royal palm. The original La Giraldilla is on show in the municipal museum. A memorial in front of the entrance to the fort commemorates Cuban sailors who died in the Second World War when German U-boats attacked commercial shipping.

On the northwestern side of the square is the city's largest **crafts market;** there is another market in Vedado near the Hotel Cohíba on the Malecón.

✷
Castillo de la Real Fuerza
🕐
Opening hours:
Daily 9am – 5.30pm

✷
◄ Giraldilla

With its beautiful colonnades, Palacio del Segundo Cabo (1772) is an impressive building. Originally serving as the Spanish military headquarters, today it accommodates the Cuban Book Institute and the Bella Habana bookshop, as well as a gallery. It is worth taking a quick look inside at the pretty two-storey patio.

Palacio del Segundo Cabo

Do make time to visit the **Museo de la Ciudad** (municipal museum) in the Palacio de los Capitanes Generales, formerly the palace of the governor general. This late Baroque building (1776 – 1791) was the seat of the US administration from 1898 to 1902, the president's palace until 1920, and after that (until 1967) the city hall.

The attractive courtyard features a sculpture of Columbus and the remains of a church that once stood here.

The ground floor contains a collection of 18th-century religious art and the original La Giraldilla, which was damaged in a storm. 19th-century uniforms and weapons are displayed on the upper floor. A portrait gallery honours the generals of the War of Independence; personal items such as Antonio Maceo's boat and the death mask of Máximo Gómez are also on view. One room is devoted to the strug-

✷✷
Palacio de los Capitanes Generales
🕐
Opening hours:
Daily
9.30am – 6.30pm

! *Baedeker* TIP

What connoisseurs know

If you always wanted to smoke banana leaves, go ahead: buy a box of cigars with ten of the finest cohíbas from an unknown »jinetero« on the street for US$ 40 instead of the shop price of around US$ 270. Often these boxes with an »original« seal (»hecho en Cuba, totalmente a mano«) contain nothing better than what was swept up from the floor of a cigar factory. Connoisseurs know how to test the goods that they are offered: they have to be able to smell the authentic aroma. The »rustle« and colour have to be right, too.

gle against Batista and American imperialism, and further rooms are furnished as a dining room, café salon, throne room for the king of Spain, ballroom, music room and chapel.

The surface of the road in front of the palace is a curious feature: it is made of wood. The story goes that a governor general ordered it to be laid so his siesta would not be disturbed by the clip-clop of horses' hooves.

✳ Calle Obispo

Calle Obispo (Bishop Street) runs right through the old quarter, from the southern end of Plaza de Armas to the Paseo. This pretty, largely restored shopping street, part of which is a pedestrian zone, is lined with a number of interesting colonial buildings, but also with examples of Art Nouveau architecture such as the wonderful **Hotel Florida**. The magnificent, salmon-pink **Hotel Ambos Mundos** is famous above all as a place of pilgrimage for Hemingway fans (►Where to Stay).

✳✳ Plaza de la Catedral

Return to Calle Obispo and enter Calle San Ignacio, which leads from the Ministry of Education straight to the cathedral square. This cobbled space is surrounded by splendid arcaded buildings. Here the restaurant **El Patio**, the Plaza gallery and the **Museo de Arte Colonial** (►below) await visitors.

✳ Catedral

☉ Opening hours: Daily 10am–3pm

Built between 1748 and 1778 with a magnificent limestone façade and two asymmetrical towers the cathedral dominates the square. Construction was begun by the Jesuits, but not completed until after their expulsion, when the Spanish king commissioned the work. In 1789 the principal church of Havana was transferred to this building from Plaza de Armas, and ten years later it was consecrated as a cathedral.

Although the façade is severely weathered, it still has an extremely imposing appearance. Cuban churches are plain, as the Catholic Church took all liturgical items and furnishings to the Vatican after the revolution. The interior is nevertheless impressive, with a high altar adorned with gold, silver and onyx. Above it is a statue of the Virgin Mary. The painting was executed by the French artist Vermay, although most of the figures are said to be the work of the Italian painter Branchini. From 1796 until 1898 the nave held the tomb of Christopher Columbus. His bones were taken to Seville after the end of Spanish colonial rule.

Arcades around Plaza de la Catedral

For insights into modern Cuban painting, go to the Centro Wifredo Lam (Calle Ignacio 22, corner of Empedrado, on the left next to the cathedral), tel. 07/861 34 19, Opening hours: Mon – Sat 8.30am – 4.30pm). The main part of the exhibition is an interesting collection of works by Lam (►Famous People).

Centro Wifredo Lam

On the opposite side of the square, Palacio Bayona, one of Havana's oldest buildings, houses the Museo de Arte Colonial, where interesting examples of art from the colonial period, glass and a few fine pieces of furniture are on display. Opening hours: daily 9am – 7pm. **Cuba's first aqueduct** used to run along the west of the museum in Callejón del Chorro; today, only a fountain serves as a reminder.

Museo de Arte Colonial

Another 19th-century aristocratic residence stands on the west side of the square: Casa de Baños (House of Baths) was named after a water reservoir that once occupied this site and is now home to the Victor Manuel art gallery.

Casa de Baños

Only a few paces further, round the corner in Calle Empedrado, discover a further **Hemingway shrine**, the Bodeguita del Medio, where the author liked to drink a mojíto, a cocktail of sugar, soda water, lime juice, white rum and fresh mint. As the bar and restaurant are usually crowded with tourists, there is often a queue to enter this place of pilgrimage. Once the haunt of artists, its walls are covered in signatures and dedications, some of them framed and under glass. The most famous of them are Ernest Hemingway's words »mi mojíto en la Bodeguita, mi daiquirí en el Floridita«.

★
Bodeguita del Medio

> ! **Baedeker TIP**
>
> **Cigar Museum and Casa del Habano**
> It is well worth visiting this museum to see all kinds of exhibits associated with the cigar and its history in Cuba, from plantations and production to the enjoyment of fine brands (more than 30 brands in the attached Casa del Habano shop, for instance). Calle Mercaderes 120, entre Obispo y Obrapía, opening hours: Tue – Sat 10am – 5pm, Sun 10am – 1pm.

Southern Old Quarter (walk)

Calle Mercaderes/Obrapía is the site of the **Casa de la Obra Pía**, built in the early 17th century and renovated in 1780. Various collections are on show in this glowing yellow Baroque building; two rooms are dedicated to the Cuban writer Alejo Carpentier, and a third is given over to an exhibition on King Carlos III of Spain. Opening hours: Mon – Sat 9am – 4.30pm, Sun 9.30am – 12 noon.

The Casa de África on the other side of the street is dedicated to Africa and Cuba's African heritage. The exhibits include a huge collection of art and cult items. The institution includes a gallery, a study centre, a library and a room for events in which performances of music and dance are held on the main holy days of Santería. Opening hours: Tue – Sat 10am – 6pm, Sun 9am – 1pm.

★
Casa de África

Walk east along Calle Obrapía for a detour via Calle Oficios to the **Casa del Árabe**, an Arab arts centre and restaurant, and the Casa del Obispo, and to take a look at the car museum.
On the opposite side of the road in the **Museo de Automobiles**, Cadillacs and Rolls-Royces, including a car that belonged to the singer Benny Moré, can be admired. Opening hours: daily 9am – 6.30pm. A few yards further on, in Calle Jústiz 21, is the **Caserón del Tango**.

Calle Oficios

⊕

← *Palacio Bayona, one of Havana's oldest buildings, dates from 1770 and now houses the Museo del Arte Colonial.*

SALSA: TAKE HEART AND SWING YOUR HIPS

Dancing salsa is quite easy, really: just keep shuffling on the spot, and the woman wobbles her breasts and buttocks, sometimes faster, sometimes slower, with an occasional »un, dos, tres« backwards, then forwards, then a 360-degree turn (but not on the wrong leg!), not forgetting to swing the hips – oh, and the arms … But non-Latinas and non-Latinos should not despair in the dance course, as they are not struggling on their own, even on Cuba.

Cuba libre, chicas and compañeros. May all the clichés continue to bring lots of tourists to Cuba. But it's high time to take leave of some musical myths. Adiós, cliché number one: all Cubans have salsa rhythm in their blood. Hasta la vista, cliché number two: the whole of the »sugar island« is one big Buena Vista Social Club, with serene old gentlemen as old as Methuselah wherever you look, all twanging their double bass day and night … **Roberto is without doubt a typical Cuban.** One who bolsters his 250-peso salary (about $ 13) with black-market dealings so he can buy his two children a hamburger and a state-produced Tropi-Cola in the Rápido fast-food chain – which costs half of his official salary, because it has to be paid for in expensive pesos convertibles. One whose favourite dish is »moros y cristianos« (rice and black beans) with pork, and **who reveres Che Guevara with all his heart**, as all Cuban comrades do. One who never fails to utter declarations of love at the sight of feminine curves. Nevertheless: Roberto can't dance salsa. At the age of 42 he hasn't even learned the basic steps!

As all the world knows, salsa is in the Cubans' blood. »That's not true at all. There are lots of Cubans who can't dance,« says our dance teacher con-

Don't believe the cliché that all Cubans have rhythm in their blood – but they can all dance at least a few steps of salsa!

solingly. Once she was a famous dancer, and now she gives lessons to supple or stiff-limbed foreigners in Havana's old quarter. »Europeans think too much when they dance,« she smiles. »I've even been asked how high and at what angle the arms should be held.« Her tip is to listen to lots of salsa music and practise all the time, for example when cleaning your teeth. People who have never listened to salsa music and tried out the Cuban style of dancing quickly get confused with all the complicated turns and figures.

One learner on the dance course compares salsa with skiing, another with driving a car. The most erotic Cuban dance is actually not salsa, but rumba . »In the guaguancó, the man approaches his partner with unmistakable sexual gestures and tries to ›inoculate‹ the woman – vacunar is what we call it. And the woman pretends to fend him off, but of course that's nothing but coquettishness.«

»Here too you get men known as ›galan de pared‹, who always stand by the wall in the dance club looking handsome and vain, but don't know how to dance,« says Tamara during the lesson. »That's not the kind of man I like!« Lazaro, her 26-year-old boyfriend, grins contentedly and adds »**For us, dancing is part of communicating**,« and every Cuban learns a bit of salsa or sees on the street how it is done. »Otherwise you simply don't get to know any women here!«

In the evening in Café Cantante on Plaza de la Revolución at a concert by Anacaona, a women's salsa orchestra, Tamara and Lazaro show us what a practised salsa looks like: the hips sway, the pelvis goes up and down, and the spine rotates so much that every joint ought to be creaking. Most of the foreign visitors are treading or hopping clumsily on the spot. Off to a dance course!

For information

about dancing and percussion courses in Havana, contact:

Teatro Nacional, tel. 07/879 60 11
Casa de la Cultura Habana Viega, Calle Aguiar
Museo del Ron, corner of Av. del Puerto and Calle Sol, tel. 07/8618051.

★ ★
Plaza de
San Francisco
de Asís

Continue south 200m/200yd to reach the Plaza de San Francisco de Asís, also known as Lion Square because of its beautiful fountain. In the course of the old quarter's restoration, the square was refurbished and the buildings of the old exchange, **Lonja del Comercio**, and the ship terminal carefully renovated. As the deepest part of the bay is in front of the plaza, this spot was an important anchorage and loading site in the 17th century. Today the buildings on Plaza de San Francisco de Asís are occupied by government offices, small shops and bars, and upmarket restaurants.

San Francisco
de Asís ▶

In the Church of San Francisco de Asís, built in 1608 and destroyed by a hurricane 200 years ago, a recent painting with a three-dimensional effect represents the old vault of the dome. The church is now used as a **museum** for religious items and some curious exhibits from the colonial period (including a mummified Franciscan monk). The tallest church tower in Havana is open to visitors, who are rewarded for the climb by a **panoramic view from a height of 40m/130ft**.

Not an unusual sight: 1950s cars are part of the street scene, and they need plenty of repairs.

The Rum Museum in the Fundación Havana Club (Av. del Puerto, also called Calle San Pedro, corner of Calle Sol) provides entertaining and tasty insights into the world of rum production, from sugar-cane fields and barrel-making to distilling. The experience finishes in the attached bar with a tasting of rum from an añejo blanco to a 15-year-old gran reserva (opening hours: Mon–Sat 9am–5pm, Sun 10am–4pm; the cocktail bar is open until midnight; gallery and souvenir shop next door).

Museo del Ron Havana Club

⏲

From the little square by the Church of San Francisco de Paula, Calle Leonor Pérez (formerly Calle Paula) leads west to the railway station. The buildings in the streets around here, mainly homes of black port workers, are in urgent need of restoration.

San Francisco de Paula

The Iglesia de Nuestra Señora de la Merced was constructed with donations from Afro-Cuban congregations. There are beautiful frescoes inside the church, but its chief sight is the **image of the Virgen de la Merced**, who is also venerated here as Obatalá (►Baedeker Special p. 28). White-clad adherents of the cult of this Afro-Cuban goddess of the head and of intelligence can often be seen here. On 24 September, the holy day of the Virgen de la Merced and Obatalá, they flock to the church in their thousands.

★

Iglesia de Nuestra Señora de la Merced

In the modest house that was the birthplace of José Martí (►Famous People), near the station at the corner of Calle Leonor Pérez (formerly Calle Paula) and Av. de Bélgica (Egido), various personal items that belonged to the freedom fighter and author, as well as photographs and first editions of his works are on display. Opening hours: Tue–Sat 9am–5pm, Sun 9am–1pm.

Casa Natal de José Martí

⏲

The convent of Santa Clara (1638–1644) between Calle Sol and Calle Luz, the first convent on Cuban soil, was built to protect noble girls and women from roaming sailors.
In 1919 it was sold by the nuns, becoming a slaughterhouse and then an office building. Today it is the seat of the National Centre for Restoration, with information about the status of the renovation works and an old convent garden containing many Cuban healing plants and trees.

Convento de Santa Clara

The 16th-century Plaza Vieja is worth a short detour. Havana's rich upper class once lived here, as evidenced by a few remaining fine **18th-century townhouses**.
Many buildings on the southeastern side, such as the **Art Nouveau Hotel Palacio**, have recently been renovated. Since the revolution most of them have been used for cultural institutions such as the State Art Fund in the Palacio del Conde de Jaruco, galleries and a school – as well as an apartment building with exorbitant rents for foreigners.

Plaza Vieja

Droguería Johnson

On the corner of Obispo and Calle Aguiar pay a visit to the Droguería Johnson, a pharmacy with a Spanish colonial interior and interesting pharmaceutical instruments.

Beyond La Habana Vieja

The sights outside the old quarter of La Habana Vieja may be far apart but are well worth a look, if enough time is available. The districts to the west are **Centro** and **Vedado**, bounded to the north by the **Malecón waterfront road**. Here you can stroll on the **former showcase boulevard Prado** (Paseo del Prado or Paseo de Martí) or the shopping street **Calle 23**, and take a look at Plaza de la Revolución, Havana's political hub, or the splendour of the graves in the Cementerio Colón. Even further to the west, discover the former high-class residential quarter of **Miramar**, the district of **Marianao** with the legendary Cabaret Tropicana (►Entertainment) and finally the exclusive Marina Hemingway.

Paseo del Prado (Paseo de Martí)

✳
Fine residences on Havana's fine boulevard

What was once Havana's showcase avenue, Paseo José Martí, also known as Paseo or Prado, runs south from La Punta fort at the harbour entrance to the Capitolio. The central strip of the boulevard is a little avenue with benches, figures of lions and fountains. Once-magnificent residences with ornate façades in the Art Deco or colonial style line both sides of the street. The central meeting point is **Parque Martí**, a shaded square with palm trees and benches.

On the Paseo and in the surrounding streets, the »old lady« Havana presents a weathered and decayed appearance, but also a morbid charm. The picturesque scene cannot conceal the poverty and social distress of this area. Originally each of these grand townhouses was planned for a single family, but after the revolution the suites of rooms were subdivided into small apartments in which dozens of families live today. In many rooms with a height of up to 5.5m/18ft, an additional ceiling was installed to create two storeys with rooms 2.5m/8ft high – **»barbacoas«**, named after Indian buildings on stilts. This trick has caused problems for the stability of the buildings, as the additional weight often means danger of collapse. Many buildings have now been demolished except for the lovely old façades, which conceal a new structure behind.

Parque de los Mártires

Between Castillo de la Punta and Castillo de la Real Fuerza lies the bustling Parque de los Mártires. At its northwestern tip a mausoleum honours students who were shot in the uprising of 1871. To the southeast of this an impressive equestrian statue represents **Máximo Gómez** (1935), a general of the Wars of Independence. To the south of this monument, Plaza 13 de Mayo is the site of a **splendid Art Nouveau palace** that now serves as the Spanish embassy.

The Museo de la Revolución in the former presidential palace of the dictator Batista

On the opposite side (Calle Capdevila), a further fine early 20th-century edifice houses the Museo de la Música with its exhibition of instruments and documentation of Cuban music. The highlight of the museum is the collection of African drums assembled by the ethnographer Fernando Ortíz. Occasionally concerts are held here. Opening hours: daily 11am – 5.30pm.

Museo de la Música

⊕

A visit to the revolution museum housed in the **former presidential palace** (1913 – 1920) is both impressive and informative. The Cuban engineer Carlos Maruri and the Belgian architect Jean Beleau designed and built the structure, which was given interior fittings by Tiffany.
The museum has an extensive collection on the recent history of Cuba (photos, documents, weapons). The second floor is devoted to ex-

★ ★
Museo de la Revolución
⊕
Opening hours:
Daily 10am – 5pm

hibitions on various historical periods, beginning with colonization and the extermination of the Indians, moving on to the introduction of slavery and the Wars of Independence, and concluding with occupation by the USA, the October Revolution and its influence on Cuba, and finally the most important section, the history of the Cuban Revolution. Famous life-size figures of Che Guevara and Camilo Cienfuegos depict them as fighting guerrillas.

The first floor gives access to the interior of the dome and the hall of mirrors, where the displays provide details of the triumph of the revolution and the ensuing campaigns to eradicate »counter-revolutionary« developments. A particularly interesting section, unusual in a museum, is the Rincón de los Cretinos (cretins' corner), where remarks made by Batista and Reagan can be perused.

Memorial Granma

A glass pavilion behind the revolution museum displays the yacht *Granma*, on which Fidel Castro, Che Guevara and 80 other revolutionaries landed on Cuba in December 1956 coming from Mexico. More weapons and vehicles (tanks, cars, planes, etc.) from Cuba's revolutionary past can be seen in the little park around the *Granma*.

✱ Museo Nacional de Bellas Artes

Opening hours:
Tue – Sat
10am – 6pm
Sun 10am – 2pm

Since the renovation of the Museo Nacional de Bellas Artes (one block beyond the revolution museum: Calle Trocadero entre Agramonte, formerly Zulueta, y Av. de las Misiones, formerly Monserrate), its exhibits have been divided between two sites: the first is a box-like modern block that does not fit well among the palacios and ruins. It houses Cuban art (Colección de Arte Cubano), starting with Arte Colonial (on the third floor), followed by Impressionism, contemporary art and 20th-century masters such as Wifredo Lam. Two blocks further south on Parque Central, masterpieces of European art, among them works by Goya, Rubens and Canaletto, are shown in a fine old building that was once known as the Centro Asturiano (Colección de Arte Universal, Calle San Rafael).

Edificio Bacardí

A tower with a huge bronze bat announces from afar that the Edificio Bacardí (Av. de las Misiones, formerly Monserrate, entre Empedrado y San Juan de Díos) was once the headquarters of the Bacardí family's rum empire. After a long and expensive restoration, this is now one of the most attractive and striking Art Deco buildings in Havana. It is used as accommodation for offices, mostly of foreign organizations, and also has a mirador (viewpoint).

✱ El Floridita

Very close to Calle Obispo, at the corner of Monserrate (Av. de la Misiones), the legendary Floridita awaits, one of Hemingway's regular drinking haunts. A bar stool is still reserved for him, and pictures recall the times he came here with Gary Cooper, Ava Gardner and Spencer Tracy (► Baedeker Special p. 234). Floridita is now one of the city's best and most expensive restaurants: paying homage to famous people means paying extra.

In El Floridita a barstool is still reserved for Hemingway. After all, it was him who made this restaurant famous. Since then, time seems to have stood still…

Parque Central on the southern section of the Paseo is a favourite rendezvous for the Habaneros. This little square with 28 palm trees grouped around a **statue of liberation hero José Martí** (1905) is an oasis for school children, couples and elderly men who discuss the latest baseball results, but there is also a noticeably large number of touts and »jineteras«. Imposing architecture such as that of the Hotel Inglaterra and Teatro Gracía Lorca give the spot its own special charm.

★
Parque Central

From here Calle San Rafael, one of the main shopping streets for Cubans, turns off west. To its south, near the corner of Calle Zanja/Galliano, the remains of Havana's old Chinatown can be tracked down in Calle Cuchillo. The scent of opium is no longer in the air, as beyond the big Chinese gateway just a few markets and restaurants with Chinese-influenced food remain in the narrow alleys.

Calle San Rafael – Calle Cuchillo

CAPITOLIO

✳ ✳ Cubans have a somewhat ambiguous relationship with this emblem of Havana, as it is the symbol of a period when their island was in an almost colonial state of dependency on the USA. Built in 1929 under the dictator Machado, the Capitolio was once the seat of the senate and parliament.

🕐 Opening hours:
9am – 5pm

① Dome
The centre of this impressive 90m/295ft-high dome, a 24-carat diamond, is the point from which all distances on Cuba are measured. The diamond belonged to the last tsar of Russia before it was sold to Cuba.

② Statue
One of the world's largest statues standing inside a building, the 14m/46ft-high *La República*, is positioned beneath the dome. It was cast in Rome and is covered in gold leaf.

③ Steps
A massive flight of steps leads up to the entrance to the Capitolio. The statues on either side represent Labour and Justice.

④ Parliament
The parliament is located exactly opposite the plenary chamber on the other side of the building.

⑤ Library
Like the former government rooms, the library is open to visitors.

The original furnishings of the semi-circular plenary chamber still convey the atmosphere of the time when it was a political arena.

Visible from afar, the dome of the neo-Classical building, which was the tallest in the city for many years, is a landmark of Havana.

Teatro Lorca

The Teatro García Lorca, also known as Gran Teatro or Teatro de la Habana, was built in 1838. Its façade has corner towers and was adorned with neo-Classical and Art Deco motifs. In the early 20th century the place where the city's Galician community met, it now houses the Teatro Lorca (2000 seats), the Cuban state opera and the world-famous Cuban National Ballet directed by Alicia Alonso. Opening hours: daily 9am – 7pm.

Capitolio

One of the showpiece buildings on the Paseo is the Capitolio, erected in 1929 on the basis of the American Capitol using light-coloured limestone. Inside it is well worth viewing the circular hall once used as a parliamentary chamber with its wonderful mosaic ceiling and marble columns, and the venerable library, where mahogany bookcases reach up to the high ceiling and a balustrade surrounds the 3000 books at a dizzying height. On the left there is a fine-looking restaurant and an internet café (Mon – Fri 8am – 8pm).

Until 1959 the Capitolio was the seat of government. History was made there in 1933, when the police opened fire on a group of demonstrators who had gathered to protest against the dictator Machado. The Capitolio recently became home to the Academy of Sciences and the Ministry for Environmental Protection.

Fábrica de Tabacos Partagás

The Fábrica de Tabacos Partagás (opposite the rear façade of the Capitolio) was built in the late 19th century as the Villar y Villar cigar factory. Visitors are admitted to the company, where the famous Partagás brand originated. Opening hours: daily 9.30am – 11am, 12.30pm – 3pm.

Palacio de los Matrimonios

The finest building of all has the address Prado 306, at the corner of Calle Animas. The registry office for this district of Havana, known as the Palace of Weddings, was constructed in 1914 as a place of assembly for the Spanish community. With a little luck you will see a newly married couple here. Opening hours: Tue – Sat 10am – 1pm.

✴ Malecón

The unofficial heart of the city

From the Castillo de la Punta, the Malecón, **Havana's multi-lane coast road**, runs west, connecting the diverse worlds of La Habana Vieja, Centro, Vedado and Miramar. It is the unofficial heart of the city, where young people stroll by day, look out to sea or try to catch fish. In the evening the waterfront promenade is taken over by courting couples, musicians, artists, peanut vendors, tourists and shady people who offer unambiguous services.

The Malecón was planned by the Cuban engineer Albear and completed in 1926. In its present form the Avenida Antonio Maceo – as it is officially called – was laid out between 1901 and 1950. It is over

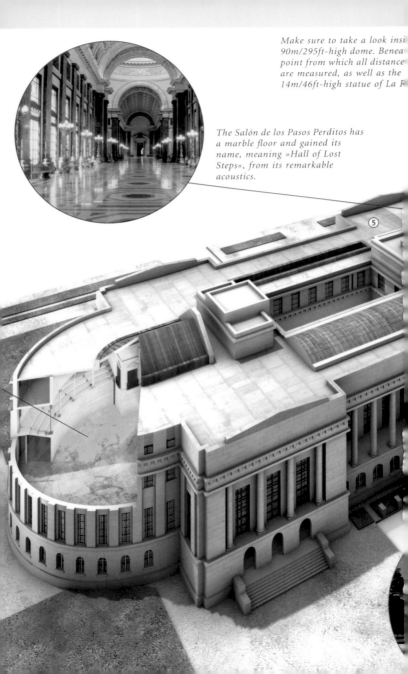

Make sure to take a look insi
90m/295ft-high dome. Benea
point from which all distance
are measured, as well as the
14m/46ft-high statue of La F

The Salón de los Pasos Perditos has
a marble floor and gained its
name, meaning »Hall of Lost
Steps«, from its remarkable
acoustics.

⑤

le the
h it is the
on Cuba
mposing
epública.

© Baedeker

The model for the Capitolio, the Capitol
in Washington, is a good deal bigger.

7km/4.5mi long and ends at the mouth of the Río Almendares. Over this distance, the Malecón changes its appearance several times, passing many interesting places of the Cuban capital. At the end near La Habana Vieja it is flanked by colonial buildings with arcades and colonnades, much weathered and just at the start of the process of restoration. The next section is modern Havana with a variety of hotels, a monument to General Antonio Maceo, the city's largest hospital, the Casa de Las Américas sport stadium and the classy Restaurant 1830 (►Where to Eat).

The Malecón, the waterfront promenade, wet by spray from the waves, is a meeting point for lovers, tourists and children.

Vedado

19th-century residential quarter

To the west of the centre lies the district of Vedado, bordered on the north by the Malecón. Before the Second World War it was an upper-class suburb, to which a new office and commercial district was added. The streets of Vedado are laid out on the American pattern and classified by letters of the alphabet.

The recommended route to the most significant sights in Vedado runs from the Malecón by the Hotel Nacional via the Rampa (Calle 32) to the university, then to the Plaza de la Revolución and the Cementerio Colón. As these places are further apart than the sights in Habana Vieja or Centro, it is advisable to travel by car or bike.

Monumento USS Maine

The Most Cuban maps don't shop the USS Maine Monument, erected in memory of 260 sailors who died when a warship of the US Navy exploded in the Bay of Havana in 1898. A plaque attached to it in 1961 reads: »To the crew of USS Maine, who were sacrificed to imperialist greed in an attempt to conquer the island of Cuba.«

Edificio FOCSAj

Havana's tallest building, the Edificio FOCSA, stands between Calles M and N. Built in the 1950s this apartment block was mainly occupied by Russian workers until the 1980s. The restaurant **La Torre** (►Where to Eat) on the top floor offers a superb view of Havana.

Calle 23 (La Rampa)

By the Hotel Nacional (►Where to Stay), the junction of the Malecón and Calle 23, is now the busiest shopping street in the city. Its lower end, called »La Rampa«, lines up commercial buildings, hotels, ministries and airline offices. Among them are the Hotel Habana Libre (previously Habana Hilton, ►Where to Stay), the headquarters of the state travel agency Cubatur and the public broadcasting corporation.

★
La Coppelia

A popular hangout of young Habaneros is situated on La Rampa. The futuristic-looking Heladería Coppelia is known throughout Latin America for the quality of its ice cream. Cineastes are only interested in the fact that Diego and David, the protagonists in the Cuban film *Strawberry and Chocolate* met here (►Baedeker Special p. 68. Tue–Sat 11am–11pm). The »foreign« department is downstairs (many flavours, paid in pesos convertible), while the Cuban department (a smaller selection in exchange for Cuban pesos) is upstairs. Cine Yara on the other side of the street is one of Havana's leading cinemas.

Universidad de la Habana

The Universidad de la Habana, a campus university with neo-Classical buildings dating from 1728, is located a few blocks further south on the Arostequi hill. A huge flight of steps leads up to the entrance, with a statue of Alma Mater in front.

South of the Castillo del Príncipe lies the gigantic Plaza de la Revolución, the political centre of Havana. At mass rallies such as the celebrations for 1 May or – in the past – speeches by the Máximo Líder Fidel Castro there is space for up to 1.5 million people.

Plaza de la Revolución

The square is oriented to the monument honouring José Martí (► Famous People), a work by Cuban artist Sicre. The 110m/360ft-high obelisk behind it stands on a star-shaped ground plan. On national holidays the stage from which Castro spoke to his people was erected in front of this monument. In the courtyard there is an exhibition about the life of the national hero Martí. A lift takes visitors up to the viewing platform, the highest in Cuba! Opening hours: Mon – Sat 9.30am – 5.30pm.

◄ **Monumento José Martí**

Clustering around the monument, modern government buildings include the seat of the Central Committee of the Communist Party of Cuba in the Palacio de la Revolución. The most impressive is the Interior Ministry, with the face of Che Guevara and the slogan »Hasta la victoria siempre« (»Until final victory«), which are illuminated after dark.

Government buildings

The Ministerio de Comunicaciones with its Museo Postal Filatélico (museum of postage stamps), the National Library and the National Theatre are also here.

This famous image of Che Guevara still adorns the Ministry of the Interior.

★★ Cementerio Colón

🕐 Opening hours:
Daily 8am – 5pm

Go several blocks northwest to see the Cementerio Colón with its magnificent gate. Three female figures symbolizing hope, faith and charity adorn the entrance; a banner with the inscription »Ianua sum pacis« (»I am the gateway to peace«) shows the way inside.

With its 800,000 graves, the Cementerio Colón (laid out in 1870) is one of the largest cemeteries in Latin America. Imposing statues and marble mausoleums give it more the air of a mythical necropolis than of a graveyard. Many famous Cubans were laid to rest here: Alejo Carpentier, Nicolás Guillén, José Lezama Lima, the Céspedes family and the parents of José Martí. One of the oldest graves is that of the Counts of Mortera on the main avenue. The mausoleum of the revolutionary forces and the monument to the firemen of Havana are particularly impressive.

Visitors will also notice the women visiting the grave of Amelia Goyre de la Hoz. **La Milagrosa** (the miracle-worker), who died in childbirth, was buried in 1901 in the area on the left in front of the chapel. According to the legend, her husband went to her grave every day. When he left, he never turned his back to it. Other visitors to the cemetery noticed his piety and also his growing wealth, and the belief arose that Amelia could work miracles for those who prayed to her. Today her grave is a place of pilgrimage, covered with flowers and votive tablets giving thanks for her miraculous deeds.

Film fans will remember the cemetery as the backdrop for the final scene of *Guantanamera* by Tomás Gutiérrez Alea (►Baedeker Special p. 68). The southwest of Cementerio Colón is occupied by the graveyard of Havana's Chinese community.

Miramar and Western Havana

Quinta Avenida

A tunnel leads under the river Almendares to Miramar, an upmarket residential district that most house-owners left after the revolution.

Havana Surroundings

Today ambassadors from all over the world live here, especially along Quinta Avenida, which is fringed with royal palms, fig trees and almond trees.

Museo del Ministerio del Interior

The Museo del Ministerio del Interior (Museum of the Interior Ministry) on the corner of Avenida 5 and Calle 14 gives detailed information about mutual spying activities of the USA and Cuba, and on the many attempts to assassinate Castro.

Acuario Nacional

Tropical and subtropical fish can be admired in the Acuario Nacional (Calle Primera, entre Calles 60 y 62). There are hourly dolphin shows, and sea lions perform their tricks. Opening hours: Tue – Sun 10am – 10pm. Calle 60 leads south from the aquarium to the district of Marianao where the legendary **Cabaret Tropicana** (► Entertainment) is hidden behind trees.

✳ Marina Hemingway

Quinta Avenida goes out to the western boundary of Havana. Directly beyond the Río Jaimanitas is the entrance to the Marina Hemingway, an exclusive anchorage for yachts with four channels. This tourist complex includes apartments, tennis courts, a dance club, various shops, restaurants and the Hotel El Viejo y El Mar (»The Old Man and the Sea«, ► Where to Stay). The water sports on offer here range from swimming to water skiing, pedalos, fishing, snorkelling and diving. Every year a renowned competition for deep-sea angling, the Torneo Internacional de la Pesca de Aguja Ernest Hemingway, starts from the Marina Hemingway. Visitors may stay in this free port for up to 72 hours without a visa.

Around Havana

Several attractive destinations for excursions close to Havana can be reached fairly conveniently on a day or half-day trip. There is something here for everyone: follow in Hemingway's footsteps in Cojímar and at Finca La Vigía, find out about Afro-Cuban culture in Regla and Guanabacoa, relax on the Playas del Este or recover from the city stress in the Botanical Garden at Lenin Park.

Around Havana: The South

Parque Lenin

About 20km/12mi south, the Parque Lenin, an enormous leisure park, covers almost 7 sq km/2.7 sq mi on the Presa Ejército Rebelde reservoir. Its facilities include an amphitheatre, an art gallery, a lending library, a pottery workshop, a riding school, a freshwater aquarium, a rodeo ground, an open-air cinema, a miniature railway and several eateries. A carefully converted sugar mill houses the Las Ruinas restaurant. In the Che Guevara Pioneer Palace Cuban children and young people have an opportunity to show and develop their talents. Opening hours: Tue – Sun 9am – 5pm.

Jardín Botánico ✷
At Havana's Botanical Garden to the south of Lenin Park, 14,000 species of plants from different vegetation zones of the earth are cultivated on an area of 6 sq km/2.3 sq mi. Highlights are the orchids and cactus departments and the Japanese Garden.

⏱ West of here is a **zoo.** Opening hours: Wed – Fri 9am – 3.30pm, Sun 9am – 4.30pm.

Around Havana: The East

Fortaleza El Morro ✷

⏱ Opening hours: Daily 8am – 20.30

From the eastern end of the Malecón, a tunnel leads beneath the harbour entrance to the El Morro fort, one of the emblems of Havana. The Castillo de los Tres Santos Reyes Magnos del Morro, to give the fort its full title, was built between 1589 and 1630 along with the La Punta fort on the other side. The two were linked by an iron chain. The work was carried out under the supervision of Italian architect Giovanni Battista Antonelli, who was succeeded from 1594 by his nephew Cristóbal de Roda. However, it was not secure enough, and after its capture in 1762 by British forces, construction began on the Cabaña fortress. The conspicuous **lighthouse** of El Morro dates from 1845. No other place has such a comprehensive **view of the skyline** of Havana. East of El Morro, the Vía Monumental leads past a hospital complex and the sports centre for the Pan-American Games of 1991 to Cojímar.

Fortaleza de San Carlos de la Cabaña ✷

Also on the east side, about 1.5km/1mi further south, the Fortaleza de San Carlos de la Cabañais the biggest colonial fort in Latin America. It was constructed between 1763 and 1774 after the withdrawal of British forces from Havana. In the Museo de Comandancia de Che Guevara, once the rebel headquarters, personal items tell Che's life story.

Every evening at 9pm (admission from 8.30pm) visitors can watch the ceremony of firing a cannon (Cañonazo de las Nueve), which back in colonial times proclaimed the closing of the city gates. Opening hours: daily 10am – 10pm.

> ❗ *Baedeker* TIP
>
> **Off to Casablanca!**
> Lots of colourful little houses give Casablanca, a small settlement south of La Cabaña, its characteristic appearance. The marble statue of Christ by Cuban sculptor Jilma Madera provides a wonderful view of Havana and the port, and, directly opposite, of the Real Fuerza fort.

Regla
Regla at the southeast end of the harbour is a lively centre of Afro-Cuban religion. It can be reached from La Habana Vieja by ferry (from the Real Fuerza fort). Black harbour workers who have kept up their rites and cults live here. Many wear necklaces in the colours of their orishas, and the beating of drums can often be heard.

Iglesia de Nuestra Señora de la Regla ✷

The main sight in Regla, the Iglesia de Nuestra Señora de la Regla, is very close to the ferry. Although the blue-and-white-clad Virgin of

These two seem to like the Fortaleza de San Carlos de la Cabaña.

Regla, the only black Madonna in Cuba, is venerated in this simple church, prayers are directed to her not only as a Catholic saint but also as the Afro-Cuban goddess Yemayá, patron of the sea and sailors (►Baedeker Special p. 28). On her holy day, 7 September, a procession with her image goes through the streets of the town, and on the seventh of every month a big Mass is held in her honour.

Travellers interested in Afro-Cuban culture should not fail to visit the historical museum in Guanabacoa, 10km/6mi east of Havana (Calle Martí 109/San Antonio y Versalles). In addition to painstakingly assembled collections on archaeology and crafts, the museum has the best exhibition about the Afro-Cuban religions Santería, Regla de Palo and Abakúa. Its most impressive department is the Munanso room with ritual items of well-known Cuban babaloás, as Afro-Cuban priests are called – large magic pots, clothes of Yoruba deities or items belonging to slaves who carried out the rites. The opening hours are a mystery in themselves, dependent on the whims of the gods. The best time to try is between 10am and 6pm, on Sundays between 9am and 1pm (closed Tue).

Museo Histórico de Guanabacoa

🕐

For about 20 years the American writer lived at Finca La Vigia, ten miles outside Havana. Cuba has profited from the great interest in Hemingway, and tourists are taken to a number of places of pilgrimage for his fans.

THE OLD MAN AND THE SEA

It is not widely known that the American writer Ernest Hemingway was very attached to Cuba. He lived on the island for 22 years – a third of his life and almost half of his time as an author.

This was the period when he wrote *Across the River and into the Trees, A Moveable Feast, The Old Man and the Sea, Islands in the Stream* and a good deal of *For Whom the Bell Tolls*.

How it all started

Hemingway made his first trip to Cuba in April 1928 when he was on his way to Key West. Four years later he returned, and from that time he spent several months every year angling off the coast of Havana. His life here – far away from his family, alone for hunting, fishing, bouts of drinking and work – seems to have reflected his idea of freedom. In this period he also discovered the bars **Bodeguita del Medio and Floridita**, to which he soon took a great liking. Hemingway often sat here for the whole of an afternoon or evening, drinking dozens of mojítos, daiquirís or »papa dobles« – the latter his own invention, consisting of a daiquirí with a double portion of rum. When he stayed ashore after such a session, he took a room at the **Hotel Ambos Mundos**, which became his permanent residence after the

Hemingway even dedicated his Nobel Prize medal to Cuba's patron saint, the Virgen del Cobre.

Spanish Civil War. In 1940 Martha Gellhorn, the third Mrs Hemingway, found a pretty country house, the **Finca La Vigia**, near Havana. Although he initially had reservations, the author soon came to love the estate with its wonderful tropical garden. He could withdraw from the world altogether here and work in peace, spending time with his dogs and cats

and breeding fighting cocks. And most important of all, he could go out in his yacht at any time and pursue his passion for deep-sea fishing.

The myth of Hemingway

Many stories are told about Hemingway. He is said to have built up a counter-espionage organization and to have cruised off the coast in his yacht *Pilar*, hunting down German U-boats. What is known for certain, however, is that he met the fisherman who was the model for the »old man« in his most famous work in the small village of Cojímar, east of Havana. His old boatman Gregorio Fuentes liked to talk about this period. Fuentes could often be seen in the restaurant La Terrazza in Cojímar, which the author immortalized in *The Old Man and the Sea*. The story is still told of how Hemingway, when invited by the owners of Cuba's biggest brewery to a party to celebrate winning the Nobel Prize for Literature for this novel (1954), brought the whole village of Cojímar with him. And the wealthy family had to mix with the fishermen if they wanted to drink and talk with Hemingway. There are many anecdotes like this, and the Cubans still love the author for his attachment to their island, its people and their traditions. Hemingway even dedicated his Nobel Prize medal to the patron saint of Cuba, the Virgen del Cobre.

But where did Hemingway, who enjoyed life's pleasures, stand on the revolution? On the one hand, he loved the fine things in life and did not want to do without them, on the other hand he had a guilty conscience

The Comandante himself had caught the biggest marlin!

because he did nothing about social evils. He was by no means ignorant of the terrible poverty and the spread of slums under Batista's dictatorship. Some passages of *Islands in the Stream* seem to have an autobiographical character: »Now they were over the bridge and going up the hill into Luyano ... This was the part he did not like on the road into town. This was really the part he carried the drink for. I drink against poverty, dirt, four-hundred-year-old dust, the nose-snot of children, cracked palm fronds, roofs made from hammered tins, the shuffle of untreated syphilis, the sewage in the old beds of brooks, lice on the necks of infested poultry, scale on the backs of old men's necks, the smell of old women, and the full-blast radio, he thought. It is a hell of a thing to do. I ought to look at it closely and do something about it. Instead you have your drink the way they carried smelling salts in the old days.«

Meeting with Fidel Castro

In 1960 he finally met Fidel Castro on the occasion of a competition for catching swordfish. Hemingway had invited Castro to present the cup to the winner. What he had not bargained on, however, was that the Comandante himself had caught the biggest marlin!

To this day the tradition of that event is kept alive in the Marina Hemingway with a competition for deep-sea fishing named Torneo Internacional de la Pesca de Aguja Ernest Hemingway. Like most of his countrymen, Fidel Castro loves Hemingway's books. When asked by an interviewer what was his favourite novel, Castro replied that it was *For Whom the Bell Tolls*, because he had learned a lot from that book. After all, the story is about a group of guerrilla fighters.

On the way to San Francisco de Paula (17km/11mi southeast of Havana), the Finca La Vigía was once the country home of the writer Ernest Hemingway. It was built in 1887 by the Catalan architect Miguel Pascual y Baguer for himself and his family. Hemingway's third wife, Martha Gellhorn, found the finca. The author lived here with interruptions from 1940 to 1960, the period when he completed *For Whom the Bell Tolls* and wrote *The Old Man and the Sea*, for which he received the Nobel Prize for Literature in 1954. The Cubans love and admire Hemingway, and the museum is regarded as a national shrine (► Baedeker Special p. 234).

Everything was left as it was in Hemingway's time, giving the impression that he has just left for a moment. He put his stamp on the house, and many personal possessions can be seen. The eye-catching items are the bar and the books in every room (even the bathroom), his hunting trophies and ubiquitous reminders of Spain (e.g. posters for bullfights). In addition to the 9000-volume library a few treasures are on show: a wall plate by Picasso and paintings by Braque and Miró.

It is unfortunately not permitted to enter and take photographs of the rooms, but there is a good view of all rooms from the circuit that leads around the house.

As her husband wanted to work undisturbed, Mary Welsh, Hemingway's fourth wife, had a three-storey **tower** built right next to the house. However, he preferred to continue writing in his library and left the tower to his numerous dogs and cats. Changing exhibitions with works by young Cuban artists are shown on the ground floor,

★ ★
**Finca La Vigía –
Museo Ernest
Hemingway**

⊘
Opening hours:
Daily 9am – 4.30pm,
closed when it rains

Hemingway caught the biggest fish (1948 with a marlin).

and photos about Hemingway's life on Cuba can be seen on the first floor. Among them are pictures of an angling contest with Fidel Castro, of the filming of *The Old Man and the Sea* with Spencer Tracy and of being awarded of the Nobel Prize.

On the top floor it is possible to visit his study. The stand-out item here is a big telescope. The view is wonderful – beautiful scenery, and you can see as far as Havana in clear weather.

The whole La Vigía estate is a delight. The finca is surrounded by a tropical garden full of palms, mango trees, frangipani, bamboo and wild orchids. Of course it would not be complete without the little pool, next to which Hemingway's yacht *Pilar* has been placed. His favourite dogs are buried here too.

✱ Cojímar
The foundation of the little fishing town of Cojímar (10km/6mi east of Havana) dates back to the 17th century. It was made famous by Hemingway's novel *The Old Man and the Sea*, which contains a lot of local colour from the town, its people and their way of life. Hemingway kept his yacht *Pilar* here. Although Havana's estates extend almost to the edge of Cojímar, it has retained the character of a small fishermen's town and seaside resort. The town was used as a set when the novel was made into a film starring Spencer Tracy (►Baedeker Special p. 234).

La Terraza ►
In the now-famous restaurant La Terraza, for many years it was possible to meet Gregorio Fuentes, Hemingway's boatman, who was happy to talk to tourists about the old days – even if his stories were not always an accurate rendering of the truth (►Where to eat).

Fortaleza La Chorrera ►
Immediately next to Cojímar's old fort, Santa Dorotea de Luna de la Chorrera y Cojímar (1643), the fishermen erected a monument in honour of Hemingway.

Holguín

Province: Holguín
Population: 262,000

Altitude: 106m/348ft
Distance: 734km/456mi from Havana
134km/83mi from Santiago de Cuba

In Cuba's fourth-largest city you can stroll from one green square (parque) to the next and immerse yourself in the island's daily life – Holguín likes to call itself the »city of squares«. Most tourists only get a bird's-eye view of Holguín as their planes land on the north coast near Guardalavaca.

What to See in and Around Holguín

Parque Calixto Garcia
Most of the sights in Holguín, including five little squares, are situated in the centre, between the streets Libertad and Maceo. One of

VISITING HOLGUÍN

EVENTS

Romerías de Mayo
At the city's biggest festival in the first week of May, the people of Holguín dance to all sorts of musical styles (a lot of rap). There are also readings and discussions, exhibitions and a procession up to ►Loma de la Cruz.

Carnaval
Music, dancing and many street stalls in the third week of August.

WHERE TO EAT

► **Moderate**
Salón 1720
Calle Frexes 190 entre Manduley y Miró
Tel. 024/46 81 50
Daily 12 noon – 11pm
International cuisine and seafood in a colonial villa with a terrace bar (until 2am), a boutique and the El Jigüe nightclub (until 5am). A small gallery sells paintings by Holguín artists.

► **Moderate/Inexpensive**
Finca and Villa Mayabe (Islazul)
Alturas de Mayabe
(8km/5mi outside Holguín)
Tel. 024/42 21 60, fax 42 54 98
www.islazul.cu
Open-air restaurant with a tourist finca campesina, beautifully situated at Loma de Mayabe for a trip out of town (daily 9am – 10pm), in a valley where thousands of royal palms grow and creole dishes taste all the better. Islazul has 24 simple rooms for an overnight stay. Pool.

► **Inexpensive**
DiMar
Calle Mártires, corner of Luz Caballero (near Plaza de la Marqueta)
No phone, daily 9am – 10.30pm
Seafood and fish in a basic restaurant that is part of a new chain.

ENTERTAINMENT

Casa de la Trova
Parque Calixto García
Local groups play traditional music such as trova and bolero (closed Mon).

WHERE TO STAY

► **Mid-range**
Hotel Pernik (Islazul)
Av. Jorge Dimitrov y Plaza de la Revolución
Tel. 024/48 10 11
fax 48 16 67
www.hotelpernik.com
The city's largest hotel, in the boxy style of the 1980s, with pool, and internet in some of the 200 rooms. Ritmo Latino disco.

the squares, **Parque Calixto García**, is named after the most important commander in the First War of Independence against Spain, and is regarded as the cultural hub of the city. Around it are the Casa de la Trova, the city gallery, the Casa del la Cultura and the historical museum of Holguín province.

La Periquera (parrot cage), a beautiful colonial building constructed between 1862 and 1868 as a barracks, is now the home of Holguín's

La Periquera

Cuban farmers lead a simple existence in the surroundings of Holguín.

historical museum. Shortly after the »Grito de Yara« (1868), the appeal by Céspedes (►Famous People) to take arms in order to gain independence from Spain, General Calixto García laid siege to this neo-Classical building, where Spanish soldiers were based.

Museo Provincial ▶
⊙
Opening hours:
Daily 9am – 5pm

The Museo Provincial tells the story of the region's historical development. Finds such as tools and weapons illustrate the aboriginal Indians' way of life. The most important exhibit in this section is the »Hacha de Holguín«, the emblem of the province. It represents an axe, with a man-shaped blade. There is also a fine display of colonial furniture. The museum also focuses on the Wars of Independence and the revolution, with special consideration of the role of Holguín at this time. Paintings by artists from the region are on show in a separate part of the museum.

Museo de Ciencias Carlos de la Torre y
⊙
Opening hours:
Daily 9am – 5pm
Sat 1pm – 5pm

Calle Maceo leads to the museum of natural history, named after Carlos de la Torre y Huerta, displaying stuffed fish and birds (including the world's smallest humming bird) and minerals. The most interesting section is an exhibition of approximately 4000 snail shells, especially those of Polymita picta (the Cuban painted snail, Baedeker Tip p. 158). In Afro-Cuban rituals these shells are still used, as magic powers are attributed to them.

The Iglesia de San Isidoro was built in 1720 in honour of the city's patron saint. It has a fine altar, originally placed in a church in ► Bayamo. When the church was destroyed by fire, Christian slaves voluntarily carried the altar a distance of 72km/45mi to Holguín. The ceiling in the Moorish Mudejar style is also beautiful.

Iglesia de San Isidoro

At the end of Calle Maceo, 450 steps lead up to Loma de la Cruz, a place of pilgrimage. The cross is said to have been erected here by citizens of Holguín in 1790. In its base is a small altar dedicated to San Lázaro, which receives donations of coins are lit candles. Each year on the Day of the Cross, 3 May, a procession makes its way up to the hill. Those who find the ascent too strenuous can go up by road. The view is truly remarkable, taking in a broad plain with fields of sugar cane on one side and the streets of Holguín on the other.

★ Loma de la Cruz

The idyllic coastal town of Gibara (33km/21mi north of Holguín) possesses three interesting museums: a museum for colonial art, a municipal historical museum and the Joaquín Fernández de la Vara natural history museum, which also has a large collection of snail shells.

Gibara

★ Isla de la Juventud

B/C 4

Province: Archipiélago de los Canarreos
Population: 80,000

Area: 2200 sq km/850 sq mi
Distance: Approx. 70km/45mi from the south coast of the main island

This island, the largest off the coast of Cuba, has already had many names, and might really have been the original of Robert Louis Stevenson's »Treasure Island« (a claim made by many Caribbean islands). One thing is known for sure: Fidel Castro was imprisoned here in 1953. Most holidaymakers come for the island's underwater treasures: 56 diving grounds of international standing with wrecks, submarine caves, colourful corals as high as cathedrals and about 500 species of tropical fish.

The Isla de la Juventud (Island of Youth), previously known as Isla de los Pinos (Pine Island), lies between Cuba and Yucatán in Mexico, about 70km/45mi from the Cuban south coast. It is the **largest island of the Canarreos coral archipelago**, a

 Baedeker TIP

Scent of citrus

In January and February the scent of citrus fruits from the extensive lemon and grapefruit plantations wafts across the island. In March at the Festival of Toronja (grapefruit), the piñerito flows. This cocktail is made from grapefruit juice, rum and ice.

group of 672 islets stretching along the southwest coast. About half of its population of 80,000 live in the main town, Nueva Gerona. The Ciénaga de Lanier, a belt of swampland, divides the Isla de la Juventud in two parts: the south is mainly forested and mountainous, while plantations and settlements dominate in the north.

The island was once a place of refuge for pirates, then a prison island, and in 1955 briefly a free-trade zone. After Cyclone Alma devastated the island in 1966, Castro called on the young people of Cuba to repair the damage. Today, more than 230 sq km/90 sq mi of plantation make the Isla de la Juventud one of the **principal areas of cultivation for citrus fruit** (especially grapefruit). For some time now marble and kaolin have been extracted here too.

History   On his second voyage to the New World, Columbus is said to have landed on the island in 1494 and named it Evangelista. As no gold was found and the island's location was not favourable, it was neglected for a long time. Only pirates and privateers frequented it,

Cuba knows where its future lies: the average age of the population is 35. In honour of the children and young people of the land, the island was renamed Isla de la Juventud.

which gave rise to stories that are said to have come to the ears of Robert Louis Stevenson, author of *Treasure Island*. The settlement **Nueva Gerona was not founded until 1830**. Later Spanish colonial rulers took advantage of the remoteness of the island by using it as **a place of exile**, for example for the Cuban freedom fighter **José Martí** (►Famous People). At the age of 17 he was imprisoned on the finca **El Abra** before being exiled to Spain in January 1871. In later decades too Pine Island was used as a place of imprisonment. In 1928 the dictator Machado built the enormous jail **Presidio Modelo** east of the main town. In 1953 Fidel Castro and 25 of his comrades were incarcerated here after the failure of their attack on the Moncada Barracks.

After the revolution, efforts to cultivate the island began. Thousands of young people were brought over for »voluntary« labour on the plantations. In recognition of this, in 1978 the island was officially given the name Isla de la Juventud. More than 60 schools and colleges were opened, registering in the peak years 20,000 students, most of them from Africa, Latin America (Nicaragua) and Asia (North Korea, Vietnam). After the start of the Special Period several schools had to be closed because of the shortage of supplies.

What to See on the Isla de la Juventud

The capital of the Isla de la Juventud, Nueva Gerona (population 35,000), was founded in 1830 on the north coast. It gained importance for the first time in the 1970s through the support of Castro's government and a programme of agricultural development. Many of the residents work on the citrus plantations and in the quarries.

The town is laid out in a grid pattern centring on Calle 39 and Calle 41, where a natural history museum and a planetarium can be visited. Nueva Gerona is known for its **marble workshops**, open to visitors in Calle 23 (between Calles 55 and 57). In the section of Calle 43 between 18 and 20 it is possible to watch woodcarvers at work.

Nueva Gerona

> ### ! *Baedeker* TIP
>
> **Liberty boat**
>
> If you are following the trail of Fidel & Co., after seeing the Presidio Modelo jail take a look at the rusty boat at the end of Calle 28 in Nueva Gerona: on board *El Pinero* Fidel Castro and his comrades returned to the mainland in 1955 after their release.

About 5km/3mi north of Nueva Gerona, the former prison is now the Museo del Presidio Modelo. After their attack on the Moncada Barracks, Fidel Castro and other leading revolutionaries served sentences here.

The enormous prison complex was based on that in Joliet in Illinois, USA, with five circular towers. Each of the wide towers has cells only around the outer walls with an empty space inside, so it could be su-

✶
Museo del Presidio Modelo

Isla de la Juventud Map

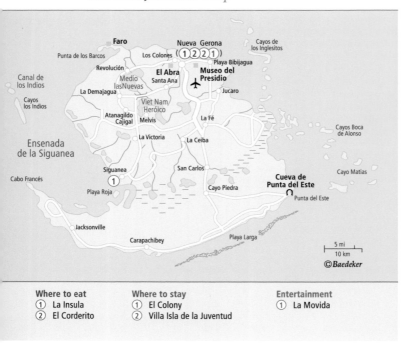

Where to eat
1. La Insula
2. El Corderito

Where to stay
1. El Colony
2. Villa Isla de la Juventud

Entertainment
1. La Movida

pervised from a shaft in the middle and only a small number of warders were needed to monitor the cells, which had no doors, only grilles on the inner side. Opening hours: Mon – Sat 8am – 4pm, Sun 8am – 12 noon

Playa Bibijagua The beach of Bibijagua, few miles east of Nueva Gerona, is remarkable for its black marble sand. Black marble is extracted in the nearby Caballes Mountains.

Museo Finca El Abra El Abra, where José Martí was imprisoned in 1870 at the age of 17, lies about 4km/2.5mi south of Nueva Gerona. The hero of liberation served time here for making rebellious speeches against the Spanish colonial government. A few of Martí's personal possessions are on show here. Opening hours: Tue – Sat 9am – 4pm, Sun 9am – 1pm.

La Fé American colonists founded La Fé, where a few well-preserved plantation houses can be seen 16km/10mi south of Nueva Gerona. Thanks to its healthy climate and mineral springs, La Fé at one time had a reputation as a spa.

◗ VISITING ISLA DE LA JUVENTUD

INFORMATION
Information point at Calle 39 (also: José Martí o. Bulevar) and corner of Calle 24, and in the Hotel Colony (for excursions to the south of the island, which is closed).

TRANSPORT
Terminal Kometa: jetfoils and large Canadian passenger catamarans run daily from the Cuban mainland (Surgidero de Batabanó), depending on the weather, their state of repair and demand (tel. in Gerona: 046/ 32 44 06, 32 44 25, terminal tel. 046/ 32 49 77). In Havana tickets are sold at the Astro bus station (incl. bus trip to Batabanó).

The town itself can easily be explored on foot, by bike or in a horse carriage; private taxis (and carriages) wait around the Parque Central for excursions around the island (negotiate the price!). The south of the island, a closed military zone, can only be seen on specially booked tours, taking visitors to a crocodile farm, caves and botanical gardens.

WHERE TO EAT
► Moderate
① *Nueva Gerona: La Insula*
Calle 39, corner of Calle 20
Cuban dishes on nicely laid tables: chicken or pork steak, lobster or fish fillet, snacks and cocktails at the bar.

► Inexpensive
② *Nueva Gerona: El Corderito*
Calle 39, corner of Calle 22
Tel. 046/32 24 00
Daily 11am – 10pm
Plain creole cooking: lamb dishes and the like.

ENTERTAINMENT
① *Nueva Gerona: La Movida*
Calle 18 (at the Río Las Casas)
Daily from 11pm
Pretty open-air disco on the river, one of four clubs in the town for dancing to salsa and other kinds of music.

WHERE TO STAY
► Mid-range
① *El Colony (Gran Caribe)*
Ctra. de Siguanea, km 46
Tel. 046/39 81 81, fax 39 84 20,
www.gran-caribe.com
Internationally known diving base, with facilities for surfing, riding and tennis, right on the beach, 77 upper mid-range rooms in a recently restored hotel and bungalows. Pool. The »Fotosub« international underwater photography competition is held annually in the hotel.

► Budget
② *Nueva Gerona: Villa Isla de la Juventud (Islazul)*
Ctra. La Fé, km 1.5
Tel. 046/32 32 90, fax 32 44 86
Pleasant little complex at the edge of town with 20 rooms in two-storey buildings around a pool.

Swing your hips in the evening – at La Movida, for example.

Cabo Francés Back in the 1950s, the divers' paradise of Cabo Francés was discovered in the west of the island. Even demanding divers enthusiastically recommend this **area of wonderful coral reefs** for its colourful marine fauna and flora. The International Scuba Diving Center runs trips to 56 recognized diving zones. A long walkway leads out to a diving station that was built in the middle of the sea with a restaurant and changing rooms.

Cueva Punta del Este In a cave at the southeastern tip of the Isla de la Juventud, Indian rock paintings, discovered in 1922, can be visited. The images on the walls and roof of the cave are thought to be connected to the measurement of time and astronomy. The superb beach nearby lacks tourist facilities.

✶ Matanzas

D 2

Province: Matanzas
Population: 127,000

Altitude: 3m/10ft
Distance: 98km/61mi from Havana
797km/495mi from Santiago de Cuba

Thanks to its many bridges, some of them pretty ancient-looking, over two rivers, the Río San Juan and Río Yumurí, Matanzas is named »city of bridges«. At the height of the sugar boom in the mid-19th century many intellectuals and artists settled here, which gives Matanzas to this day a second title: »the Cuban Athens«. In the old quarter many wonderful colonial façades remain from this era – some of them restored, others decaying without respite.

What to See in Matanzas

The town centre, situated between the rivers Yumurí and San Juan, has extremely pretty, elaborately decorated houses with balustrades, wrought-iron railings and tiles. Tankers and cargo ships anchor in the bay.

Parque Libertad Various cultural and political institutions are grouped around Parque Libertad, the cultural hub of the town: the town hall, now seat of the Poder Popular, the Biblioteca Gener y del Monte, the Hotel Louvre and the Pharmacy Museum.

✶ Museo Farmacéutico The interesting Pharmacy Museum is located on Avenida Milanés (Calle 83, south side of the square). It began life as a pharmacy that was very carefully fitted out in 1882 by one Dr Triolet and his wife. Cupboards and drawers were made from expensive wood; porcelain crucible, distilling tubes and other equipment was imported from Europe. Opening hours: Mon – Sat 10am – 6pm, Sun 10am – 2pm.

On Parque Milanés stands the neo-Classical **Cathedral of San Carlos Borromeo**. It was built in 1693 and remodelled in the 19th century. The wall and ceiling paintings are highly impressive.

The Teatro Sauto, a splendidly designed theatre on Plaza de la Vigía seating an audience of 750, dates to 1862–63 and is regarded as one of Cuba's most important examples of neo-Classical architecture. Sarah Bernhardt herself is said to have trodden the boards here. The building next door belongs to the local fire brigade.

✷
Teatro Sauto

! *Baedeker* TIP

Festival del Bailador Rumbero
Matanzas is inconceivable without rumba. Well-known groups such as Los Muñequitos de Matanzas play at the ten-day festival in the Teatro Sauto and on the streets (from 10 October).

A beautifully equipped pharmacy dating from 1882 is one of the sights of Matanzas.

Matanzas Map

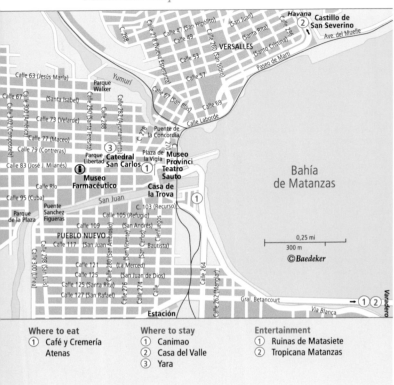

Where to eat
① Café y Cremería
   Atenas

Where to stay
① Canimao
② Casa del Valle
③ Yara

Entertainment
① Ruinas de Matasiete
② Tropicana Matanzas

Museo Histórico Provincial
⊕

The 19th-century Palacio del Junco (Calle 83 y 272) opposite the Teatro Sauto houses the Museo Provincial Matanzas, which casts light on the history of the town and province of Matanzas. Opening hours: Tue – Sat 10am – 12 noon, 1pm – 6pm, Sun 8am – 12 noon.

★
Castillo de San Severino

To the north of the historic centre, the Castillo de San Severino was constructed in the 17th century. The purpose of this eye-catching fort, probably the oldest building in Matanzas, was to afford protection against pirate raids (entrance on Calle 230).

Around Matanzas

★ ★
Cuevas Bellamar

The Cuevas Bellamar, about 5km/3mi south of town, were discovered by chance in the mid-19th century. Many stories are told of the **largest accessible complex of caves** in Cuba. Exploration did not

VISITING MATANZAS

INFORMATION

Infotur
Calle 83 (previously José Milanés),
corner of Calle 290 (previously Santa
Teresita, at the Parque Libertad)
Tel. 045/25 35 51

WHERE TO EAT

► **Inexpensive**

① **Café y Cremería Atenas**
Calle 83 on Plaza de la Vigía
Daily 10am – 11pm
Basic dishes such as pizza, spaghetti
and grilled chicken, ice-cream as
dessert.

WHERE TO STAY

► **Mid-range**

① **Canimao (Islazul)**
Ctra. Via Blanca, km 4.5, Canímar
district
Tel. 045/26 10 14, fax 26 22 37
www.islazul.cu
Several miles out of town in the
direction of Varadero on the Río
Canímar, a modern two-star hotel
(near the Tropicana complex) with
120 basic rooms, some with a balcony.
Pool.

② **Valle de Yumurí: Casa del Valle
(Horizontes)**
Ctra. de Chirino, km 2, approx. 7km/
4.5mi out of Matanzas in the direction of Havana
Tel. 045/25 33 00?, tel./fax 25 33 27
www.horizontes.cu
In a pleasant, leafy location, 40 well-
equipped rooms and a few bungalows
(fridge, satellite TV). Pool, restaurant,
massage and skittles.

► **Budget**

③ **Yara (Islazul)**
Calle 79 (previously Contreras) entre
Calles 288 y 282 (near Parque
Libertad)
Tel. 045/24 44 18
www.islazul.cu
Restored colonial hotel in the town
centre with basic rooms.

ENTERTAINMENT

① **Ruinas de Matasiete**
Calle 129 (outside the old quarter,
south of Puente Calixto García near
the Bahía de Matanzas)
Fri – Sun from 9pm
At the weekend the old walls vibrate
to the sound of live music for
dancing; small open-air restaurant.

② **Tropicana Matanzas**
Autopista Matanzas-Varadero
Tel. 045/26 55 55, 26 53 80
Wed – Sun from 10pm
Branch of the famous cabaret in
Havana.

---

begin until 1948 due to superstitions that this subterranean world
was the realm of evil. A stream flows through the 2.5km/1.5mi-long
cave system past its bizarrely shaped stalagmites and stalactites.
The largest cave, called the Gothic Chamber, is 80m/250ft long and
25m/80ft wide. Opening hours: daily 9am – 5pm.

Some 8km/5mi west of Matanzas lies the stunning Valle de Yumurí.
The river Yumurí has cut through this limestone gorge and flows in-

★ ★
Valle de Yumuri

to the Bahía de Matanzas – a sight that delighted Alexander von Humboldt long ago.

The longest bridge in Cuba, the **Puente de Bacunayagua**, crosses the wide valley of palms, with turkey vultures circling overhead. The marvellous view can be enjoyed from an observation point with a bar.

★ Península de Zapata

C–E 3

Province: Matanzas
Distance: 140 – 190km/85 – 120mi
southeast of Havana

Altitude: Sea level

The Zapata Peninsula and National Park are a paradise for fish, crocodiles and birds. However, mangroves and swamps, marshes and idyllic lakes attract not only animals but also two-legged creatures looking to fish or sunbathe. Beach lovers too find the right habitat here on the south coast: Playa Larga, a narrow strip of sand on the Bahía de Cochinos, and Playa Girón on the Caribbean Sea, the site of the historic Bay of Pigs invasion in 1961.

What to See on the Península de Zapata

Gran Parque Natural Montemar

Cuba's largest area of swamp (almost 5000 sq km/1930 sq mi, protected by Unesco since 2001) is home to crocodiles, iguanas and other reptiles, as well as being a habitat where tens of thousands of migratory birds from the USA spend the winter. It is an eldorado for ornithologists and anglers. Among the strange primeval animals here watch out for a fish with a crocodile mouth, the **manjuarí** or alligator gar. Tours and information in the national park office (on the west side of the road when entering from the north towards Playa Larga) or at the finca Fiesta Campesina north of Guamá (▶ Baedeker Tip). Bring binoculars and protection against mosquitoes!

According to a legend, Indians placed all their gold in the Laguna del Tesoro (Treasure Lagoon) to conceal it from the Spanish. Guamá got its name from an Indian chief who led one of the last uprisings against the conquistadors and

!

Baedeker TIP

Finca Fiesta Campesina

A pretty, typical farm for day trips: stretch your legs beneath hibiscus, mango and avocado trees, see the crocodiles in the miniature zoo, take photos of Cuban cattle, and watch cocks performing a kind of show fight in their arena, if this appeals to you. There is also accommodation on site in the idyllic bohíos of Batey de Don Pedro (eight basic but pleasant double bungalows) and a terrace with rocking chairs where you can watch the sun go down.

Smile for the camera! The crocodiles in Guamá are now bred for tourists.

is today commemorated by one of the 32 bronze sculptures in the open-air museum on the hotel island Guamá.

★ **Guamá–Laguna del Tesoro**

The complex consists of a resort, a crocodile farm, a pottery studio and various restaurants and souvenir shops.

More than 8000 reptiles live on the crocodile farm founded on the initiative of the revolutionary Celia Sánchez, originally as a conservation measure. Today the reptiles are bred for profit. The smaller animals are caught to pose for photos with tourists, and those not then consigned to the grill of the adjoining restaurants, are eventually made into bags and shoes that are sold here. Opening hours: daily 9am – 4.30pm.

◄ La Boca crocodile farm

🕐

Travel 15km/10mi south of Guamá to reach Playa Larga, a beach with a small hotel on the beautifully situated Bahía de Cochinos (Bay of Pigs). This is a particularly good place for a family holiday, as children can safely play in shallow water and on the shaded beach.

Playa Larga

The Australia sugar factory, which Castro used as his headquarters during the Bay of Pigs invasion (►Playa Girón), lies about 13km/8mi

Australia sugar factory

▶ VISITING

WHERE TO STAY

► Mid-range

Laguna del Tesoro: Villa Guamá (Horizontes)
Tel. 045/91 55 51
www.horizontes.cu
This complex built on the lines of a Taíno village spread over ten artificial islands consists of 50 wooden bungalows on stilts with double rooms, a restaurant, grill and bar, reception, souvenir shop and disco. Boat trips, angling and bird watching are organized. Not suitable for those who are sensitive to mosquito bites and dance music at night. The complex is also known for the 32 bronze sculptures by Cuban artist Rita Longa that have been installed there.

Playa Larga: Hotel Playa Larga (Horizontes)
On the road to Playa Girón
Tel. 045/98 71 99, 98 71 06
Fax 98 72 94
www.horizontes.cu
Located between a beautiful narrow beach and the country road, the facility offers hotel rooms and cottages of lower mid-range quality. Pool, international diving school, tennis court.

Playa Girón: Villa Playa Girón (Cubanacán)
Tel. 045/98 41 10, fax 98 41 17
recepcion@hpgiron.co.cu
www.cubanacan.cu
On a meadow by the sea and beach, some 300 rooms in a hotel and bungalows (some with a kitchen). Pool, international diving school.

WHERE TO EAT

► Moderate

Laguna del Tesoro: Restaurante La Boca de Guamá
At the ferry pier car park
No phone
Thatched restaurant, where there is usually a Cuban band playing for dancers.
The speciality is crocodile meat. Lots of coach groups.

Playa Larga: La Cueva de los Peces
Ctra. a Playa Girón, 15km/9mi south of Playa Larga
No phone
Daily 9am – 5pm
Restaurant on a little lake with underwater caves at depths of up to 70m/230ft and colourful fish which can be seen using the snorkelling equipment that is available here.

Punta Perdiz
Further south, also on the country road to Playa Girón
Daily 11am – 10pm
Restaurant on a long sea bay. After enjoying lobster, fish and chicken from the grill and taking a break on the sun deck to digest it, you can dive and snorkel in the sea.

Playa Girón: Restaurant Caleta Buena
About 8km/5mi southeast of Playa Girón
Daily 10am – 5pm
Restaurant and terrace bar in the pretty little bay of the same name with a mini-beach of coral sand suitable for sunbathing, snorkelling and diving. The admission fee includes the cost of the buffet.

north of Guamá. A small museum in the sugar refinery and a row of memorials to those who fell in the battle commemorate the repulse of this attack.

A museum commemorates the repulse of the American-backed invasion at the Bay of Pigs.

In April 1961 Playa Girón, a beach on the forgotten south coast of Matanzas, or to be exact on the **Bahía de Cochinos (Bay of Pigs)**, was the scene of one of the most important incidents of the post-revolutionary period. A force of Cuban exiles, the self-styled Brigade 2506, attacked Cuba with the support of the USA in order to topple the revolutionary government. The attempt failed, as popular resistance was much greater than expected. Within 24 hours the invasion force of 1300 was surrounded by 20,000 Cuban soldiers led by Fidel Castro. On the morning of 19 April almost all the Cuban exiles had been captured. They were sent back to the USA in exchange for medicines and food worth US$ 60 million.

★ **Playa Girón**

On the road from ► Guamá to Playa Girón, **80 memorials** were set up to those who died in the attempted invasion. Giant posters depict Fidel Castro in combat gear with a Kalashnikov, defending revolutionary Cuba.

A monument serves as a reminder of these events, and a museum (Museo de la Intervención) tells the story of the Bay of Pigs invasion with a display of photographs, newspaper articles and weapons. A captured plane stands in front of the museum in Playa Girón. Opening hours: daily 9am – 12 noon and 1pm – 5pm.

★ ◄ Museo de la Intervención ⊙

A lovely quiet beach near the village is suitable for diving and snorkelling.

◄ Beach

★ Pinar del Río

B 3

Province: Pinar del Río
Population: 150,000

Altitude: 30m/100ft
Distance: 147km/91mi from Havana

Pinar del Río is the tobacco capital and »city of columns«. Situated in the middle of the wonderful tobacco-growing region of Vuelta Abajo at the edge of the Sierra de los Órganos mountain range, this tranquil small town presents a picture of arcaded, slightly decayed-looking colonial villas and sleepy charm.

Pinar del Río Map

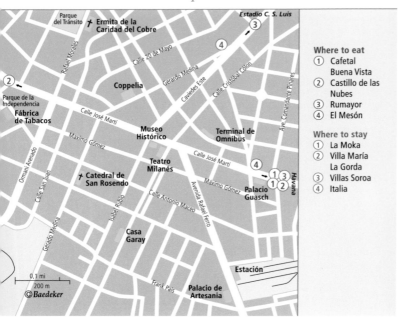

This is not really surprising, as tobacco cultivation requires time and leisure, and the best place to puff on a cigar is a cosy rocking chair on the veranda. Most tourists pass through this provincial capital only on their way to the Valle de Viñales, and visit the famous tobacco factory in the town.

What to See in Pinar del Río

★
Palacio Guasch

The most interesting colonial building in town is without doubt Palacio Guasch (Calle Martí 202), dating from 1914. The striking architecture of this mansion, home to the town's natural history museum, combines many styles. The former owner is said to have been a globetrotter, who collected all kinds of souvenirs to decorate his home. Egyptian hieroglyphs can be seen next to Gothic gargoyles Greek columns and Art Nouveau features.

Museo de las Ciencias Naturales ►

The Museo de las Ciencias Naturales illuminates the natural history of the region. As in other collections of this kind, birds, fish, mammals and shells are exhibited, but the most remarkable sight is a concrete dinosaur in the courtyard, where a rare specimen of the cork palm also grows. Opening hours: Tue–Sat 9am–4.30pm, Sun 9am–12 noon.

► VISITING PINAR DEL RÍO

INFORMATION
Cubatur
Calle Martí 51, corner of Calle Rosario

WHERE TO STAY
► Mid-range
① *Candelaria: La Moka*
Complejo Turístico Las Terrazas, Autopista Havana -Pinar del Río, km 51
Tel. 082/77 86 00?, fax 77 86 05
www.lasterrazas.cu
Small »ecohotel«, overpriced but with an original touch: a tree grows in the lobby, and from the bathtub guests have a panoramic view of the model village Las Terrazas (►p. 258) Pool, tennis court.

② *Península Guanahacabibes: Villa María La Gorda (Gaviota, Centro Internacional de Buceo María la Gorda)*
Sandino (approx. 60km/37mi west of Pinar del Río)
Tel. 082/77 81 31, 77 30 72, -75
Fax 77 80 77
comercial@mlagorda.co.cu, mlagorda@mlagorda.co.cu
www.gaviota-grupo.com
20 rustic wooden cabañas and two-storey hotels with a total of 35 rooms on a beautiful white beach, some with a sea view. International diving school (take passport!)

③ *Candelaria: Villas Soroa (Horizontes)*
Ctra. de Soroa, km 8
Tel. 082/35 34, 35 12 and 35 56
Fax 38 61
arturo@hvs.pr.minaz.cu
www.horizontes.cu
Pleasant but simply furnished bungalow in a row on the edge of the woods around a big pool.

► Budget
④ *Italia*
Calle Gerardo Medina Norte 213
Tel. 082/77 61 20
Basic three-storey hotel on the northern border of town.

WHERE TO EAT
► Moderate
① *Candelaria: Cafetal Buena Vista*
Complejo Turístico Las Terrazas, Autopista Havana-Pinar del Río, km 51
Tel. 082/33 55 16
Restaurant in the former planter's mansion on a coffee plantation, approx. 5km/3mi uphill from the hotel ►La Moka. Excellent food.

② *Soroa: Castillo de las Nubes*
El Salto
Tel. 082/21 22
Daily 8am – 4pm
The »castle in the clouds« is a tower with a restaurant serving creole chicken dishes, and a stunning view!

③ *Rumayor*
Ctra. Viñales (about 1km/0.5mi north of the centre)
Tel. 082/76 30 50, -51
Daily 10am – 11pm
Tourist eatery decorated in Afro-Cuban style at the north end of town with a terrace and bar, cabaret show from 9pm every night except Mon.

► Moderate/Inexpensive
④ *El Mesón*
Calle Martí 205, corner of Calle Comandante Pinares y Pacheco
Tel. 082/75 28 67
Mon – Sat 12 noon – 10pm
Old-established paladar with lots of regular guests, serving delicious grilled chicken, pork and fish in a in colonial residence.

Teatro Milanés

The Teatro Milanés (Calle Martí, corner of Colón), built in 1845, is an outstanding example of the columned architecture in Pinar del Río. It is worth visiting the interior of the 500-seat theatre, as the citizens spared no expense when furnishing it, and used the finest kinds of wood.

✳
Fábrica de Tabacos
🕐

Opening hours:
Mon – Fri 10am – 12 noon
1pm – 4pm
Sat 9am – 12 noon

The Francisco Donatien tobacco factory is close to Plaza de la Independencia. The building, constructed in 1868, has served as a hospital, a prison and since the 1960s as a cigar factory. It is an opportunity to observe the different steps in the production of cigars: first the tobacco leaves are sorted, then the cigars are rolled, and finally the bands are placed on them.
The factory is geared up for crowds of tourists, with souvenir shops, a bar and of course a salesroom for cigars. The production here is not for export. Six different brands are made for consumption in Cuba. These, and also export cigars, are on sale in the shop.

Many steps on the way to a Havana cigar.
The main area of tobacco cultivation is around Pinar del Río.

Another typical local product is made in the Casa Garay liqueur factory (Calle Isabel Rubio). Guayabita, a liqueur made from small guavas, is produced, bottled and sold there. Two kinds (sweet and dry) are sold in the tasting room. Opening hours: Mon – Fri 9am – 4pm.

Casa Garay

Around Pinar del Río

Cuba's largest national park, a Unesco biosphere reserve, situated to the west of Pinar del Río on the Guanahacabibes Peninsula, is named after an, Indian tribe who lived here at the time of the Spanish conquest. It mostly consists of mangrove forests, where many native plants and animals thrive. From November to March it is an important habitat for migratory birds.

Parque Nacional Guanahacabibes Península

The south side of the peninsula with its superb beach is the semicircular **Bahía de Corrientes**.

From the diving resort **María La Gorda** fascinating trips to coral reefs and wrecks very close to the coast are possible. The resort takes its name from a Venezuelan woman, »fat Maria«. She is said to have been abducted by pirates whose ship foundered here and to have sold drinking water (and possibly her body) to passing sailors, after buying her freedom from slavery. In La Bajada payment for admission to the national park has to be made at a road block (8 – 10 CUC, hotel guests excepted). Access is permitted only with official guides, who are hired at the Estación Ecológica.

> ! **Baedeker** TIP
>
> ### Vegas Robaina
>
> What is probably the most famous private tobacco plantation, run until his death in 2010 by a legend of the business, Don Alejandro Robaina (»el Viejo«), is a place of pilgrimage for true »aficionados«, who come from as far away as Arabia. Here it is possible to see a tobacco enterprise, take a look inside the »secadero« drying huts and buy first-class products. Robaina was the only remaining living person after whom a cigar was named in his own lifetime: the Vegas Robaina. About 15km/10mi southwest of Pinar del Río, via the village of San Juan y Martinez (open on weekdays).

The La Güira National Park is situated about 50km/30mi northeast of Pinar del Río in the Sierra de los Órganos. Many tropical trees and plants grow on this area of 20,000 sq km/8000 sq mi. Birdwatchers can spot several rare species of Cuban birds here. From the heights of the Sierra La Güira the view of the surrounding country is wonderful. Che Guevara stayed in the **Cueva de Los Portales** (11km/7mi west of Pinar) during the Cuban Missile Crisis in October 1962.

Sierra de los Órganos

◄ National Park La Güira

San Diego de los Baños(55km/34mi northeast of Pinar del Río) in the Sierra de los Órganos is known for the healing properties of its thermal springs. Since the late 19th century people have been coming here for their health, and after the revolution a clinic was built.

San Diego de los Baños

The unique landscape around Pinar del Río: red earth, mogotes and tobacco sheds.

Hunting

South of the autopista lies one of the best-known hunting grounds on Cuba. Trips are run by the **Maspotón** Club, a hotel for anglers and hunters.

Sierra del Rosario

The Sierra del Rosario, renowned as a Unesco biosphere reserve and destination for eco-tourism, is less than two hours by car from the capital. Visitors can wade in streams and splash about under waterfalls, see orchids and birds, and explore the scenic mountain country around the village of Soroa on horseback or by bicycle.

In the **Las Terrazas** artists' colony craft work is sold and there are hiking trails. Farmhouse accommodation is available in green surroundings.

✳ Soroa

✳

Orquideario ▶

Soroa is located in a long, narrow valley 16km/10mi south of Las Terrazas. A recommended visit is the orchid garden in an extensive park, where more than 700 kinds of orchid, of which some 250 are endemic to Cuba, can be admired, in addition to an abundance of begonias, bromeliads and tropical trees. The best time to go is between November and April, when the orchids are in full flower. This colourful bloom has given Soroa the nickname »Cuba's rainbow«. Opening hours: daily 8am–5pm.

⏲
◀ El Mirador de Venus

El Mirador de Venus, which is reached after a climb of about 30 minutes, is an outlook point with a stunning view across the whole valley. In clear weather you can see as far as the Gulf of Mexico in the north and the Caribbean Sea in the south.

✸
◀ El Salto del Arco Iris

Just before the entrance to the gardens, a narrow, in places slippery path leads 500m/550yd to the El Salto del Arco Iris waterfall. Go here in the morning ideally, as the falls look best in direct sunlight. After a walk in hot, steamy conditions, the crystal clear water of the pool is the perfect place to cool off. At the entrance a masseur waits for customers in the Baños Romanos with fango and sulphur treatments.

Las Barrigonas

Approximately 60km/35mi northeast of Pinar del Río, halfway to ▶ Havana, the hut and the small estate of the farmer Umberto with animals and a tobacco shed near Las Barrigonas is open to visitors. As almost all tour buses stop here, a bar, snack bar and souvenir stands have been set up.

Playas del Este

C 2

The Habaneros' »bathtub«: 18km/11mi east of the capital a coastal strip extends over 9km/6mi of little bays and long sandy beaches shaded by palms, the Playas del Este. Admittedly, the beaches and sea are not in pristine condition everywhere, but to make up for that you get real beach life à la cubana, more than anywhere else in Cuba.

The Cubans come here to swing a »beisbol« bat and their hips as well (they sometimes practise salsa without music when the batteries have run out). A bottle of rum is always circulating somewhere, and instead of sand castles, families make sea turtles that look almost alive.

The names of the beaches, from west to east, are: **Bacuranao, El Mégano, Santa María del Mar, Boca Ciega, Guanabo, Jibacoa** and **Tropico**. At the quieter and pleasanter

! *Baedeker* TIP

Cook your own meals

The Mercado Agropecuario at Calle 494 entre Av. 5ta. B y Av. 5ta. C in Guanobo sells everything that's in season: papayas and cooking bananas, cucumbers, onions, eggs, sometimes even lobsters (»langostas«) at very low prices – unofficially, offered in a whisper, of course.

◉ VISITING PLAYAS DEL ESTE

INFORMATION
Santa María del Mar
Infotur offices in the Tropicoco Hotel and Las Terrazas Hotel as well as on Av. del Sur (Av. de las Terrazas entre Calles 11 y 12)

Guanabo
Infotur at Av. 5ta. entre Calles 468 y 470, tel. 07/96 68 68, www.infotur.cu

TRANSPORT
A trip with the Hershey train
The electric Hershey train dating from 1917 stops in Guanabo and Jibacoa Pueblo on its four-hour journey between Casablanca (district of ▶Havana) and ▶Matanzas. It rumbles through the sugar-cane fields, stops near the former sugar-cane factory at Central Camilo Cienfuegos (also known as Hershey) and crosses the Valle del Yumurí (▶Matanzas), which Alexander von Humboldt thought was »the most beautiful valley in the world« when he saw its lush tropical vegetation and thousands of royal palms.

WHERE TO EAT
▶ **Moderate**
Boca Ciega: El Cubano
Av. 5ta. entre Calles 454 y 456
Tel. 07/96 40 61
?daily 10am – midnight
Excellent food in a grill-bar-restaurant run by the Palmares chain: delicious shrimps in tomato salsa, chicken in wine sauce, grilled fish or steak, served in the dining room or the garden.

Guanabo: Pizzeria Italiana Piccolo
Av. 5ta. entre Calles 502 y 504
Tel. 07/96 43 00
Daily 12 noon – midnight
An almost genuine Italian in Cuba: rustic paladar with crispy pizza from the wood-burning oven and Cuban dishes.

▶ **Inexpensive**
Guanabo: Tropinini
Av. 5ta. A entre Calles 492 y 494
Tel. 07/96 45 17
Daily 8.30am – 11pm
Long-established mini-paladar for breakfast and comida criolla. The twelve seats are almost always occupied.

WHERE TO STAY
▶ **Mid-range**
Santa María del Mar: Santa María del Mar Atlántico (Gran Caribe)
Av. de las Terrazas
Tel. 07/97 10 85, -87, fax 80 39 11
virtudes@complejo.gca.tur.cu
www.club-atlantico.com
www.gran-caribe.com
The best-equipped of the hotels that lie right on the beach at Santa María del Mar.

Santa María del Mar: Villa Los Pinos (Gran Caribe)
Av. de las Terrazas 21
Tel. 07/97 13 61, -67, fax 97 15 24
www.gran-caribe.com
Two-storey buildings with modern fittings, approx. 300m/300yd from the sea, with kitchen, bathroom, satellite TV and little imperfections here and there.

▶ **Budget**
Guanabo: Estrella Diliz
Calle 468 Nr. 714 entre Calles 7 y 9
Tel. 07/96 28 19
More of a mansion than a private house: enormous, with four rooms, a modern living room and satellite TV, an almost Olympic-standard pool with loungers, about 300m/300yd from the beach.

beach of Santa María del Mar, accommodation is in hotels right by the sea or behind the dunes, but there is not much going on outside the hotels. Further east in Boca Ciega and Guanabo, guests stay in small hotels in the town or with Cuban families who make rooms by the sea and in the town available to Cuban sun-seekers (especially in July and August) and foreigners. This area is good for families who prefer self-catering or can eat at the many small restaurants and paladares. About 60km/35mi east of Havana lie the less frequented and smaller beaches of **Jibacoa** and **Tropico**. Close by, in the former fishing village **Santa Cruz del Norte**, the world-famous Havana Club is produced in Cuba's biggest rum factory.

On the idyllic Laguna Itabo in Santa María del Mar, holidaymakers can row on the lake and hire kayaks to explore the mangroves. The open-air restaurant Mi Cayito on a small island in the lake serves low-price Cuban meals (daily 10am – 6pm, at weekends show at 3pm).

Santa María del Mar

At the Playas del Este no one is averse to a little showing-off –
for example with lovingly tended old-time cars. A sight for sore eyes!

★ Sancti Spíritus

F 4

Province: Sancti Spíritus   **Population:** 105,000
Distance: 348km/216mi from Havana
513km/319mi from Santiago de Cuba

The charm of one of Cuba's oldest cities derives from its historic centre of cobbled alleys and low houses painted in pastel shades, plazas with colonial mansions and horse-drawn carriages – and from the fact that it sees few tourists.

History

As early as 1514 Sancti Spíritus was founded on the Río Tuinicú, but a few years later plagues of insects and pirate raids prompted a move to the Río Yayabo. As the town had no harbour, the pillar of the economy was **cattle breeding**, which was to dominate the whole region. The economy grew slowly, and as little labour was required each farm had a maximum of three slaves. To this day 80% of the population is white. After fires and devastation on several occasions during the Wars of Independence, the city prospered in the early 20th century thanks to the involvement of investors from the USA in the sugar industry.

After the revolution, when counter-revolutionaries gathered their forces in the Sierra del Escambray, Sancti Spíritus became a **command centre for Fidel Castro**. In later years the Jehova's Witnesses who lived here repeatedly refused to cooperate with the system. In order to convert them and the other farmers of the region to the revolution, the **Escambray theatre ensemble** toured the villages to educate them in revolutionary ideas by staging plays.

> ❗ *Baedeker* TIP
>
> **On horseback**
> Sancti Spíritus has its own characteristic version of carnival celebrations: a big parade with floats and many horses. Even the conga drummers go through the streets on horseback.

What to See in and Around Sancti Spíritus

Parque Serafín Sánchez

Parque Serafín Sánchez with its carefully restored buildings and pretty glorieta is the hub of the city. The most imposing architecture on the square is that of the provincial library.

★
Parroquial Mayor del Espíritu Santo

At the corner of Calle Menéndez stand the main parish church (parroquial mayor), Espíritu Santo, begun in 1522 and thus one of the oldest on Cuba. According to tradition the Spanish missionary and chronicler Bartolomé de Las Casas preached here. During the 17th century the church had to be rebuilt twice, and the tower and dome date from the 18th and 19th centuries. The ceiling of ornately

VISITING SANCTI SPÍRITUS

INFORMATION

Cubatur
Calle Máximo Gómez 7
Tel. 041/285 18

WHERE TO EAT

▶ Moderate

Mesón de la Plaza
Plaza Honorato
Tel. 041/285 46
Daily 10am – 10pm
Small restaurant with the usual Cuban pork and chicken dishes, served with lots of rice, beans and tostones.

Quinta Santa Elena
Calle Padre Quintero 60
Tel. 041/291 67
Daily 10am – 11pm
Small patio restaurant by the river, with live music to accompany chicken, shrimps and pork.

ENTERTAINMENT

Casa de la Trova Miguel Companioni Gómez
Calle Máximo Gómez 26 (near Plaza Honorato)
This typical Cuban institution is a rendezvous for both professional and amateur trovadores. At weekends don't miss the well-known local groups, Coro de Clave and the elderly musicians of La Parranda. They play traditional rustic music (»musica campesina«).

WHERE TO STAY

▶ Mid-range

Carrusel Rancho Hatuey (Cubanacán)
Ctra. Central, km 383 (4km/2.5mi north of Sancti Spíritus)
Tel. 041/283 15, -17
fax 283 50
www.cubanacan.cu

The hotel is located a little way outside Sancti Spíritus and has two-storey cottages with a total of 74 rooms. Bar, restaurant, swimming pool. Friendly staff and a pleasant atmosphere.

▶ Mid-range/Budget

Hostal del Rijo (Cubanacán)
Calle Honorato del Castillo 12, corner of Calle Máximo Gómez (on Plaza Honorato)
Tel. 041/285 81, -88
tel./fax 285 77
www.cubanacan.cu
Pretty, two-storey, 19th-century colonial-style residence of a doctor, wonderfully restored with a mini-pool and bar on the roof terrace, excellent value for money. Some of the 16 pleasant rooms (satellite TV, phone, mini-bar) have a balcony. Restaurant on the patio.

▶ Budget

Plaza (Islazul)
Calle Independencia, corner of Av. de los Martíres (on Parque Sanchéz)
Tel. 041/271 02
Fax 269 40
www.islazul.cu
Colonial hotel with 28 simply furnished but cosy rooms (don't leave money in the room safe!).

Lago Zaza: Hotel Zaza (Islazul)
Finca San José, km 5, 10km/6mi southeast of Sancti Spíritus
Tel./fax 041/254 90
fax 283 59
www.islazul.cu
Right by the presa (reservoir) with 128 basically equipped rooms. Trout fishing and hunting in the Coto de Caza Sur del Jíbaro.

carved, expensive Cuban wood is noteworthy. Like the bridge over the Yayabo, this church has been declared a Cuban national monument.

Museo de Arte Colonial

On the opposite corner (Calle Plácido) in the direction of the Río Yayabo is the former **mansion of the Iznaga family**, now home to a museum of colonial art. Furniture and other domestic items from the colonial period are on display there, and the house has a wonderful patio. Opening hours: Tue – Sat 9am – 5pm, Sun 9am – 12 noon.

Puente Yayabo

The Puente Yayabo, which spans the Yayabo in three broad arches, seems medieval in its plain and massive style, but was actually built between 1817 and 1825.

Callejón de Llano

Just before the bridge is reached, Calle Padre Quintero branches off left and leads to the Callejón de Llano, the oldest street in Sancti Spíritus. With its uneven paving and shingle-roofed cottages, this is a trip back into the early colonial period.

SE ASIGNA AL COMANDANTE
RNESTO GUEVARA LA MI.
ION DE CONDUCIR DESDE
A SIERRA MAESTRA HASTA
A PROVINCIA DE LAS VILLAS
NA COLUMNA REBELDE

In Santa Clara the history of the revolution is present as nowhere else.

Follow Calle Plácido to get to the oldest square in the city, Plaza de Jesús, around which there are various second-hand shops and money-changers' offices.

Plaza de Jesús

In Calle Independencia on Parque Honorato, the Museo de la Esclavitud (Museum of Slavery) uses documents and exhibits such as instruments of torture to tell the story of slave-owning in the region.

Museo de la Esclavitud

The Zaza Reservoir lies on the southeastern edge of Sancti Spíritus. It is the largest water reservoir of its kind in Cuba. A variety of leisure facilities have sprung up on its banks, but to use them or to go angling in its well-stocked waters it is absolutely essential to be resistant to mosquitoes.

✱
Presa Zaza

✦ Santa Clara

F 3

Province: Villa Clara
Population: 210,000

Altitude: 200m/655ft
Distance: 272km/169mi from Havana

This provincial capital is beautifully situated in the foothills of the Sierra del Escambray. Everything in the city revolves around one man: Che Guevara is the undisputed hero here. It was in Santa Clara in late 1958 that he was victorious in the decisive battle that caused the revolution to triumph. Today, an armoured train of the Batista regime and the bullet-holes on the high-rise Santa Clara Libre Hotel bear silent witness to the historic battle, and Che Guevara's grave is a shrine for Cubans and tourists from all over the world.

Santa Clara was originally founded by conquistadors on the north coast near ►Remedios. Some researchers believe this was the site of the Indian settlement Cubanacán, which gave the island its name and was the centre of government. Santa Clara was not moved to its present location until 1689. As the soils are suitable for cultivating tobacco, this was the region's source of income for a long time; cattle farms were a later development.

History

Santa Clara is famed in song and story as a **symbol for the end of the Batista dictatorship**. It was here that on 29 December 1958, Che Guevara derailed an armoured train, which had been sent to reinforce Batista's troops. Weapons and ammunition fell into the hands of the revolutionaries, many soldiers who were taken prisoner went over to Che's side, and the captured weapons helped the revolutionaries to victory in the skirmishes over the following days. Fulgencio Batista left the country on New Year's Eve.

Santa Clara Map

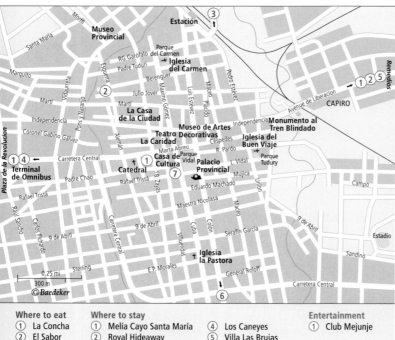

Where to eat
① La Concha
② El Sabor Latino

Where to stay
① Meliá Cayo Santa María
② Royal Hideaway Ensenachos
③ Carrusel La Granjita
④ Los Caneyes
⑤ Villa Las Brujas
⑥ Hanabanilla
⑦ Santa Clara Libre

Entertainment
① Club Mejunje

What to See in Santa Clara

★
Monumento al Tren Blindado

Near the northern exit out of the city, on Carretera de Camajuaní (the continuation of Calle Independencia), the Monumento al Tren Blindado (armoured train monument) commemorates a decisive event in the victory of the revolution. At this relatively exposed spot in Santa Clara, where the railway line and the main road meet, the rebels led by Che Guevara derailed the armoured train in 1958 (▶ History). Two railway wagons, equipped with bunk beds, hammocks, weapons and ammunition, have been converted into a small museum. Documents and pictures furnish information about the events and their consequences. Opening hours: Tue–Sat 8am–12 noon, 2pm–6pm, Sun 8am–12 noon.

★
Plaza de la Revolución

In honour of the darling of the Cuban revolution, an enormous square with an over-lifesize statue of Che Guevara was laid out on the eastern edge of the city in 1987 on the 20th anniversary of his death. He is depicted carrying a machine gun and pointing towards the Sierra Maestra, the rebels' hideout for a long period. Beneath the figure is the slogan of the revolution: **»Hasta la victoria siempre«** (»Until the final victory«). Next to the monument stand reliefs of scenes from his life, complemented by quotes from his letters. Since 1997 an attached mausoleum has harboured the mortal remains of Che Guevara, following their recovery from Bolivia. A small museum tells the story of his life and the history of Santa Clara. Opening hours: Tue–Sun 9am–9pm.

The main square of Santa Clara, Parque Leoncio Vidal, is named after a general who lost his life fighting here in 1896. The city's most important cultural institutions, the library, theatre, colonial museum, arts centre and high school, surround the square.

Parque Leoncio Vidal

The Teatro de la Caridad (Theatre of Charity) was donated to the city in 1885 by the philanthropist Doña Marta Abreu, honoured by a small memorial on the square. It is worth taking a look inside the theatre to see the murals by Cuban painter Camilo Zalaya.

Teatro de la Caridad

A fine colonial building on the northeastern side of the square is home to the Museo de Artes Decorativas, which has a collection of 18th and 19th-century furniture.

Museo de Artes Decorativas

The Iglesia de Nuestra Señora del Buen Viaje (1775) on Parque Tudury to the east of Parque Vidal is notable for the craftsmanship of its wooden ceiling.

Iglesia de Nuestra Señora del Buen Viaje

Beautiful scenery around the Hanabanilla Reservoir

⏵ VISITING SANTA CLARA

INFORMATION

Cubatur
Calle Marta Abreu 10, entre Calle
Gómez y Villuendas
Tel. 042/20 89 80, -81
villaclara@cubatur.cu
director@cubaturvc.co.cu
(also moped hire)

EVENTS

On 8 October, the day of Che
Guevara's death is commemorated
more reverently in Santa Clara than
anywhere else in the country.

SHOPPING

Part of Calle Independencia is a
»bulevar«, i.e. a pedestrian zone. The
stores here include craft shops.

TRANSPORT

From Caibarién a 48km/30mi-long
causeway with 45 bridges (passport
required, modest toll) leads to Cayo
Santa María.

WHERE TO EAT
► Moderate/Inexpensive
① La Concha
Ctra. Central, corner of Calle Danie-
lito Benitez

Tel. 042/20 81 24
Simple palmares on the main street;
the menu ranges from pizza to lobster.

► Moderate
② El Sabor Latino
Calle Esquerra 157, entre Calle Julio
Jover y Berenguer
No phone, daily 12 noon – 11pm
This recommended paladar serves
various fixed menus with all imaginable variations of pork, chicken and
fish.

WHERE TO STAY
► Luxury
① Cayo Santa María: Melía Cayo
Santa María (Melía)
Tel. 042/35 20 00, 35 05 00

Fax 35 05 05?
www.solmeliacuba.com
One of the best resorts in Cuba at the
end of the island that has not yet been
completely built up with hotels.
Rooms with every amenity, some
including a sea view.

② Cayo Ensenachos: Royal Hideaway
Ensenachos (Occidental/Gaviota)
Tel. 42/35 03 00
www.royalhideaway.com/ensenachos
On the neighbouring island of Ensenachos, too, so far only one resort has
been built on the mile-long beach.
Designed in the Caribbean colonial
style, it is more exclusive than anything else in Cuba: 50,000 sq m/over
half a million square feet of Cuban
marble were lavished on the 506
rooms and »royal« suites. Guests are
spoiled with all-inclusive service and
the last word in luxury, from designer
furniture and gourmet dining (including Thai and vegetarian) to butler
service.

Baedeker recommendation

► Mid-range
③ Carrusel La Granjita (Cubanacán)
Ctra. Maleza, km 2.5
Tel. 042/21 81 90, -91, fax 21 81 49 ?
www.cubanacan.cu
Pretty wooden bungalows in the style of a
Indian village on the edge of town, among
palm trees and tropical plants, plus a hotel
for relaxing by the swimming pool and at
the bar. 65 rooms, excellent restaurant.

▶ Mid-range

④ *Los Caneyes (Horizontes)*

Av. de los Eucaliptos y Circunvalación
Tel./fax 042/21 81 40
www.horizontes.cu
As with La Granjita, wooden bungalows in a garden paradise, but some of
the rooms have much plainer furnishings and are overpriced. Swimming pool, and a top restaurant.

⑤ *Cayo Las Brujas (west of Cayo Santa María): Villa Las Brujas Gaviota)*

Farallón de las Brujas, Playa La Salina
Tel. 042/35 00 23, -4
fax 35 05 99
brujagav@enet.cu
www.gaviota-grupo.com
Lower mid-range complex with a
family feel: 23 small rustic cabañas in
rows on a bay with a beach (the
rooms have air-conditioning, satellite
TV, some a terrace and sea view) and
a large restaurant.

▶ Budget

⑥ *Manicaragua: Hanabanilla (Islazul)*

Lago Hanabanilla
Tel. 042/20 85 50
fax 20 35 06
www.islazul.cu
What is special about this hotel is its
unique location on the shores of the
Hanabanilla Reservoir with a wonderful view across the water and the
surrounding fertile hills of the Sierra
del Escambray. The Soviet-style hotel
finds its clientele mainly among
Cuban families, but is also suitable for
nature lovers, anglers and bird
watchers. Boat excursions are on
offer, as well as trips to the Río Negro
restaurant (book at the hotel), serving
outstanding creole food.

*Che Guevara and Camilo Cienfuegos,
heroes of the battle for Santa Clara*

⑦ *Santa Clara Libre (Islazul)*

Parque Vidal No. 6 entre Padre Chao
y Tristá
Tel. 042/20 75 48, -50
fax 68 63 67
www.islazul.cu
Situated on the main square of the
city, this ten-storey hotel with 168
rather dark rooms has seen better
days, but is popular with Cuban
guests. The restaurant on the top floor
provides a fine view of the city and its
surroundings. Bullet holes from the
fighting between the revolutionaries
and Batista's forces on 28 December
1958 are still visible on the façade.

ENTERTAINMENT

① *Club Mejunje*

Calle Marta Abreu 107, entre J. B.
Zayas y Rafael Lubián
Tue – Sun 4pm – 1am
This club in a decaying building is a
venue for an afternoon disco as well
as live music, dance shows and
cultural events from salsa to jazz and
rock (alcohol served only in the
evening).

Around Santa Clara

Presa Hanabanilla

The journey out to the Hanabanilla Reservoir (48km/30mi south of Santa Clara) makes an enjoyable excursion. The reservoir lies in the Sierra del Escambray between green hills still sheltering a few privately run farms. Boat trips are run along the Río Negro to a rustic restaurant serving delicious Cuban food. Another option is to go hiking in the mountains or visit one of the small farms. With a length of over 30km/20mi, Presa Hanabanilla is Cuba's second-largest reservoir, supplying cities such as Cienfuegos and Santa Clara with water and the region around Hanabanilla with hydroelectric power.

Remedios
Map F 3 ►

To experience the original charm of colonial days with uneven paving in the alleys, and Baroque churches, completely free from crowds of tourists, go to Remedios, 53km/33mi northeast of Santa Clara. One of the first places founded on Cuba by Spanish settlers (1514), Remedios is only 5km/3mi from the north coast. Frequent attacks by pirates caused several families to move away from the coast in 1689, to found Santa Clara. Today Remedios is still the very picture of a Spanish colonial town with one-storey, shingle-roofed houses and narrow, winding streets. As in the past, the inhabitants live mainly off sugar cane and breeding cattle.

Pray for a good journey: Iglesia del Buen Viaje on the south side of Plaza Martí.

The main sights of the town are grouped around attractive Plaza Martí, the focal point of life in Remedios. It is the only square in Cuba boasting two churches. **San Juan Bautista** is an impressive building. First constructed in the 1550s, it is one of Cuba's oldest churches. Its highlights are the altar of gilded cedarwood and a ceiling of carved mahogany.

◀ Plaza Martí

The **Iglesia del Buen Viaje** on the south side of the plaza is dedicated to the Virgin of Good Voyage.

The **Museo Alejandro García Caturla** close by is a music museum devoted to the Cuban avant-garde composer and named after him. Personal memorabilia and items related to his work are on display.

> ## ! *Baedeker* TIP
>
> ### Carnival competition
>
> Each year the »Parrandas« are held in and around Remedios. This festival with competing carnival and musical groups and colourful floats starts in December with a children's parade and fireworks and features dancing, music and food stalls. It comes to an exuberant climax on the evening of 24 December with processions attracting hundreds of natives of Remedios from all over the country. On 25 or 26 December the winner presents the loser with a »coffin« ...

When in Remedios, a visit to the Museo de las Parrandas in Calle Máximo Gómezis is a must. Costumes and other items serve as reminders of the »Parrandas« – big parades with music, dancing and decorated floats which are held every year. Opening hours: Tue – Sat 9am – 12 noon, 3pm – 6pm, Sun 9am – 1pm.

★
◀ Museo de las
Parrandas

5km/3mi further north, the port of Caibarién is the point of departure for boats running to Cayo Conuco and the causeway to Cayo Santa Maríá and Cayo Las Brujas.

Caibarién

Recently a new ultra-inclusive island opened for visitors on the doorstep of the fishing port of Caibarién and the little colonial town of Remedios: a total of 10,000 hotel rooms with every comfort are planned on this previously virgin island, which is part of the Archipiélago Sabana-Camagüey. A brand-new causeway (»pedraplén«) crosses 48km/30mi of blue sea, and a modest fee has to be paid at a checkpoint. In contrast to the causeway leading to Cayo Coco (▶ p. 175), which is proven to have damaged the environment, the causeway to Cayo Santa Maríá is broken up by about 45 bridges and is thus intended to be less harmful to flora and fauna, by allowing currents of seawater to flow and swarms of fish to move unhindered for instance. The road to Cayo Santa Maríá passes **Cayo Las Brujas** and the new international airport, as well as **Cayo Ensenachos** beyond it to the east. On these two unspoilt islands with their lonely, pristine beaches, **sea turtles** come to lay their eggs in the nesting period between May and September. However, energetic construction work is under way, and every new hotel leaves these primeval ocean creatures less space to lay their eggs – as has already happened on Cayo Largo in the south of Cuba, one of the main nesting places in the Caribbean ▶p.180).

Cayo
Santa Maríá

⋆⋆ Santa Lucía

H 4

Province: Camagüey
Distance: 630km/390mi from Havana
112km/70mi from Camagüey

Altitude: Sea level

A large coral reef with 500 spectacularly colourful species of fish and 35 diving grounds with a varied flora, fauna and ships' wrecks once brought the legendary undersea explorer Jacques-Yves Cousteau to Playa Santa Lucía, which today is largely a hotel destination. The maritime experiences and attractions on offer here now include feeding sharks, which are generally harmless, and watching the mantas and dolphins that inhabit the waters off the miles-long beach on the north coast.

In Santa Lucía itself there are no sights as such, but the hotel agencies run tours into the surrounding area. For those who would like to get to know this part of Cuba, tours are offered to ▶Santiago de Cuba, ▶Baracoa, ▶Trinidad, ▶Camagüey and ▶Cayo Coco.

⋆
Coral reef ▶ The coral reef off the coast, said to be the world's third largest, is a veritable paradise for divers. Coral gardens, sunken wrecks and submarine caves make for a colourful and exciting underwater world.

A shady spot beneath the palm trees

VISITING SANTA LUCÍA

WHERE TO EAT

► Moderate

Bon Sai
Tel. 032/33 61 01
Pleasant little eatery specializing in Chinese food in the town centre (east of the hotels).

Playa Los Cocos: El Pescador
About 6km/3.5mi west of the hotels in La Boca
Take a lovely walk along the coast (or a trip in a horse-drawn carriage) to this restaurant to enjoy fresh seafood on a wonderful beach. Further west, towards the river estuary and the village of La Boca is the more expensive but excellent grill and fish restaurant Bocana (Playa Los Coquitos).

WHERE TO STAY

► Mid-range

Brisas Santa Lucía Cuatro Vientos (Cubanacán)
Tel. 032/33 63 17, -60
Fax 36 51 42
www.cubanacan.cu
Colonial architecture with wonderful detailing, bars and extremely tasteful rooms in the style of bohíos lend this resort its own special atmosphere. The 400 rooms and suites all have a terrace, and a full range of water sports are on offer on the well-tended sandy beach.

Club Amigo Mayanabo (Cubanacán)
Tel. 032/33 61 84, -5
Fax 33 51 76
www.cubanacan.cu
Newly renovated mid-range all-inclusive hotel, suitable for families (club for children, health club), fans of water sports and sun worshippers. Dancers love the disco built right into the sea. All the usual sports facilities, excellent food. 213 rooms, twelve suites.

Club Amigo Caracol (Cubanacán)
Tel. 032/33 63 02, fax 36 53 07
www.cubanacan.cu
This attractive complex with diverse and in some cases extremely spacious two-storey chalets extends along a palm-fringed beach. Pool, tennis court.

Around Santa Lucía

Gentle waves and a broad sandy beach are the trump cards of **Playa Los Cocos** (6km/3.5mi west of Santa Lucía) on the Bay of Nuevitas. Close by, some beach cafés can be found in the fishing village of La Boca.

The causeway to Nuevitas and boat trips take visitors to the dream beaches of **Cayo Sabinal** (9km/5.5mi west of Santa Lucía), with its open-air restaurant plus a number of basic bungalows. Deer, wild boar and a variety of waterfowl live on the peninsula, which is wooded in parts. With a little luck you will spot flamingos and pelicans.

In the plains around Camagüey, which has an aura of the Wild West with its cowboys and herds of cattle, trips on horseback are a favourite activity.

Rancho King

The Farm Rancho King (26km/16mi southwest of Santa Lucía) belonged to a Texan until he was dispossessed in 1959. Today guests in the restaurant here can enjoy specialities from the grill and watch a genuine Cuban rodeo.

★ Santiago de Cuba

K 5

Province: Santiago de Cuba
Population: 444,000

Altitude: 36m/118ft
Distance: 860km/535mi from Havana

No Cuban city exudes more Caribbean flair than Santiago de Cuba: this is undoubtedly because most of its residents are Afro-Caribbean, but is also due to its hot climate and wonderful location between the Caribbean Sea and the tallest mountain in Cuba, the Sierra Maestra.

The roots of **son**, the classic Cuban beat, and also of the revolutionary ideas behind all Cuban struggles for liberation are to be found in Santiago. »The cradle of the revolution« delights visitors with sites where history was made, and colonial atmosphere at every turn.

1515	Foundation, capital of Cuba	**History**
Late 18th century	30,000 Haitians flee to the Santiago area after a revolt of slaves.	
1898	Decisive naval battle between Spanish and American fleets	
26 July 1953	Failed attack on the Moncada Barracks by the »Movement of 26 July«	
1 January 1959	Fidel Castro proclaims the victory of the revolution on Parque Céspedes.	

At its foundation in 1515 by Diego Velázquez, Santiago de Cuba was the **fifth Spanish settlement** on Cuba. Thanks to its favourable location and natural harbour, Santiago was the capital city of the island from 1522 to 1553, before having to cede this status to Havana. Conquistadors such as Hernán Cortés and Francisco Pizarro prepared their campaigns of conquest in Mexico and South America in Santiago de Cuba. Cheap labour was always required in the copper mines

← *Lots of wood, and music of course: Isabélica is Santiago's best-known café.*

of El Cobre. As time passed, Santiago prospered and became a **centre of the slave trade**. In the 17th and 18th centuries the city was repeatedly attacked by pirates, and in 1662 even briefly occupied by English forces. In the late 18th century, after the first revolt of slaves on Haiti, about 30,000 Haitians fled to the Santiago area, which had previously only had a population of 10,000. Among the refugees were many families of French planters, who brought with them their **knowledge of sugar processing and coffee cultivation**, as well as their lifestyle, which has left its mark on the culture of the region.

Santiago played an important role in the War of Independence, but a different event was to herald the end of 386 years of Spanish colonial rule on Cuba: in 1898 the coastal waters off Santiago were the scene for a decisive naval battle between the Spanish and American fleets. This had been preceded in February of the same year by the explosion of an American battleship in Havana harbour.

The city also gained great historical significance through **Fidel Castro's first revolutionary attack**, the attempted storming of the Moncada Barracks on 26 July 1953. Although the attack failed, today it is seen as the start of the popular uprising (»Movement of 26 July«). History was on the rebels' side: on 1 January 1959 Fidel Castro was finally able to proclaim the victory of the revolution.

Since then, Santiago has changed a great deal and become a modern industrial city. With Soviet help, a big power station, oil refinery, ce-

Golden atmosphere in the city seen as the cradle of the revolution

Santiago de Cuba *City Centre*

Where to stay
① Casa Granda
⑤ Hostal San Basilio
⑥ Casa Particular of Radamés Fiol Pantaleón y Mabel Llanes

Entertainment
② Casa de la Trova
③ Patio de los dos Abuelos
④ Quitrin

ment factory and the largest textile factory in Latin America were built near the port. The growth of tourism in Santiago has also benefited people in this part of Cuba.

Parque Céspedes

The heart of Santiago is Parque Céspedes, with most of the historic sights in the immediate vicinity. A **monument at the centre of the square** commemorates freedom fighter Carlos Manuel de Céspedes (►Famous People). Pretty benches and shade-giving trees make this a good place to linger and watch the bustle of the square. Or take a walk through the side streets of the city, which is laid out on a grid plan, to discover typical architectural details: projecting balconies with ornate wooden or wrought-iron grilles and beautiful patios. Parque Céspedes is also important to Santiago de Cuba as the scene of significant historical events.

The Cathedral of Nuestra Señora de la Asunción stands on the south side of the square. A wooden church built here as early as 1516 fell victim to fire. A succession of later buildings were also destroyed by fire or earthquake; today's church was completed in 1922. Notable features inside are the 19th-century carved choir stalls and the tomb of Diego Velázquez. The large figure of an angel can be seen between the twin towers. Cuba's only church museum, the Museo Arquidiocesano, adjoins the cathedral. Opening hours: cathedral at Mass times; museum Mon–Fri 9am–5pm, Sat 9am–2pm, Sun until 12 noon.

★
Catedral Nuestra Señora de la Asunción

Casa Diego Velázquez is one of the earliest colonial buildings in Latin America and the oldest surviving house on Cuba. Between 1516 and 1530 this residence of the first island governor was constructed in the Mudéjar style, a blend of Moorish and Gothic elements. The house's most eye-catching features are the balconies enclosed by a grille (miradores), and carved wooden roofs (alfarjes).

★ ★
Casa Diego Velázquez

Since 1971 it has been home to the **Museo de Ambiente Historico Cubano**, which casts light on life in colonial times. The main exhibits are pieces of furniture and other household items, which come from the 16th and 17th centuries. The lower floor holds examples of the crucibles in which gold was smelted into ingots before being shipped to Spain. Opening hours: Mon – Thu, Sat 9am – 12.45pm, 2pm – 4.45pm, Fri 2pm – 4.45pm, Sun 9am – 12.45pm.

The conspicuous white building with balconies and windows painted a radiant blue was once the town hall (**ayuntamiento**). Today the Communist Party of Santiago is based here. It was from this balcony that Fidel Castro made his first speech as head of state on 1 January 1959 following dictator Batista's flight from the country. Thousands gathered on the square that day, and millions more listened on the radio.

Enramada (José A. Saco) Right next to the ayuntamiento, the shopping street Enramada (José A. Saco) leads towards the harbour. To stroll past colourful advertisements, horse-drawn carriages and veteran cars is to feel transported back to the 1950s.

Calle Heredia

Casa de Vino A variety of regional wines, including one made from grapefruit (!), can be sampled in the Casa de Vino.

Museo Municipal Emilio Bacardi Morau ⏲ The Bacardí Museum on Calle Pío Rosado displays archaeological finds from various Indian cultures, Egyptian works of art, weapons from the Wars of Independence in the 19th century, Cuba's only Egyptian mummy in the basement and interesting European and Cuban paintings. Opening hours: daily 10am – 6pm.

Cafetería Isabélica On the corner of Porfirio Valiente (previously Calvario) is the Cafetería Isabélica, Santiago's most famous café. Take a break here to try one of its coffee specialities.

✳ Museo de Carnaval A sight not to be missed is the carnival museum at Calle Heredia 303. Santiago's carnival celebrations, the most famous in Cuba, were originally called Fiesta de los Mamarrachos (roughly translatable as

Festival of Idiots). Influences from Spain, Africa, France and Haiti are obvious here, as Catholic processions and courtly minuets are joined by ritual Haitian dances and the sound of yoruba drums. The big parades of the cabildos and tumbas (Cuban carnival societies) with colourful floats, figures shaped from papier-mâché and costumed dancers are typical elements of the carnival festivities.

An interesting exhibition explains all the diverse influences on the carnival traditions of Santiago. The collection of costumes and masks is impressive. Opening hours: Tue–Sun 9am–5pm, folklore shows: Mon–Sat 4pm, Sun 11am. ◷

A flight of many steps flanked by little houses, **Padre Pico** connecting the lower and upper parts of town. It is worth making the steep climb for the fine view of the roofs of Santiago from the top. There are usually men playing dominoes in this street.

Close by, the remains of the **Balcón de Velázquez** fort command a good view of the harbour.

★ **Viewing points**

Near the harbour, at the corner of Avenida J. Menéndez and Aguilera, the Cesar Escalante tobacco factory is an opportunity to watch Romeo y Julieta cigars being made. Opening hours: Mon–Fri 9am–11am, 1pm–3pm. ◷

Fábrica de Tabaco Cesar Escalante

Highlights Santiago de Cuba

Casa Diego Velázquez
A visit to the oldest surviving house in Cuba is a trip back into the 16th century.
► page 277

Roof terrace of the Casa Granda hotel
From the fifth floor of this splendid colonial building you get a 360-degree view across the Bay of Santiago, the Caribbean Sea and the Sierra Maestra.
► page 283–284

Casa de la Trova
Shades of Buena Vista Social Club: to go dancing in this traditional music club has become a must for tourists.
► page 283

Basílica del Cobre
Make a pilgrimage with the Cubans to the patron saint of the island, the Vírgen de la

Caridad (Virgin of Charity) – ideally on 8 September, when the faithful flock to their national saint, some of them shuffling on their knees.
► page 287–288

The Casa de la Trova caters for every age group and level of skill.

Santiago de Cuba Map

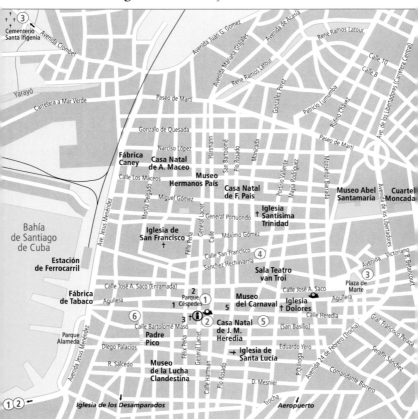

✴ ✴ Moncada Barracks

Famous attack by Fidel Castro

To the northeast of the city centre, what used to be the Moncada Barracks now houses a school and a museum of Cuban history. The yellow building with its reconstructed bullet holes was the target of a famous attack by Fidel Castro and his supporters on 26 July 1953.

The barracks, constructed in 1859 and the second-largest in Cuba, had already been the **starting point for Batista's coup** in 1952 and were thus a symbol of his dictatorship. The attack on the day of carnival in 1953 was planned in three stages: Fidel led the storming of the barracks, Abel Santamaría the attack on the hospital and Raúl Castro a raid on the attached courts of law. However, Fidel accidentally fired a shot too early, the soldiers had advance warning, and the

Plaza de la Revolucion

1   Casa Diego Velázquez
2   Ayuntamiento
3   Catedral
4   Museo Emilio Bacardi

Where to eat
①   El Cayo
②   El Morro
③   Zun Zún
④   Salón Tropical

Where to stay
①   Casa Granda
②   Melía Santiago
③   Los Galeones
④   Villa El Saltón
⑤   Hostal San Basilio
⑥   Casa particular of Radamés
     Pantaleón y Mabel Llanes
     Rodriguez

Entertainment
①   Cabaret Tropicana Santiago
②   Casa de la Trova Pepe Sánchez
③   Patio de los dos Abuelos
④   Quitrín
⑤   Casa del Caribe

© Baedeker

0.1 mi
200 m

whole plan miscarried. Most of the rebels, including Fidel and Raúl Castro, were captured, many of them tortured and murdered. Only a few were able to escape back to the Granjita Siboney (► Santiago, Surroundings), from where the attack had been planned, but they too were taken by surprise and executed.

Immediately after the triumph of the revolution in 1959, the »Movement of 26 July« primary school was set up in the barracks. Part of the building is now the Museo Histórico 26 de Julio, which presents the revolutionary history of Cuba in an extremely detailed and interesting manner – starting with the first uprisings against Spain led by the cacique Hatuey and continuing through to the achievements of recent decades. Naturally, the main focus of the exhibition is the at-

 **
Museo Histórico 26 de Julio

● VISITING SANTIAGO DE CUBA

INFORMATION

Cubatur
Parque Céspedes (opposite the Hotel
Casa Granda), old quarter
Tel. 022/68 60 33, 65 25 60
Av. Victoriano Garzón 364 entre Calles
3ra. y 4ta. (opposite Av. de Céspedes),
Reparto Sueño district
Tel. 022/65 25 60

EVENTS

Carnaval
Carnival in the last week of July,
around 25 July, with competitions
between dance groups (comparsas)
and musicians from different districts
of the city, is a colourful, hot-blooded
and noisy affair. The locals get in
practice for the carnival in early July
with the equally hot Caribbean-style
Fiesta del Fuego.

SHOPPING

On Calle Heredia, souvenir dealers
and craftsmen display their wares on
stalls and tables; if you prefer not to
haggle, rummage through the goods in
the state-run Artex shops (e.g. opposite the Museo del Carneval in the
Patio Artex or next to the Casa de la
Trova).

WHERE TO EAT

► Moderate
① *El Cayo*
Cayo Granma
Tel. 022/69 01 09
Daily 9am – 9pm
Built on stilts on Granma Island, this
restaurant is known for its fresh fish.
The view of the city and harbour is
fantastic.

② *El Morro*
Ctra. del Morro, km 8.5
Tel. 022/69 15 76

Daily 12 noon – 10pm
This restaurant terrace near El Morro
spoils diners with a stunning sea view,
enjoyed with outstanding creole
dishes.

Baedeker recommendation

► Moderate
③ *Zun Zún*
Av. Manduley 159, Vista Alegre district
Tel. 022/64 15 82
Daily 12 noon – 10pm
An elegant Palmares restaurant in a colon
residence. Attentive service in a variety of
small rooms furnished with antiques and
paintings, or on the terrace facing the stre
Cuban specialities such as ajiaco stew, or
international cuisine such as steak in red
wine sauce, tapas, lobster or fillet of fish –
of the very best quality.

► Inexpensive
④ *Salón Tropical*
Calle Fernández Marcané 310, entre
Calles 9 y 10, Santa Bárbara district
Tel. 022/64 11 61
Mon – Fri 6pm – midnight, Sat – Sun
12 noon – midnight
One of the best paladares in Cuba,
offering a wide choice: soups, salads,
spaghetti, grill platters, lamb, beer and
wine are served on the roof terrace
with its 360-degree city panorama.
The prices might give the impression
that the portions are small – but that is
not the case! Book in advance.

ENTERTAINMENT

① *Cabaret Tropicana Santiago*
Autopista Nacional, km 1.5
Tel. 022/64 25 79, 68 70 90
Shows Thu – Sat from 10pm
This show has more Caribbean style

Party mood at the Cabaret Tropicana

than the one in Havana's famous nightclub, and finishes in a carnival atmosphere. Afterwards the place to go dancing is the adjacent El Tropical (until 5am).

② *Casa de la Trova Pepe Sánchez*
Calle Heredia 208, old quarter
Daily 11am – midnight
All day and all night, the sound of music emanates from this traditional club: sometimes its is amateurs practising, sometimes the musicians are real professionals, but they all know how to put their audience in the mood.

③ *Patio de los dos Abuelos*
Plaza de Marte, eastern old quarter
Daily 4pm – 7pm
Live music 10pm – 2am
In this narrow courtyard beneath orange trees, two grandfathers may well be present from time to time, as the name says, but usually a mixed crowd comes to listen to trova singers and dance. Cheap snacks, beer and cocktails are served.

④ *Quitrín*
Calle Sánchez Hechavarría (previously San Jerónimo) 473, entre Porfirio Valiente y Pio Rosado, old quarter
Tel. 022/62 25 28
On Fridays and Saturdays from 10pm the lovely patio of this colonial building hosts fashion shows by the Quitrín brand and concerts of trova, boleros and salsa for a mixed Cuban and foreign audience, with acts such as Septeto Santiguero. A good vibe is guaranteed! During the day the small boutique sells white-only cotton and knitted evening dresses and blouses, as well as menswear such as typical Cuban guayabera shirts.

⑤ *Casa del Caribe*
Calle 13 no. 154, corner of Calle 8, Vista Alegre district
Tel. 022/64 22 85
Live music is played daily from 5pm in the garden of this pretty villa. At weekends a folklore show with rumba and Santería influences is held (3pm). Visitors can even learn to play the drums.

WHERE TO STAY

▶ **Luxury**
① *Casa Granda (Sofitel/Gran Caribe)*
Parque de Céspedes
Tel. 022/68 66 00, 65 30 21, -4
Fax 68 60 35
recep@casagran.gca.tur.cu
www.gran-caribe.com
The centrally located colonial-style Casa Granda has an enormous terrace on the upper floor with a wonderful view of the cathedral and the city. The cafeteria with outdoor seating on the ground floor is a good spot for watching what's going on in the park.

Casa Grande is worth a visit for the bar alone.

With its bags of atmosphere, the hotel is a favourite with independent tourists. 58 rooms.

② *Meliá Santiago (Meliá/Cubanacán)*
Av. de las Américas, District Sueño
Tel. 022/68 70 70, fax 68 71 70
melia.santiago@solmeliacuba.com
www.solmeliacuba.com
This giant modern glass tower is a conspicuous building, and has all the comforts of a 5-star hotel, including a nightclub, good restaurants and three pools. The terrace at the top commands a superb view of the city and the surrounding mountains. 270 rooms, six suites.

► **Mid-range**
④ *Santiago province: Villa El Saltón (Cubanacán)*
Ctra. Puerto Rico a Filé, III. Frente
Tel. 022/563 26, fax 56 492
economia@salton.scu.cyt.cu
www.cubanacan.cu
Nestling amidst green surroundings in remote mountains, this is truly an »anti-stress hotel«. Rooms with a terrace (phone, satellite TV, fridge).

Instead of a pool, the natural basin of the Saltón waterfall is available for swimming. Massage, in-house psychologist, hiking, birdwatching, horseriding, etc.

Baedeker recommendation

► **Luxury**
③ *Chivirico: Los Galeones (Cubanacán)*
Ctra. Chivirico, km 72
Tel. 022/261 60, fax 291 16
www.cubanacan.cu
One of Cuba's most beautiful hotels: 36 cottages and rooms nestling on a hill in an idyllic location between the Caribbean Sea and the Sierra Maestra. Small beach reached via steps, pool, sauna, diving base.

► **Mid-range/Budget**
⑤ *Hostal San Basilio (Cubanacán)*
Calle Bartolomé Masó 403 (previously Calle San Basilio), old quarter
Tel. 022/65 16 87
www.cubanacan.cu
Tiny colonial guesthouse with eight delightful little rooms on the ground floor (TV, mini-bar, bathtub), their windows looking onto the corridor and small patios. Excellent value for money.

► **Budget**
⑥ *Casa particular owned by Radamés Fiol Pantaleón y Mabel Llanes Rodriguez*
Calle Padre Pico 354 entre Bartolomé Basó (previously San Basilio) y Santa Lucía, old quarter
Tel. 022/65 53 17
rfiolp@yahoo.es
The architect has created an attractive apartment for guests on the second floor of his house, with kitchenette, phone and a great view of the historic city centre.

tack on the Moncada Barracks and the fighting in the Sierra Maestra. Opening hours: Mon – Sat 9am – 5pm, Sun 9am – 1pm.   ⏲

The Parque Abel Santamaría was laid out west of the barracks, on the site where the hospital once stood. Here, a modern monument and a small museum honouring Castro's comrades, who died after being captured and tortured, can be viewed.

Parque Abel Santamaría

Plaza de la Revolución

Avenida de los Libertadores, flanked by busts of heroes of the wars of liberation, leads to Plaza de la Revolución, which was laid out for the Pan-American Games in 1991 and is the site of the Sala Polivalente school and the Teatro Heredia, one of Cuba's most modern theatres and a venue for assemblies, congresses and cultural events. Revolution Square is the political centre of the city. Fidel Castro used to make an annual speech to the Cuban people here on 26 July, the anniversary of the attack on the Moncada Barracks, but today, the top salsa bands also get the acclaim of the masses here – today perhaps more than the Castros.

Political centre

The whole of the Plaza de la Revolución is dominated by an imposing monument to Antonio Maceo, a native of Santiago. Constructed of bronze and green marble, it commemorates the freedom fighter and the machetes he and his followers used in the struggle. The steps leading up to the monument are flanked by an eternal flame and a small museum.

★
Monumento Antonio Maceo

Continue north along Avenida Las Americas to reach the baseball stadium and the Tropicana (►Entertainment), the »little sister« of the famous nightclub in Havana.

★
Tropicana

★ Cementerio Santa Ifigenia

The late 19th-century Cementerio Santa Ifigenia is situated on Avenida Crombet to the north of the Bay of Santiago. Like most Cuban cemeteries, it has the appearance of a small city of marble graves with angels and crosses.

Graves of prominent Santiagueros

Many eminent citizens of Santiago were buried here, but the most impressive tomb, a rotunda supported by columns, is that of the poet and hero of the liberation struggle José Martí (►Famous People). Inside is a statue of Martí, and the room below contains a coffin decorated with the Cuban flag. The mausoleum was designed so that a ray of sunlight always falls on the coffin – a reference to one of his poems, in which Martí wrote that he wished to be buried with his face towards the sun.

Close to this spot are a memorial to those who attacked the Moncada Barracks and a mausoleum for Santiagueros who fell in Angola.

There is also a monument to Carlos Manuel de Céspedes.
Further graves preserve the memory of the Bacardí family, the family of Frank País and Cuba's first president, Tomás Estrada Palma. Opening hours: daily 8am – 6pm.

✳ ✳ El Morro (San Pedro de la Roca del Morro)

Fort At the entrance to the Bay of Santiago, construction of the El Morro fort (Castillo de San Pedro de la Roca del Morro) began in 1640 –

The resemblance to the fort of the same name in Havana is no coincidence.
One architect built them both.

1642 but was not completed until around the year 1700. The similarity with the fort of the same name in Havana is no coincidence, as both were designed by the architect **Giovanni Battista Antonelli**. Now a Unesco World Heritage site and restored in exemplary fashion, during the Wars of Independence it was used as a prison for rebels. From the fort (about 7km/4.5mi from the centre) visitors enjoy a **wonderful view** across the Bahía de Santiago, the Caribbean coast and the wooded heights of the Sierra Maestra. Beyond the drawbridge that gives access to the fort, a different era awaits: in the nooks and corners between massive stone walls and imposing cannons, the fort feels like the set of a pirate film.

⏱ Opening hours: Daily 9am – 8pm

Ten of the rooms of the fort have been made into a pirate museum. Old navigation charts, weapons and pictures of ships are on display. Interestingly the CIA is cited as a modern example of piracy, an assertion backed up by a rubber boat and various weapons which were seized in the bay. Opening hours: same as fort.

★ **Museo de la Piratería**

⏱

In the middle of the Bay of Santiago, the small island of Cayo Granma (Cayo Smith before the revolution) is occupied by boatyards, wooden houses and small harbour. It once belonged to a slave trader, who found it a secure place for his dealings. The island is reached by boat from Punta Gorda.

Cayo Granma

Around Santiago de Cuba: The West

Nestling on the green slopes of the Sierra Maestra, about 20km/12mi northwest of Santiago, the pilgrimage church of El Cobre with its three yellow towers can be seen from afar.

El Cobre

According to a legend, the Virgin Mary appeared to fishermen in 1606, when they were in danger of drowning in the Bay of Nipe (► Guardalavaca, Surroundings), and held out a wooden plank to them. After their rescue the fishermen, who came from El Cobre, built a small chapel to hold an image of the saint and the plank. The Virgin became **the patron saint of the slaves** working in the nearby copper mines. Over the course of time the church was enlarged again and again, and in its present form dates from the 1920s. In 1916, the Catholic Church finally recognized the Caridad del Cobre as the Cuban Virgin.

★ ★ ◄ Pilgrimage church
⏱ Opening hours: Daily 6.30am – 6pm

In the room behind the altar many **valuable votive offerings** can be admired. One of them even derives from Ernest Hemingway, who donated to the Caridad del Cobre the Nobel Prize medal that he won in 1954 for *The Old Man and the Sea*. It was stolen, then returned, but is unfortunately no longer on display. An amulet dedicated to the Virgin by the mother of Fidel Castro for the safety of her son is also among the gifts that are kept in the safe. Many of the offerings are related to supplication for good health or for success in fleeing from Cuba to Miami.

The Valle de la Prehistoria is said to have inspired Spielberg's film Jurassic Park.

Steps lead up to a small audience room, which is decorated with flowers, usually yellow. Here the figure of the Virgin, clad in a yellow robe, stands in a glass case. During services the figure is turned to face the congregation. Although most Cubans are atheists, the Virgin of Cobre is generally revered and prayers are directed to her. »Caridad« forms part of the name of almost all Cuban women. She is not only a Catholic saint but also a representation of the **Afro-Cuban goddess Ochún**, whose colour is yellow.

Chivirico Chivirico is a small place on the coast road south of the Sierra Maestra, 47km/29mi west of Santiago. Although the south coast lacks the beaches of fine white sand that are found in the north, a coastline of pebbles and rocks has its own charm. At the few sandy beaches basic accommodation is available. Below the Los Galeones hotel complex (►Where to Stay) a diving station has been opened, and a wide range of sports (tennis, volleyball, angling, surfing, etc.) is available.

Around Santiago de Cuba: The East

★
Granjita Siboney Granjita Siboney (14km/9mi southeast of Santiago) lies only a short distance along the main road to Baconao Park. This chicken farm

(granjita) was a **hideout for Fidel Castro's rebels** while they were planning the attack on the Moncada Barracks. Along the route that the rebels then took, stones commemorate those who died in the attack. Each of the 26 memorials has a different design and bears an inscription with the first name and profession of each. Abel Santamaría, who led the attack together with Fidel and Raúl Castro, hired the farm. Vehicles, uniforms and weapons were concealed in its garden.

After the failure of the attack, some of the rebels returned here, but none survived the storming of the farm on 28 July 1953. When the revolutionaries took power, Granjita Siboney gained the status of a national monument and was made into a museum. Pictures, documentary material and personal items belonging to the rebels illustrate the events. Opening hours: Tue – Sun 9am – 5pm.

Playa Siboney to the south of Siboney is one of the most beautiful beaches around Santiago.

Playa Siboney

About 28km/17mi east of Santiago, the **Parque Nacional de Gran Piedra** shelters the Jardin Botánico and La Isabélica, one of the first coffee plantations, which should not be missed.

Parque Nacional de Gran Piedra

Continue on the road and turn off left before reaching the village of Siboney on the way to the Parque Baconao (40km/25mi southeast of Santiago), which is a **Unesco-protected biosphere reserve** thanks to the diversity of trees that grow there. A great variety of leisure facilities are spread across a distance of 52km/32mi: a kind of prehistoric valley, a collection of veteran cars, an automobile and doll museum, botanical gardens, a crocodile farm, an aquarium with a dolphinarium, a cactus garden and an exhibition of Mexican art, as well as a hotel (►Where to Stay).

Parque Nacional de Baconao

Since Steven Spielberg's film, the Valle de la Prehistoria has also been known as »Jurassic Park«. It's not hard to understand why, as visitors suddenly find themselves surrounded by dinosaurs, mammoths and Stone Age humans.

Valle de la Prehistoria

The Museo Nacional de Transporte has a collection of lovingly looked-after veteran cars, including a Cadillac owned by the singer Benny Moré and a Cuban car named Maya Cuba (1960), a tiny single-cylinder vehicle. Opening hours: daily 8am – 5pm.

Museo Nacional de Transporte

A number of beaches, for example Siboney, Cazonal and Baconao, offer an opportunity to swim within the national park. USA forces landed on **Playa Daiquirí** in 1898 after their victory in the naval battle against Spain. The story goes that an American soldier christened the famous cocktail after this beach, which is no longer accessible to the public.

Beaches

Slave labour portrayed as an idyll: harvesting sugar cane on Cuba, by Victor Patricio de Landaluze.

NO SUGAR WITHOUT SLAVES

Slavery was common on Cuba for more than 350 years – from 1531, when citizens of Santiago first petitioned for its introduction, until its final abolition in 1886. The period of the sugar boom, which lasted from 1792 until 1886, was Cuba's principal era as a slave-owning society.

Initially the forcible transportation of African labourers only took place on a small scale, but later it became a thriving business. It has been shown that 1.3 million slaves were taken to Cuba, i.e. about 10% of the 10 to 15 million who were shipped across the Atlantic in the centuries of the slave trade. It was English merchants who began the triangular trade: they exchanged textiles and iron goods for humans with traders in Africa, then sold the slaves in the Caribbean to purchase sugar, molasses or rum, which they could exchange in turn for finished or half-finished manufactured goods in France or Britain. However, the more the economic prosperity of Cuba depended on slavery, the more eager the Cubans themselves became to take their share of its considerable profits. The aristocracy, the Church and the bourgeoisie all took part in this.

As Spain, in contrast to other colonial powers, held on to slavery and the slave trade for a relatively long time, thanks to the low prices for its sugar Cuba was easily able to catch up with Jamaica and Haiti, which had had a lead in this business. With increasing wealth, the self-confidence of the Cubans in relation to their colonial rulers grew. Liberal ideas gained popularity in the fields of politics and economics. However, there was no desire to abolish slavery, the basis of prosperity, and therefore the colonial hierarchy remained untouched: the upper class, consisting of landowners, clerics and government officials headed by the governor, were born in Spain. The next group were Spaniards born on Cuba: »Criollos«, who as planters and merchants often had power and wealth. Below these two groups were the mulattoes and freed slaves, who in turn looked down on the class of slaves.

Black slaves led a humiliating existence on the sugar-cane plantations, with 20 hours of labour each day in the fields and the sugar mills, crammed into barrack-like huts to vegetate there. As the slave-owners believed female black workers were not tough enough, there were few women. However, this was only one

of the reasons why black slaves on Cuba had few children. Although this was officially attributed to the »polygamous nature of the blacks«, in reality female slaves did not want to bear children in these conditions of lack of freedom and preferred to resort to abortions and sterilization. About 20% of slaves died young, and few lived into old age.

There were practically no opportunities to escape this hard life. Although a slave could buy his freedom if he saved up for long enough, this was usually not possible until he was of no further use to his master. As these »emancipados« were prohibited from doing many kinds of job, they generally entered other forms of dependency. The other options were violence or flight. Some slaves fled to the woods to live as cimarrones, but this way of existence was by no means pleasant, as they were constantly on the run from slave-catchers who wanted to claim the price put on their heads, and when caught they were punished severely. In the early 19th century political pressure on colonial rulers increased – in 1817, at the insistence of the British government, Madrid even signed an agreement to end the slave trade – but in practice little changed. It took the »Grito de Yara« in 1868, which triggered off the First War of Independence, to initiate the end of slavery, when the leader of the revolt, **Carlos Manuel de Céspedes**, set free his own slaves.

Abolition of slavery through industrialization

Although Spanish forces regained power in 1878, times had changed. In the end neither political nor moral reasons were decisive in the abolition of slavery on Cuba, but economics pure and simple: the work of slaves could be done more quickly and cheaply by machines. Before long there were only 400 large factories with machines driven by steam engines instead of the 1500 smaller sugar mills in which slaves did the work. Finally, on 7 October 1886, this sad chapter in the history of Cuba was officially closed.

Trinidad

F 4

Province: Sancti Spíritus
Population: 50,000

Altitude: 40m/130ft
Distance: 335km/210mi from Havana
77km/48mi from Sancti Spíritus

Hidden away behind the Escambray mountains on the south coast, Trinidad is a colonial gem which has enjoyed Unesco protection as a World Heritage site since 1988. This picture-book town and its magnificent colonial mansions from the age of the sugar barons have a place on every tourist's itinerary.

In the afternoon, things get quieter again in the unevenly paved alleys. Women can chat to their neighbours behind wrought-iron window grilles without being photographed, and goat carts carrying schoolchildren get a clear run again. A bout of time travel back into the era of slavery involves a trip on a little railway from Trinidad into one of Cuba's loveliest scenic areas, Valle de los Ingenios.

1514	Foundation of the town	**History**
1886	After the abolition of slavery, sugar production comes to a halt.	
1988	Unesco declares Trinidad a World Heritage site.	

In 1514 Diego Velázquez, the first Spanish governor of Cuba, founded the town, one of the first on the island, hoping to find gold in the nearby Agabama and Tayabo rivers. As very little gold was found, however, Hernán Cortés set off with a large band of Trinitarios to seek his fortune in Mexico. The result was that Trinidad went into a long slumber. In the course of the 17th century, families from Sancti Spíritus settled here. Its favourable location for overseas trade made Trinidad a busy **port for goods and slaves**, who were in increasing demand as the sugar-cane plantations became more important to the economy. The sugar boom, supplemented by the slave trade and cattle farming, saw Trinidad into its golden age. When the abolition of slavery brought sugar production to a halt, however, the town fell into neglect. Since the 1950s the historic centre has been a protected landmark, and extensive restoration work began after the revolution. In 1988, Unesco declared the old quarter to be a World Heritage site, as alongside Havana and Camagüey, Trinidad boasts the **largest ensemble of colonial architecture** in Cuba.

← *The beautiful Palacio Cantero was built for a plantation owner.*

Cannons and songbirds A conspicuous sight on many streets are the barrels of cannon, which have been rammed into the ground. Brought to Trinidad as ballast on ships, the cannons were then used to protect pedestrians and buildings from the heavy coaches of the sugar barons with their high wheels.

A second peculiarity of Trinidad is the residents' fondness for songbirds. People can be seen going for a walk with a birdcage, and on Sunday mornings the owners of songbirds meet for a chirruping contest.

What to See in and Around Trinidad

✶ ✶
Colonial-architecture A walk through the colonial quarter in the north of Trinidad with its cobbled streets, horse-drawn carriages clip-clopping past and **colour-ful single-storey houses with window grilles and verandas** takes you back to the early colonial days. Part of the town is closed to motor vehicles. Everywhere you look it is evident that the Trinitarios, whose wealth came from cattle farming and sugar-cane plantations, were once very prosperous.

18th-century charm in Trinidad: restored colonial architecture from the age of the sugar boom, awarded World Heritage status by Unesco

Parque José Martí (also Parque Trinidad or Plaza Mayor), surrounded by the cathedral and a few townhouses converted into museums, is the focal point of Trinidad. With its palm trees, white fences and bronze greyhounds, the square has its own particular charm.

★
Parque José Martí

The former townhouse of the sugar baron Nicolás Brunet y Muñoz, built in around 1740, is now home to the Museo Romántico. The absolutely exquisite furnishings of the museum make a visit very rewarding. The furniture made from expensive types of wood, objets d'art such as Bohemian crystal glass, Meissen and Sèvres porcelain, and many more items, are not however family possessions but have been gathered from all over Cuba. In addition to various especially fine exhibits (including a bed frame with mother-of-pearl inlay work), the kitchen and bathroom are worth a visit.
The balcony on the second floor has an excellent view of the square and the Convent of San Francisco (1745) with its impressive bell tower. Opening hours: Tue – Sun 9.30am – 5pm.

★ ★
Museo Romántico (Palacio Brunet)

⊙

The Iglesia de la Santísima Trinidad (Church of the Holy Trinity, 1884 – 1892) occupies the east side of Parque Martí. A wooden predecessor of the present building was constructed in the 17th century on the same site. Note the Gothic altar, made from 18 different kinds of wood. The **figure of Christ** (»Cristo de Veracruz«) in a small chapel was originally intended for a church in Mexico. The ship that was taking it there sailed into a severe storm three times when leaving the harbour, which was interpreted as a sign that the statue should stay in Trinidad.

Iglesia de la Santísima Trinidad

Highlights Trinidad

Trinidad Map

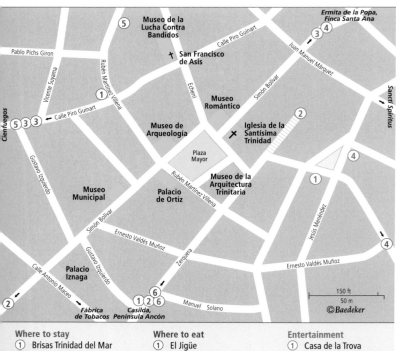

Where to stay
1. Brisas Trinidad del Mar
2. Costasur
3. Escambray Spa Hotel
4. Las Cuevas
5. Villa María Dolores
6. La Ronda

Where to eat
1. El Jigüe
2. Grill Caribe
3. La Coruña
4. Plaza Santa Ana
5. Taberna La Canchánchara
6. Trinidad Colonial

Entertainment
1. Casa de la Trova
2. Casa de la Música
3. Ayala disco cave
4. Ruínas de Segarte

✳
Museo de la Arquitectura Trinitaria

Devoted to the characteristics of colonial architecture in Trinidad, this museum displays a selection of the **imaginatively designed adornments of window and door grilles** that catch the eye on a walk through the town. Round-arched windows are another genuinely Trinitarian architectural detail. The semi-circle is not decorated with colourful pieces of glass, as in Havana, but is subdivided by radiating slats that allow the wind to cool the house but keep out the sun. With its patio and colonnade, the single-storey house (1738) that accommodates the museum is itself an excellent example of colonial architecture. It once belonged to one of Trinidad's richest citizens, sugar baron Sánchez Iznaga. Opening hours: Sat–Thu 9am–5pm.

VISITING TRINIDAD

INFORMATION
In the hotels and at
Cubatur
Calle Antonio Maceo 447
corner of Calle Zerquera
(formerly Calle Rosario)
Tel. 04 19/63 10, 63 14
Tours of the surrounding country and
mountains; twice daily a shuttle bus
runs to the beach and back.

TRANSPORT
In the town of Trinidad itself, many
streets are closed to cars, horse-drawn
carriages and taxis with meter. For the
Valle de los Ingenios, the valley of the
sugar mills, the best means of transport from Trinidad is a bike, horse,
taxi or the normal train from Trinidad to Manaca-Iznaga (the tourist rail
link, tren turístico, no longer operates!). To reach Topes de Collantes
take a hire car, taxi, tour bus or bike
(it's ideal for mountainbikers). If you
don't like pedalling, take a motorized
trip, maybe the popular »Rambo
tour« on army trucks, because the
road from Trinidad is extremely steep.

EVENTS
Fiestas Sanjuaneras
For three uproarious days on the last
weekend in June, a carnival is celebrated in the lanes of the old quarter.
Wild, often drunken »cowboys« ride
around on their horses.

SHOPPING
Open-air market
In Calle Jesús Menendez (near the
Casa de la Trova) in the old quarter,
and in Callejón de Peña, round the
corner to the right of the Museo
Histórico (Calle Simón Bolívar),
many traders sell crochet-work and
lace, souvenirs and crafts.

Taller Alfarero
Calle Andrés Berro Macías 9, old
quarter
Mon – Fri 8am – 12 noon
2pm – 5pm
A long-established business run by
the Santander family, this pottery has
a small souvenir shop.

Colonial style at El Jigüe

WHERE TO EAT

▶ Moderate

① *El Jigüe*
Calle Rubén Martínez Villena no. 70, corner of Piro Guinart
Tel. 04 19/64 76
One of the town's best restaurants: creole food in a central location in the historic quarter.

② *Playa Maria Aguilar: Grill Caribe*
2km/1.25mi north of the Costasur Hotel
Tel. 04 19/62 41
Daily 9am – 2am
A beach rendezvous at sunset for cocktails and lobster, shrimps and fish, Tropi-Cola and pork steak, chicken and snacks.

③ *La Coruña*
Calle José Martí 430, entre Fidel Claro y Santiago Escobar
No phone
Daily 11am – 10.30pm
Walk through the living room of this colonial house to the beautiful green

*Music everywhere –
part of the Cuban way of life*

patio to eat creole food to the sound of the resident rooster crowing.

④ *Plaza Santa Ana*
Plaza Santa Ana
Tel. 04 19/64 23
Daily 9am – 10pm
This colonial villa with a big, airy patio was once a prison. After enjoying delicious creole dishes (the speciality is pork escalope stuffed with cheese and ham), play pool or browse through the CDs in the in-house souvenir shop.

⑤ *Taberna La Canchánchara*
Calle Rubén Martínez Villena
Tel. 04 19/41 36
Don't leave this bar without trying the drink of the same name, made from rum, lime juice and honey, while tapping your feet to Cuban rhythms.

▶ Moderate/Inexpensive

⑥ *Trinidad Colonial*
Calle Antonio Maceo 51
Tel. 04 19/64 73
Daily 9am – 10pm
Genteel-looking restaurant in a venerable 19th-century house. Creole dishes, lunch buffet accompanied by a live trio (and lots of tourist groups), in the evening à la carte, also with música.

ENTERTAINMENT

① *Casa de la Trova*
Calle Echerrí 29, old quarter
Daily 10am – 1.00am
This has now become a tourist bar that attracts organized groups. Modest admission fee in the evening and a few Cubans who show how to dance to son and salsa.

② *Casa de la Música*
Plaza Mayor (above the steps), Calle Juan Manuel Márquez, old quarter
Traditional live music such as danzón

and trova or readings in the patio (lots of good CDs on sale in the shop). In the evenings, tourists, Cubans and some dubious characters come for a salsa concert and show with dancing on the big square below the steps.

③ *Disko-Höhle Ayala*
The German name gives a clue to the clientele, but this vault above the Las Cuevas Hotel is a good place for dancing under party lights – every night except Monday from 10.30pm.

④ *Ruínas de Segarte*
Calle Jesús Menendez, old quarter
Small bar with patio and live music, open round the clock, Afro-Cuban shows, also salsa. Snacks and cocktails.

WHERE TO STAY
► **Mid-range**
② *Peninsula Ancón: Costasur (Horizontes)*
Playa María Aguilar
Tel. 04 19/61 72, 61 74, tel./fax 61 73
www.horizontes.cu
Beach hotel with tennis court and the full range of water sports, 131 rooms, restaurant, tourist office.

③ *Topes de Collantes: Kurhotel Escambray (Gaviota)*
Sierra del Escambray
Tel. 042/54 02 72, fax 54 02 28
www.gaviota-grupo.com
A spa hotel in the mountains of the Sierra del Escambray, restored in 2003. Professional service and treatments: pool, sauna, steam bath, massage, acupuncture, hydrotherapy, cosmetic treatments and anti-stress therapy with trained psychologists etc.

④ *Las Cuevas (Horizontes)*
Santa Ana

Tel. 04 19/613 35, fax 61 61
www.horizontes.cu
Standing on high ground with a fine view of Trinidad, the hotel is a good alternative to the beach hotels. 114 rooms.

⑤ *Villa María Dolores (also Casa del Campesino, Cubanacán)*
Ctra. a Cienfuegos, km 1.5
Tel./fax 04 19/64 81
www.cubanacan.cu
A rambling green complex in the style of a country estate (1.5km/1mi out of town): bungalows with simple furnishings (but satellite TV) on the Río Guaurabo, some with a terrace and river view. Pool, restaurant. Excursions by boat, on foot, and on horseback.

► **Budget**
⑥ *La Ronda (Islazul)*
Calle José Martí 238 (near Parque Céspedes/Central), old quarter
Tel. 04 19/40 11
www.islazul.cu
Beautiful, rather noisy colonial house with 16 small, basic rooms (but equipped with phone and satellite TV) around a patio. Bar on the roof terrace.

Baedeker recommendation

► **Luxury/Mid-range**
① *Peninsula Ancón: Brisas Trinidad del Mar (Cubanacán)*
12km/7mi to the beach
Tel. 04 19/65 00, 65 07, fax 65 65
reservas@brisastdad.co.cu
www.cubanacan.cu
Wonderful four-star (all-inclusive) resort in the style of a colonial town with plazas and church tower. Fantastic beach, pool, tennis court, massage.

Galería de Arte Universal (Palacio Ortíz)
Formerly the Museo Alejandro de Humboldt, a yellow building with blue windows, now houses a gallery mainly exhibiting work by young artists from Trinidad. The natural history collection can be seen next door in the Archaeological Museum.

✳ Museo de Arqueología y Ciencia naturales Guamuhaya
When Alexander von Humboldt spent three days in Trinidad in 1801, he stayed in the building that now houses the Archaeological Museum.
Finds such as tools, ceramics and skeletons as well as visual displays illuminate the **life of the aboriginal Indians** and the era of slavery.

Trinidad's Iglesia de la Santísima Trinidad has the superb backdrop of the Sierra del Escambray, whose foothills extend down to the city.

One of the exhibits is a toothbrush said to have belonged to a conquistador – possibly Hernán Cortés, who lived in a previous building on the site of this townhouse before he left for Mexico.
The natural history collection taken over from the former Humboldt Museum displays Cuban plants and animals that are now extinct or are endemic to Cuba.

⏱ Opening hours: Mon – Sat 9am – 5pm, reopened after a decade of restoration

The cobbled Calle Simón Bolívar is Trinidad's best-restored street. Many souvenir shops, little restaurants, cafés and the truly fascinating Museo Municipal can be found here.

Calle Simón Bolívar

The finest building in Trinidad originally belonged to the Borel family. It is now called Palacio Cantero, as this was the married name of a daughter who inherited the house.

★★ **Museo Municipal (Palacio Cantero)**

The first owner, who had the house constructed between 1827 and 1830, was not only a wealthy plantation owner but also a poet, doctor and lover of the beautiful things in life. His marble bathroom is said to have been equipped with putti that spouted gin and eau de Cologne.
The municipal museum which now occupies the building displays beautiful colonial furniture, pretty mural paintings and various luxury items made from glass and porcelain. The patio, partly decorated with paintings, has a well and many plants. The rooms around it are dedicated to different periods in the town's history since 1514: **colonization, the sugar boom and slavery, the Wars of Independence** and the **revolution**. Bells that were rung on the plantations and instruments of torture are reminders of the era of slavery.
There is a stunning view of the town and its surroundings from the upper storeys and the roof.

⏱ Opening hours: Sat – Thu 9am – 5pm

Further south, at the corner of Calle General Izquierdo and Calle General Hugo Robert, discover one of Trinidad's most splendid residences, the newly restored house of the Iznaga family.

Palacio Iznaga

Close by in Calle Antonio Maceo, a tobacco factory is open to visitors. Beneath the gaze of Che Guevara and Camilo Cienfuegos the tobacco is prepared and the cigars are rolled, fitted with bands and packed.

★ **Fábrica de Tabacos**

To the north of Parque Martí the bell tower of the former Franciscan monastery stands out. Inside is an exhibition on a special theme: the Museo de la Lucha contra Bandidos tells the story of battles that the Cuban militia fought in the 1960s against counter-revolutionary groups in the Sierra del Escambray. Opening hours: Tue – Sat 9am – 5pm.
The view from the yellow and white **bell tower**, a landmark of Trinidad which belonged to the Iglesia de San Francisco de Asís that once stood here, is superb.

Museo de la Lucha contra Bandidos

⏱

Iglesia de la Popa

From the hill-top ruins of the Iglesia de la Popa, Trinidad's first church, northeast of the town centre, visitors have a fantastic view of the town and the coast. Take Calle Simon Bolívar from Parque Martí to get there.

✷
Playa Ancón

About 12km/7.5mi southwest of Trinidad, the Ancón Peninsula points into the sea. So far not many hotels have been built on its 5km/3mi-long Caribbean dream beach.

Diving expeditions to the Jardines de la Reina, an archipelago further offshore to the southeast, and tourist trips on a catamaran, including to Cayo Blanco, are on offer here.

✷ ✷ Valle de los Ingenios (Valle San Luís)

»Valley of sugar mills«

East of Trinidad the main road leads into the scenic Valle de los Ingenios, so called because almost 50 sugar mills were in operation

Life outside the colonial towns: alongside the cultivation of tobacco and sugar cane, cattle raising dominates the existence of inhabitants of the »Valley of Sugar Mills«.

here in the late 19th century. This valley was the source of Trinidad's wealth, which could never have been earned without slave labour. During the First War of Independence freed and runaway slaves burned down all the plantations and sugar mills, which means most of them survive only as ruins.

A **mirador** with an open-air restaurant on the road to Iznaga is a lookout point allowing to view this beautiful countryside with palms, fields and little farms. The Sierra del Escambray on the horizon forms its boundary. Like the town of Trinidad, the valley is protected by Unesco.

In the 19th century, the **village of Manacas Iznaga** in the middle of the valley was surrounded by Cuba's largest sugar plantation, owned by the Iznaga family. The 50m/165ft-high Torre de Iznaga (12km/ 7.5mi northeast of Trinidad) is a **Cuban national monument**. It is

★
Torre de Iznaga
🕐
Opening hours:
9am – 5pm

possible to climb the seven-storey tower, though this is rather a wobbly ascent. A splendid view of the valley from the top is the reward. Originally towers like this were used for **supervising slaves** who worked on the sugar-cane planta- tions. Bells called them to work and a watchman could scan the whole valley for signs of revolt or bands of men. The tower goes back to a wager between sons of the Iz-

> ❗ **Baedeker TIP**
>
> **Overwhelming panorama**
> The most stunning view in all of Cuba can be enjoyed from a steep hill about 4km/2.5mi east of Trinidad, where there is also a bar that serves light meals (Mirador de la Loma del Puerto, Ctra. a Sancti Spíritus. Daily 8am – 9pm).

naga family. The sugar aristocracy had a habit of meeting after the harvest and spending their gains in as extravagant a fashion as possi- ble. One of the Iznagas decided to dig the deepest well far and wide. Not to be beaten, his brother built a tower next to the well, planning it to be taller than the well was deep. Nothing has survived of the well.

Next to the tower travellers may visit the Iznaga family hacienda, which now includes a very attractive restaurant. A small exhibition tells of the history of the regional sugar industry, illustrating it with relics such as slaves' chains and tools. The five recesses of varying size at the back of the house served for chaining up and mistreating slaves.

◄ Hacienda Iznaga

Topes de Collantes

Trippers come to Cuba's second-highest chain of mountains after the Sierra Maestra to see its waterfalls, to bathe in wonderfully refreshing pools, to visit coffee fincas and agricultural cooperatives and to ad- mire lush green valleys full of eucalyptus trees and pines. In the Par- que Nacional Topes de Collantes, hikes at the foot of Pico San Juan (1156m/3793ft) make a change from seeing the colonial sights in Tri-

Spa tourism ►

nidad, and guests at the Stalinist-looking mountain spa hotel can indulge in a few days' rest and professional treatments.

The treatments on offer here range from hydrotherapy and physiotherapy to »green medicine«. The spa guests mainly come from Latin America. The Clínica Central Cira García has state-of-the-art equipment and is specialized in plastic surgery, hepatitis and lung complaints.

Salto de Caburní

One of the most popular tours through the beautiful scenery of the Sierra del Escambray goes to the 65m/213ft-high Caburní Waterfalls. This three-hour hike heads east from the spa hotels for some 7km/4.5mi, along a rock wall. It is tough in places, especially when the steep paths are slippery after rain, and involves managing a height difference of 400m/1300ft!

Salto Javira

Although the Javira waterfall in El Cubano National Park drops a mere 10m/33ft, its curtain of water conceals a wonderful stalagmite cave into which you can swim from the emerald-green pool. This walking tour and rough-and-ready trips in »camiones« (trucks) can be booked at the travel agencies in Trinidad.

✳
Finca Codina

Finca Codina, founded in 1910 by a Catalan coffee planter, can be reached in off-road military trucks. The estate, now a restaurant for daytrippers with bands playing music and souvenir stalls, is regarded as an insiders' tip for birdwatchers, but walks in this area are also an opportunity to see butterflies, hummingbirds and a great variety of plants – even the Cuban national flower, the mariposa. After a trip, guests relax with the special house cocktail, made from ginger, honey and rum.

✳✳ Valle de Viñales

B 3

Province: Pinar del Río

Distance: 160km/100mi from Havana
28km/17mi from Pinar del Río

The scene in the valley of Viñales in the heart of the Sierra de los Órganos is as pretty as a picture: humpy limestone hills (»mogotes«) rise like elephants' backs from the rust-brown soil of the tobacco plantations, and at first light the tips of royal palms rise above the morning mist that lies on the fields.

This is one of the most beautiful parts of Cuba and protected by Unesco. Day-trippers from Havana and holidaymakers flock to the

The valley at its best, where tobacco grows →
between the steep walls of limestone hills, the mogotes.

Valle de Viñales Map

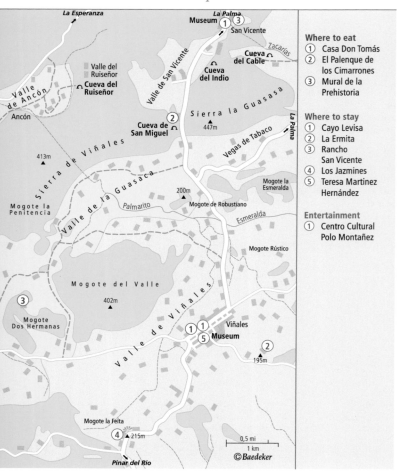

Where to eat
1. Casa Don Tomás
2. El Palenque de los Cimarrones
3. Mural de la Prehistoria

Where to stay
1. Cayo Levisa
2. La Ermita
3. Rancho San Vicente
4. Los Jazmines
5. Teresa Martínez Hernández

Entertainment
1. Centro Cultural Polo Montañez

village, where the latest trend is climbing the vertical rocks – an activity that comes with a fantastic panorama!

Mighty mogotes These heavily eroded and overgrown rocks were once the pillars of a massive cave system that was formed 160 million years ago. As the limestone eroded, many cave roofs collapsed. Some of the valley floors, where today tobacco, maize, malangas and beans are grown, mark the course of ancient cave passages. Several caves can be explored on foot or by boat on organized tours. This is now a thor-

oughly marketed source of income – many groups are bussed in – and has nothing to do with green tourism: there are motor boats and a disco in the Cueva de Viñales and Cueva del Indio!.
Excursions to the Gran Caverna de Santo Tomás, a cave system covering 46km/29mi approx. 16km/10mi southwest of Viñales, the **biggest cave in Cuba** and the second-biggest in Central America, are a different matter. Here visitors are given a hard hat and guided by a caving expert through unlit tunnels to view impressive stalagmites and stalactites; tours range across varying levels of difficulty. Information: Escuela Nacional de Espeleológia in Viñales (Granja Moncada, near the cave entrance, tel. 08/77 10 14, 79 31 45).

◄ Gran Caverna de Santo Tomás

Tobacco is grown in the fertile red earth, dried in sheds and then processed to make cigarettes and cigars. Small farmyards with green fields and palm trees nestle in amongst the tobacco crops. For the best view of the Valle de Viñales, head for the **mirador** (viewpoint) near the Los Jazmines Hotel (► Where to Stay, hotel car park with souvenir stalls).

Tobacco cultivation

What to See in the Valle de Viñales

Viñales, a small town at the heart of the valley, takes its name from a vineyard (viña) that immigrants from the Canary Islands planted here in the 19th century. It is an absolutely idyllic place with a sleepy plaza, a pretty church, single-storey houses with shingle roofs and a small avenue of pines along the main street. Viñales is a protected conservation zone as an example of Cuban rural colonial architecture.

★
Viñales

In the unspoiled natural surroundings of the Valle de las dos Hermanas (Valley of the Two Sisters), 5km/3mi west of Viñales, a gaudy work of art, the Mural de la Prehistoria, is a startling sight.
The **Mural de la Prehistoria** was created in the early 1960s on the initiative of Celia Sánchez, a former guerrillera and later Fidel Castro's secretary. Leovigildo González Morillo, a pupil of the famous

★
Mural de la Prehistoria

! *Baedeker* TIP

Heaven for climbers

Active visitors to Viñales don't only go below ground – fearless climbers also tackle precipitous heights and hang upside down from the rocks, with a view to die for. It was only a matter of time before climbers discovered the Valle de Viñales. They have to bring their own equipment, however. Information: www.cubaclimbing.com.

▶ VISITING VALLE DE VIÑALES

INFORMATION

Parque Nacional de Viñales (Centro de Visitante)

Ctra. a Pinar del Río, 2km/1.25mi south of Viñales (near ▶Los Jazmines Hotel)

It is obligatory to hire one of the guides who await visitors here. Tours can also be booked through the tourist offices, e.g. in hotels and next to the restaurant ▶Casa de Don Tomás on the main road or at Cubanacán, Calle Salvador Cisneros 63 (main road opposite the church), tel. 08/79 63 93 (here also pricey hire of bikes and mopeds, internet).

WHERE TO EAT

▶ Moderate

① Viñales: Casa Don Tomás

Calle Salvador Cisneros 140 (main road)
Tel. 08/79 63 00

Creole dishes (fish, chicken, lobster) at a paladar in a beautiful house dating from 1889, in the patio at the back, on the terrace or on a balcony with a view of the comings and goings in Viñales.

② EL Palenque de los Cimarrones

Ctra. de Puerto Esperanza, km 36
Tel. 08/79 62 90
Daily 12 noon – 4pm, groups only in the evening

Hidden behind the Cueva de Viñales (cave, also called Cueva de San Miguel), this is an open-air eatery for trippers at the foot of one of the giant mogotes. Tourist groups come here for creole cooking with »slave« waiters, and to see a folklore show and drink the »slave spirit« chinguerito. Disco at the cave entrance: Fri – Sun from 10pm, with Afro-Cuban show, Sun also in the afternoon.

Swimming with a fine view: Hotel La Ermita

③ *Mural de la Prehistoria*
Valle de Viñales
Tel. 08/79 33 94, 79 62 60
Daily 11am – 7pm
The speciality in the Mural restaurant right by the prehistoric rock paintings is cerdo asado y ahumado, estilo Viñales: pork in a delicious marinade, braised in a wood-burning oven and served with a creole sauce and »viandas cocidas« (malanga, yuca, boniato).

ENTERTAINMENT

Most clubs for music and dancing are close together along the main street of Salvador Cisneros (at 9pm or 10pm you can hear and see where the action is, at Patio del Decimista for instance, and opposite in El Viñalero).

① *Viñales: Centro Cultural Polo Montañez*
Calle Salvador Cisneros (main road on the church square)
Daily 10am – midnight
Small bar in a colonial villa on the main plaza, named after a popular »guajiro natural« singer who died in 2002 at the height of his career. Live music from 10.30pm and other cultural events, art gallery next door.

WHERE TO STAY
► **Mid-range**
① *Cayo Levisa: Cayo Levisa (Cubanacán)*
Ferry from Puerto Palma Rubia to Cayo Levisa, going out daily at 10am and 6pm, returning at 9am and 5pm)
Tel./fax 082/77 30 15, tel. in Havana 07/690 10 05, -6
www.cubanacan.cu
Well-equipped but overpriced bungalows (e.g. satellite TV) in two rows on a beautiful and narrow beach (3km/2mi long) between mangroves, the azure sea and a visible coral reef.

② *La Ermita (Horizontes)*
Ctra. de La Ermita, km 1.5
Tel. 08/79 60 71, fax 79 60 91
www.horizontes.cu
Blending harmoniously into the countryside, this hotel has a magical view. 64 rooms, restaurant, swimming pool.

③ *Rancho San Vicente (Horizontes)*
Ctra. de Puerto Esperanza, km 33 (7km/4.5mi north of Viñales)
Tel. 08/79 62 01, fax 79 62 65
www.horizontes.cu
53 pleasant rooms in log cabins and little concrete houses, scattered across wooded terrain around a big pool.

► **Mid-range**
④ *Los Jazmines (Horizontes/ Cubanacán)*
Ctra. de Viñales, km 2.5
Tel. 08/79 62 05
Fax 79 62 15
www.horizontes.cu
www.cubanacan.cu
The unique location of this hotel on higher ground in the Valle de Viñales guarantees a wonderful view over fertile countryside. The 62 rooms and 16 bungalows are being renovated step by step. Pool. Guests can explore the surroundings on horseback. Book in advance for the high season.

► **Budget**
⑤ *Viñales: Teresa Martinez Hernández*
Calle Camilo Cienfuegos Nr. 10
Tel. (neighbour) 08/79 32 67
Guests of this family, who speak only Spanish, have quiet accommodation in small en-suite rooms and take their breakfast in a charmingly overgrown garden with banana plants and an orange tree. There are now casas particulares everywhere in the town – their number is said to be 160.

Tobacco is vital to the economy: Cuba sells well over 100 million cigars per year, with France and Spain as important export markets. More than 20,000 people are employed in the tobacco fields, and a further 5000 have jobs rolling cigars in the tobacco factories.

FOREIGN CURRENCY FOR CASTRO: HAND-ROLLED HAVANAS

Travellers are often offered »genuine« Havanas, which have supposedly been smuggled out of the tobacco factory in mysterious ways, at knock-down prices on the street in Cuba. These items are usually machine-made cigars which are in no way comparable to the original hand-rolled Havanas (►3D graphic, p. 36).

It is better to buy cigars in one of the officially recognized tobacconists in the Castillo de la Real Fuerza, in the Partagás factory or on Quinta Avenida in Havana. Cigars sold under the major brand names, for example **Cohiba, Bolívar, Partagás, Punch, Hoyo de Monterrey, Montecristo, Romeo y Julieta and H. Upmann**, are rolled by hand in nine tobacco factories that survived the revolution. For connoisseurs, to smoke a genuine Havana with its dry scent, spicy, complex aroma and special character is a sensual treat, though admittedly not a particularly cheap one. The guiding principle is quality at all stages of the process.

The conditions for growing tobacco plants are ideal in the Vuelta Abajo, in the western province of **Pinar del Río**.

The El Llano district there has the best areas for cultivation, with its famous red earth and a highly suitable climate. Between the Vuelta Abajo and Havana province, the Semi Vuelta produces a tobacco with a coarser structure and a stronger aroma. By contrast the leaves from the Partido district in Havana province have a more refined quality, meeting the high standards required for a hand-rolled export cigar. The two other tobacco-growing regions, Remedios in the centre of the island and Oriente out in the east, are of no importance for the premium-quality sector.

Cultivation

The individual stages in the process of growing tobacco and making cigars were laid down in the early 19th

century and have essentially remained unchanged since then. Close attention is paid to every phase. This starts with taking care of the seed, which is produced by scientists in state-owned agricultural institutions and distributed to the »vegueros« (farmers). A distinction is made between two kinds: **corojo** for the wrappers and **coriollo** for the fillers and binders.

The season starts with preparing the fields between June and August. About 45 days after sowing (October to January) the seedlings, by now 15–20cm/6–8in high, are planted out on the farms (»vegas«). Immediately after planting, the corojos are covered with gauze cloth (»tapados«) so that the young tobacco plants grow in the shade. This is done to ensure that they have the suppleness and even appea-

rance required for wrappers. Coriollos, however, are exposed to the sun. Their leaves develop various kinds of taste, as is desired and also necessary for the filler and binder leaves of a perfect Havana blend. As with vines, there are good and bad years. The most favourable conditions for tobacco plants, which are extremely sensitive to the climate, are lots of warm days and cool nights in summer, ideally without rain.

The harvest lasts from January to March. As soon as the bottom leaves are tender green in colour, the farmers start to harvest at the lowest level and then work upwards in weekly cuts, depending on the degree of ripeness. A tobacco plant usually yields 16 to 18 leaves. Sorted according to the stages of cutting, the

With practised movements, the cigar roller selects leaves (it is said that more than 800 colours can be distinguished), cuts them to size, puts three leaves as the filler, rolls them in a fourth leaf and finally adds the wrapper leaf, the capa, which is smoothed using a flat piece of metal.

Careful finishing of the product is a mark of the quality of a genuine Havana cigar.

harvested leaves are taken to **Casas del Tabaco**, well-ventilated sheds in which the leaves are hung up in pairs on poles for air curing. The drying sheds are constructed so that their two doors, oriented to the east and west, admit the sun's rays only when it is low in the sky, in the morning and evening. In order to control the temperature and humidity, the tobacco leaves are regularly moistened and aired.

The drying phase concludes after 50 days. The golden-brown leaves are packed in bundles (»gavillas«), and taken to fermentation houses, where they are piled up one on top of the other for storage. The future taste and aroma of the cigars develop here because it is here inside the piles (»pilones«) that the heat (32–42°C/ 90–108°F, depending on the cut) needed for the fermenting process is generated. The first fermentation, of about 30 days, is followed by a second, which lasts 60 days. Between these two stages the leaves are sorted according to their size, colour and characteristics, and the middle vein is removed. The leaves are then left for a

few days in a wood-lined temporary store known as a »picadero«. After that they are taken in balls (»tercios«) to storehouses where they remain for several months, often even years, until transportation to the cigar factory takes place.

Nimble-fingered torcederos

The highly elaborate production of »puros«, as the cigars are known, begins at the factory. The wrapper, binder and filler leaves are treated with extreme care before the »torcedor«, the cigar maker, rolls them into a cigar. Following a special moistening process (for wrapper leaves only) the leaves are halved and sorted once again according to size, colour and structure. The blending master makes the mixture (»ligas«) for the cigars on the basis of recipes that are kept strictly secret, before the leaves, once again packed into bundles, arrive at the cigar rollers.

In the workshop (»galera«), the heart of the factory, workplaces are arranged in rows as if in a large classroom. The **torcederos**, who make about 120

cigars per day, are permitted to smoke as many cigars as they want during their working day. While they are on the job, a »**lector de tabaquera**« reads to them: current affairs from the daily newspaper in the morning, and stories or novels in the afternoon.

To roll a perfect Havana demands remarkable manual dexterity of the cigar makers. There are **fixed rules** for the structure of a cigar. The first part is to make the bunch, which consists of the filler mixture and the binder. The bunch is now pressed in a wooden form, which consists of two halves, each with ten cigar-shaped depressions. The bunches are then rolled in high-quality wrapper leaves, and a cap is added at the end, or head, of the cigar.

After the finished cigars have spent between three weeks and several months in an air-conditioned room clad with cedarwood, the colour sorter (»escogedor«) classifies them into 65 different shades and packs them into cigar boxes. These boxes, made of cedarwood, allow the cigar to continue to breathe.

Finally the warrany seal of the Cuban government, »hecho en Cuba, totalmente a mano«, is affixed. Now the Havana can be sent on its way to a lover of cigars, an aficionado.

Visits

The oldest cigar factory still in operation, the **Fábrica de Tabacos Partagás** behind the Capitolio, makes the brands Bolívar, La Gloria Cubana and Ramón Allones (Calle Industria 520 entre Dragones y Barcelona, Habana Vieja), tours Mon – Fri 9.30am – noon and 1pm – 3.30pm.

At **La Corona** near Plaza de la Revolución, practised torcederos roll the Hoyo de Monterrey and Punch brands of Havanas (Av. 20 de Majo 520 entre Línea del Ferrocarril y Marta Abreu, Cerro), tours Mon – Fri 9am – 3pm.

The **Romeo y Julieta** tobacco factory is housed in a shining blue Belle Époque palace. Its well-known products include El Rey del Mundo Cuaba and Saint Luis Rey (Calle Belascoaín 852 entre Peñalver y Desagüe, Centro), tours by appointment: tel. 07/870 47 97, Mon – Fri 9am – 3pm.

Mexican muralist painter Diego Rivera, designed this representation of the evolution of humankind. Local farmers and workers helped him carry out the work on a wall 120m/400ft high and 180m/600ft long. The work is touched up with fresh paint every five years.

✳ Cueva del Indio

The valley of Viñales is full of caves, amongst them the Cueva de Viñales with its discotheque and restaurant **El Palenque** (► Where to Eat) and the Cueva del Indio 5km/3mi north of Viñales, which is said to have been the hideout of the son of a chieftain who eloped with the daughter of another chief. Parts of the cave, which was carved out by a river, can be visited on foot and by boat. It contains beautiful stalagmites and stalactites, which with a little imagination can be interpreted as a snake, a sea horse and Columbus's three ships.
To avoid the tourist buses, don't go in the morning. At quieter times, with a little luck it is possible to spot rare plants and animals such as the Cuban national bird, the tocororo, the archaic cork palm or the mariposa.

✳ Cayo Levisa

Many day trippers from Havana and Viñales come to Cayo Levisa for the snorkelling, and divers enthuse about the 23 diving spots off the coast. Others prefer to have a lazy time, as sightseeing is not on the agenda here, and just one single bungalow hotel caters for those in search of a Robinson Crusoe experience (► Where to Stay). This tiny island is home to tree rats, called jutías. There is no need to be afraid of these cat-sized rodents, which appear on the paths between the bungalows at night. To the west the islet of Mégano, where Hemingway once anchored, is within sight.

✳ ✳ Varadero

D 2

Province: Matanzas
Population: 10,000

Altitude: 0 – 5m/16ft
Distance: 144km/89mi from Havana
835km/519mi from Santiago de Cuba

The beach seems to be endless here – and so does the number of hotels. Cuba's number one holiday town on the Hicacos Peninsula pulls in sun-seekers from all over the world. It is the realm of the »todo incluído« holiday, where almost everything is included in the price: 20km/12mi of beach, entertainment round the clock in numerous comfortable hotel resorts, and activities such as diving, parachuting and parasailing for those who are so inclined. To ensure that no Cubans stray onto their homeland's finest beaches, checkpoints monitor access to the peninsula and the police patrol the beach from time to time in their buggies.

Bacardí feeling: the peninsula almost 150km/100mi from Havana has become a holiday paradise, but Cubans are present only as extras.

Foreign visitors meet Cubans here only in their capacity as service personnel, or as »heroes of labour« who are allowed to spend a holiday in Varadero – in the lower-category hotels, of course. In order to get at least a fleeting impression of Cuban everyday life, leave the poolscape for a day and make a trip to ►Matanzas, the nearest sizeable provincial capital, or to ►Cárdenas.

The Hotel Varadero opened in 1910. In 1930 the DuPont family, fabulously rich American industrialists, bought a huge estate and built a luxurious holiday home there. Other wealthy Americans followed their example – and some influential Cubans, including President Batista. During the first wave of tourism in the 1950s, the Hotel Internacional and its casino were built with American money. After the victory of the revolution on 1 January 1959, the new government confiscated properties built along the beach. Villas abandoned by their owners were converted to hotels and holiday flats, to open up the dream beach of Varadero for the Cuban people and tourists from the Soviet bloc.

History

⏵ VISITING VARADERO

INFORMATION
In all large hotels
Cubatur
Av. Primera, corner of Calle 33
Tel. 045/66 72 17
varadero@cubatur.cu

TRANSPORT
The bright red open-top bus on the Varadero Beach Tour links 42 stops serving the widely scattered hotels and the small town. The entire journey takes two hours, and passengers can hop on and off as often as they like (9am – 9pm, www.trans-turcuba.-com). There is also a kind of mini-train running around the centre of Varadero, as well as metered taxis and horse-drawn carriages (negotiate the price!)

SHOPPING
A big market for crafts, souvenirs, paintings, etc. sprawls along Av. Primera between Calle 44 and Calle 46. Plaza América between the Melía Las Américas and Melía Varadero hotels is a shopping centre with a range of stores, boutiques, a small supermarket, bars and cafés, a post office, travel agencies and a congress centre (Autopista del Sur, km 11, daily 10am – 8.30pm).

Casa del Ron
Av. Primera entre Calles 62 y 63
Daily 9am – 11pm
Lovers of high-class (and high percent) liquor are in heaven here: all kinds of Havana Club rum and other spirits; there is a shop and a bar with a model of the old distillery. Next door, the Casa del Habano caters to cigar aficionados (daily 9am – 7pm).

WHERE TO EAT
▶ **Expensive/Moderate**
① **Las Américas**
Ctra. de la Américas, km 8
Tel. 045/66 73 88
The restaurant of choice for a celebration – in the Villa DuPont, with good French cuisine. The lobster is overpriced though.

▶ **Moderate**
② **Antigüedades**
Av. Primera, corner of Calle 59
Tel. 045/66 73 29
Daily 11am – 11pm
This restaurant is jam-packed with antiques, plants and kitsch but is one of the few places with no background music. Reasonably priced menus with modest portions of meat, fish, lobster etc.

③ **Esquina de Cuba**
Av. Primera, corner of Calle 36, centre
Tel. 045/61 40 (7pm – 9pm)
Daily 10am – midnight
Bar, café and open-air restaurant on the main street, decked out in 1950s style. Good Cuban home cooking at premium prices, for example »old washing« (»ropa vieja«: beef braised till it falls apart), grilled chicken or pork steak, also fish and seafood. Thursday is »old fashion night« with live music.

At the Parque Retiro Josone in the town centre three more excellent restaurants dish up creole, Italian and international meals.

ENTERTAINMENT
① **Tropicana Matanzas**
Autopista Matanzas – Varadero
Wed – Sun from 10pm
On the Canimar River (half an hour by

bus from Varadero) in an eye-catching building, lively entertainment based on the performance in the well-known club in Havana, with long-legged revue dancers and a folklore show.

Similar cabaret shows are regularly staged in Varadero in the Cueva del Pirata club (near the Sol Elite Palmeras Hotel), in the Hotel Internacional and the Hotel Kawama (at the western end of the peninsula), and less regularly on holidays and feast days in the Anfiteatro Varadero (on the western edge of the town).

② *Club Mambo*
Avenida de las Américas (near the Sandals Royal Hicacos)
Tel. 045/66 85 65

Daily from 11pm
Trendy nightclub with a high admission price (which means that tourists have the place to themselves), live bands.

WHERE TO STAY
► Luxury
① *Sol Elite Palmeras (Sol Melía)*
Ctra. de las Morlas (Autopista del Sur)
Tel. 045/66 70 09, fax 66 70 08
jefe.recepcion.sep@solmeliacuba.com
www.solmeliacuba.com
Enormous luxury beach resort in the shape of a half-moon with a lush green poolscape, 407 large rooms, 200 bungalows and every amenity to make guests comfortable.

At leisure in the Sandals Royal Hicacos Resort

② *Varadero Internacional
(Gran Caribe)*
Ctra. de las Morlas (Autopista del Sur)
Tel. 045/66 70 38
Fax 66 72 46
director@gcinter.gca.tur.cu
www.gran-caribe.com
Varadero's oldest four-star hotel on one of the nicest stretches of beach has had a thorough refurbishment. Elegantly fitted with 1950s charm, 163 double rooms and 66 pretty bungalows, cabaret.

③ *Sandals Royal Hicacos
Resort & Spa*
Ctra. Las Morlas (Autopista del Sur), km 15
Tel. 045/66 88 44
Fax 66 88 51
www.sandals.com
A hotel village to dream of (»ultra-all-inclusive«) with 404 imaginatively furnished suites (some with concierge service) and a spa. Wedding arrangements with a »personal wedding coordinator«, but the indulgence here is not just for honeymooners. Three pools, four superb restaurants, six bars, gym etc.

▶ **Mid-range**
④ *Brisas del Caribe (Cubanacán)*
Ctra. de las Morlas (Autopista del Sur)
Tel. 045/66 80 30
Fax 66 80 05
ventas@bricar.var.cyt.cu
www.cubanacan.cu
Extensive all-inclusive facility 6km/3.5mi from the centre of Varadero. 440 comfortably furnished rooms and seven suites with balcony, some of them suitable for guests with disabilities. Daily programme of activities and entertainment, gym facilities, tennis courts, jacuzzi and water sports.

▶ **Budget**
⑤ *Pullman (Islazul)*
Av. Primera entre Calles 49 y 50
Tel. 045/66 74 99
Fax 61 27 02
recepcion@dmares.hor.tur.cu
www.horizontes.cu
Small castle-like hotel on the main street in the town centre: some of the 15 rooms have handsome four-poster beds. Shared terrace, pretty patio, 200m/200yd from the beach. At the same address: the equally reasonably priced Dos Mares Hotel, diagonally opposite and a little closer to the sea.

What to See in Varadero

★ ★
Playa de Varadero
Playa de Varadero, a gently shelving beach over 20km/12mi long, with fine-grained sand and shaded by pine trees, is one of the most beautiful in the whole Caribbean.

Many luxurious residences once belonging to the rich testify to the splendour of past times, when Varadero was the stamping-ground of the American financial elite. Today holidaymakers can linger in small cafés and palm-roofed bars over a cup of real Cuban coffee or a mojíto, yield to the tempting aroma of shrimp skewers and sample other delights from the restaurant grills.

*A few palm trees give shade on one of the Caribbean's loveliest beaches, →
Playa de Varadero, which is over 20km/12mi long.*

Avenida 1 Varadero's main drag, Avenida Primera, runs down the middle of the peninsula. This road is lined with holiday houses dating from the late 19th century boasting particularly fine decorative features. Not only that: along the main street visitors will also find shops, restaurants, cafés and galleries, sometimes a long way apart, as well as a hospital, the police station and a pharmacy. It is a good place for watching the comings and goings in a typical tourist town: holidaymakers and Cubans, souped-up American cars and horse-drawn carriages.

Museo Municipal Even the Museo Municipal, dedicated to the history of Varadero, is situated on this road by the beach. Opening hours: Mon – Sat 10am – 7pm, Sun 2pm – 6pm.

★
Parque Retiro Josone The estate that once belonged to the dictator Fulgencio Batista (Av. 1, corner of Calle 58) is now the leisure park Retiro Josone with its small lake. Shops, restaurants, a guarapo bar serving freshly squeezed sugar-cane juice and lots of souvenir stalls are scattered around the somewhat plain park. Opening hours: daily 9am – midnight.

Mansión Xanadú The former estate of the DuPont tycoons, now known as Mansión Xanadú, houses one of the most expensive and exclusive restaurants in Varadero: **Las Américas** (▶ Where to Eat). From the top floor of the mansion, the Sunset Bar, the view of Varadero, the beach and the sea is breathtaking. In the elegant house accommodation is available in six rooms with high-class furnishings, and a generously designed 18-hole golf course rounds off the facilities on the estate.

Delfinario El Laguito Near the Marina Chapelín (close to the Sandals Royal Hicacos Hotel & Spa) three shows daily are staged in the dolphinarium, and visitors

Varadero Map

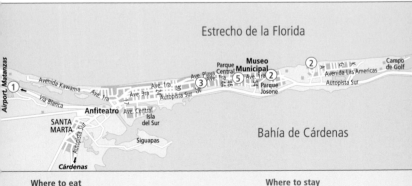

Where to eat
① Las Américas
② Antigüedades
③ Esquina de Cuba

Where to stay
① Sol Elite Palmeras
② Varadero Internacional

can swim with the dolphins afterwards. Opening hours: daily 9.30am – 5pm.

At the eastern end of Varadero the Cueva de Ambrosio was discovered in 1961. Rock drawings found here demonstrate that the peninsula was already inhabited in the pre-Columbian era.
African figures were also found in the cave, suggesting that slaves used it for secret religious ceremonies. Opening hours: daily 9am – 4pm.

✱
**Cueva
de Ambrosio**

Around Varadero

Northeast of the Hicacos Peninsula, the Archipelago of a chain of islets and cliffs off the north coast, Sabana is fringed by coral reefs. Its extremely diverse western end attracts fans of sailing, angling and diving.

✱
**Archipiélago
de Sabana**

From the Marina Chapelín and Marina Gaviota, the catamarans *Seafari* and *JollyRoger* make daily trips to this island with its white beach and the neighbouring islets. Passengers can sunbathe on deck, then snorkel around the coral reefs. The daytime tour includes a creole lunch (lobster, shrimps, chicken) and cocktails served on the island or on board, and a side trip to the dolphin show is thrown in as well. There is also a sunset tour that sets off in the afternoon.
The »jungle tours« are not to be recommended: jet skis roar through the mangrove channels, disturbing the birds that nest here and other animals.
The Japanese **glass-bottomed boat** Varasub and a genuine »submarino« hover above the coral reefs, allowing tourists to observe swarms

Cayo Blanco

◄ Varasub

③ Sandals Royal Hicacos
Resort & Spa

④ Brisas del Caribe
⑤ Pullman

Entertainment
① Tropicana Matanzas
② Club Mambo

of fish and count the starfish. This is also a way to see some submerged wrecks without getting wet. The underwater tour lasts 90 minutes, starting from Marina Chapelín in the west of the peninsula.

Cárdenas
Map D 2 ▶

Although this town of 100,000 residents is only a stone's throw to the south from the holiday mecca Varadero, there is hardly a less touristy place anywhere in Cuba. Indeed, there is not much to see here: horse-drawn carriages and a few veteran cars rumble along the streets, laid out in a checkerboard pattern. Nevertheless, Cárdenas is not an insignificant place: rum and bicycles are made here, two products without which Cuba is unthinkable, and there is a small shipyard. It is also the hometown of a tragic figure of recent history. In 1999 Cárdenas made global headlines when a woman from the town fled from Cuba with her five-year-old son Elían in an overloaded boat heading for Florida. She died, but her son was rescued by the US coastguard and a political drama between Cuba and the USA ensued. The tug-of-war over the child ended in 2000, when Elían returned to his natural father in Cárdenas. A **museum** opened especially for the purpose presents the tragedy from the Cuban point of view (Museo Batalla de las Ideas, Av. 6 entre Calles 11 y 12).

> **! Baedeker TIP**
>
> **Into the jungle**
> The jungle tour goes to the Río Canímar tourist park: first into the densely overgrown country on the banks of the Río Canímar by kayak or motor boat; then, those who like the idea, can jump on horseback at a tourist farm or have a swim in the river. The lazy option is to hang around in a hammock or occupy one of the rocking chairs. This four or five-hour trip with a creole meal in the restaurant can be booked through all hotels in Varadero.

Parque Colón ▶

The focal point of the town is Parque Colón, with a statue of Christopher Columbus (1862) by the Spanish artist Piquier. In 1850 the Cuban flag was raised for the first time on this spot.

In the mid-19th century Cuba's first sugar shipment facility, La Dominica, was built on the site. Today, carriages offering a tour of the town wait here. Follow the main street, Av. Céspedes, towards the Bahía de Cárdenas to get to a monument in the form of a huge flagpole which commemorates the first raising of the Cuban flag here in 1850. There is a good view across the sea to Varadero.

Parque Colón is the site of the **cathedral** (1846), which has notable stained-glass windows.

Plaza Molokoff ▶

Plaza Molokoff's major eye-catcher is the market hall with its Art Nouveau adornments. The iron-built market has a 16m/52ft-high dome.

Sculptures ▶

On the road to Varadero (18km/11mi), some strange sculptures (e.g. a crab) date back to an artists' competition of the 1960s on the theme of »sun, sand and sea«.

Museo Oscar María de Rojas ▶

Opened in 1900, the Museo Oscar María de Rojas (on Parque Echevarría, corner of Calle 4), is one of the oldest museums in Cuba. Its

Highlights *Varadero*

**Villa DuPont
(aka Mansion Xanadú)**
Happy-hour cocktails (5pm – 7pm) with sunset panorama in Bar Mirador
► page 316, 320

Delfinario El Laguito
Expensive but unforgettable: swim and surf with dolphins
► page 320

Trip to the Cayos
Take a catamaran or sailing boat to Cayo Blanco for snorkelling and sunbathing
► page 321

Expedition in a submarine
Marvel at the underwater flora and fauna in a glass-bottomed boat or a submarine
► page 321

home is the former town hall, built in 1861. The interesting exhibits on history and natural history include coins, butterflies and shells, as well as weapons and documents from the Wars of Independence. Opening hours: Tue – Sat 10am – 6pm, Sun 9am – 12 noon. ⏲

From the main street, turn onto the airport road and follow it for 2.5km/1.5mi to a large car park with a restaurant on the left. Here wooden steps lead to the Cueva Saturno, a wonderful dripstone cave with crystal-clear water in which you can swim and snorkel. **Cueva Saturno**

From here it is 5km/3mi to the white sands of Coral Beach and the small bar operating there. The fantastic underwater world here is perfect for snorkelling – but take care not to be injured on the rocks; snorkelling here is only advisable when the weather is right. **Coral Beach**

INDEX

a

Abakúa **233**
Abra **244**
Abra, El **243**
Academy S. Alejandro **61**
accommodation **82**
active holidays **123**
agaves **166**
Agramonte **172174**
Agramonte, Ignacio **171**
agriculture **34, 41, 43**
airport **177**
ajiaco **99**
Alea Gutiérrez **230**
Alea, Tomás Gutiérrez **69**
Alea, Tomás Gutiérrez **69**
Alfonso, Gerardo **65**
almiquí **23**
Alonso, Alicia **226**
Alonso, Fernando **173**
Altos de Malones **190**
Alturas de Sancti Spíritus **17**
Alturas de Trinidad **17**
Alturas del Sur **16**
Alturas Pizarrosas del Norte **16**
Álvarez, Adalberto **65**
Álvarez, Santiago **68**
Ancón Peninsula **302**
animal husbandry **43**
animals **22**
antelopes **195**
Antilles **40**
Antonelli, Giovanni
   Battista **232, 287**
archipelagos **15**
Archipiélago de los
   Canarreos **15**
Archipiélago de los Jardines de
   la Reina **15**
Archipiélago de Sabana **321**
architecture **59**
arrival **84**
arroz congrí **99**
athletics **78**
Australia sugar factory **251**
avocados **21**

b

Bacardí **286**
Baconao **289**

Baconao Park **166**
bagasse **35**
Bahía de Bariay **193**
Bahía de Cochinos **251, 253**
Bahía de Corrientes **257**
ballet **226**
bamboo **166, 189**
bananas **21, 192**
Banes **192**
Baracoa **43, 158**
Baracoa Mountains **21**
barbacoas **220**
Bariay **193**
Barrigonas, Las **259**
barrotes **60**
bata **63**
Batista **265, 280, 315**
Batista regime **49**
Batista, Fulgencio **48, 73, 320**
bats **23**
Bay of Corrientes **257**
Bay of Jagua **186**
Bay of Pigs **51, 73, 251, 253**
Bayamo **43, 74, 155, 163**
bays **15**
Beaches **138**
beans **21**
beer **100**
Beleau, Jean **221**
Bernhardt, Sarah **186**
Bevölkerung **24**
bike **142**
bike tours **124**
biosphere reserve **289**
birds **2223**
black vulture **23**
boa **22**
Bobadilla, Ines de **211**
Boca de Dos Ríos **78**
bohío **42, 59**
bohíos **192**
Book Institute **211**
bougainvillea **21**
Breu, Doña Marta **267**
Brunet y Muñoz, Nicolás **295**
bus **142**

c

Cabaña, La **232**
Cabo Francés **246**
Caburní Waterfalls **304**
cacique **43**
cacique **41**

cacti **168, 190, 232**
Cafe Cantante **65**
caguama **22**
Caibarién **271**
Caimanera **190**
Calle Heredia **282**
Camagüey **147, 168**
camellos **131**
camiones **143**
camper van **143**
canaries **23**
caney **41**
caneyes **59**
Cangilones del Río Máximo **174**
cannons **294**
Caonao **169**
Cárdenas **148, 322**
Caridad del Cobre **287**
carnival **63, 262, 278**
Carpentier **215, 230**
Carpentier, Alejo **73**
Carreno, Mario **62**
Caruso, Enrico **186**
Casa de la Trova **64**
Castillo de Jagua **188**
Castro **20, 55, 73, 75, 166,
   168, 229, 238, 243, 251,
   262, 276, 278, 280, 289**
Castro **243**
Castro Ruz, Fidel **73**
Castro, F + R. **49**
Castro, Fidel **23, 32, 35, 236,
   285**
Castro, Fidel Ruz **49**
Castro, Raúl **49, 73, 75, 280,
   289**
cattle **23**
cave **321**
caves
   – Cueva de Los Portales **257**
   – Cueva de Viñales **314**
   – Cueva del Indio **314**
   – Cuevas Bellamar **148, 248**
   – Gran Caverna de Santo
     Tomás **307**
   – Mayarí **195**
Cayo Blanco **321**
Cayo Cantiles **183**
Cayo Coco **38, 175**
Cayo Conuco **271**
Cayo Ensenachos **271**
Cayo Guillermo **175, 178**
Cayo Iguana **183**
Cayo Largo **38, 180**

LIST OF MAPS AND ILLUSTRATIONS

PHOTO CREDITS

PUBLISHER'S INFORMATION

Illustrations etc: 186 illustrations, 28 maps and diagrams, one large map
Text: Beate Szerelmy, Martina Miethig, Jutta Buness, Heidi Engelmann, with contributions by Bettina Lutterbeck, Dr. Hedwig Nosbers, Siegfried Schäuble and Andrea Wurth
Editing: Baedeker editorial team (Kathleen Becker)
Translation: John Sykes
Cartography: Christoph Gallus, Hohberg; Franz Huber, Munich; MAIRDUMONT/Falk Verlag, Ostfildern (city plan)
3D illustrations: jangled nerves, Stuttgart
Design: independent Medien-Design, Munich; Kathrin Schemel

Editor-in-chief: Rainer Eisenschmid, Baedeker Ostfildern

1st edition 2013
Based on Baedeker Allianz Reiseführer »Kuba«, 7. Auflage 2010

Copyright: Karl Baedeker Verlag, Ostfildern
Publication rights: MAIRDUMONT GmbH & Co; Ostfildern

Printed in China

BAEDEKER GUIDE BOOKS AT A GLANCE
Guiding the World since 1827

DEAR READER,

We would like to thank you for choosing this Baedeker travel guide. It will be a reliable companion on your travels and will not disappoint you.
This book describes the major sights, of course, but it also recommends hotels in the luxury and budget categories, and includes tips about where to eat or go shopping and much more, helping to make your trip an enjoyable experience. Our authors ensure the quality of this information by making regular journeys to Cuba and putting all their know-how into this book.

Nevertheless, experience shows us that it is impossible to rule out errors and changes made after the book goes to press, for which Baedeker accepts no liability. Please send us your criticisms, corrections and suggestions for improvement: we appreciate your contribution. Contact us by post or e-mail, or phone us:

▶ **Verlag Karl Baedeker GmbH**
 Editorial department
 Postfach 3162
 73751 Ostfildern
 Germany
 Tel. 49-711-4502-262, fax -343
 www.baedeker.com
 www.baedeker.co.uk
 E-Mail: baedeker@mairdumont.com